FORENSICS

True stories from Australian police files

For Dalia.

VIKKI PETRAITIS

FORENSICS

True stories from Australian police files

'Forensic evidence is the silent witness'

LAKE PRESS

**LAKE PRESS**

Lake Press Pty Ltd
5 Burwood Road
Hawthorn VIC 3122 Australia
www.lakepress.com.au

These stories were first published in 2006.

This edition first published 2021

Printed in Australia by McPhersons Printing Group 5 4 3 2
LP22 016

 A catalogue record for this
book is available from the
National Library of Australia

CONTENTS

PREFACE

When *Forensics* was first published in 2006, it seemed like every show on TV was about some kind of forensic investigation. Gorgeous forensic cops with perfect hair solved crimes in no time at all, using the most modern scientific techniques. Some were so modern, they hadn't been invented yet. I wanted to write a more realistic version of how Australian police used forensics in their investigations. While the science can be impressive, what was always more impressive was the way everyday cops did their jobs with a dogged pursuit for the truth. We owe them a great debt.

Chapter One

✦

POISON IVY

Joanna Jones was housekeeper to a 73-year-old vision-impaired man. She had worked for him for over a year when she decided to move on. To help the old man find someone else to take care of him, on 7 July 1987, she placed an advertisement in a Melbourne newspaper for a replacement.

One of the respondents was a woman who gave her name as Sandra Arnold. At the job interview, Sandra read out a reference that she had with her, saying that she had worked as a housekeeper for ten years for a couple who had recently moved to England. Sandra explained that the couple had wanted her to accompany them overseas, but she wanted to stay in Melbourne. She seemed like a good choice and Joanna and her elderly boss offered her the position to start straightaway. Joanna would stay on for a while to show her the ropes. Carrying a large suitcase, Sandra returned the next day around lunchtime and moved into the spare bedroom.

Shortly after Sandra arrived at the house, Joanna went out and did some shopping, leaving the new housekeeper with her boss. When she returned, Sandra was gone and her boss said that he had given her $50 from his wallet to go and pay some bills. Later in the afternoon, when Sandra had returned, Joanna showed her where everything was kept – especially the most important things like her boss's sleeping tablets and prescription painkillers.

After dinner that night, Sandra washed the dishes and suggested that Joanna have an early night, but she refused – she never went to bed early. It was then that she noticed that her boss's bottle of sleeping tablets wasn't on the shelf where it was normally kept. Around 8 pm, Sandra offered to make Joanna a cup of tea, but the conscientious housekeeper didn't want to stop until she had finished her chores. Later, Joanna noticed that the sleeping tablets were back in their normal place on the shelf. But she didn't think much of it at the time.

Around 10.30 pm, Sandra offered Joanna a Butter-Menthol lolly and had one herself, and then made her a cup of tea. When Joanna screwed up her face after taking a sip of her tea, Sandra quickly said, 'Does your tea taste funny? Mine does. It must be the Butter-Menthol.'

There was something odd about the whole situation. Joanna didn't want to finish her cup of tea despite the urgings of the new housekeeper.

'I'll take it with me when I have a shower,' she told Sandra. Not to be put off, Sandra followed Joanna into the bathroom.

'You're not drinking it, are you?' accused Sandra from the doorway.

'Yes I am,' replied Joanna. But instead, she turned away from Sandra and secretly tipped the tepid tea down her chest as she showered.

When Joanna had finished her shower and was putting on her pyjamas in her bedroom, Sandra came in several times to ask her if she was feeling sleepy. Joanna's suspicions were more than aroused. She put two and two together and realised that Sandra must have taken the bottle of sleeping tablets from the shelf and put one in her tea. She decided to be blunt about it.

'Why did you put the sleeping tablets in my tea?' she asked.

'How could you say such a thing? I'm really hurt,' declared Sandra, marching out of the room in indignation.

As a safety precaution, Joanna jammed the bedroom door shut. The next thing she heard was Sandra calling out goodnight and then some noises from the adjacent bedroom. Joanna then heard the side gate bang. Joanna had locked the gate and put the key in the kitchen before going to bed. When the gate banged, Joanna climbed out of bed and ran outside just in time to see their new housekeeper running off down the street carrying her suitcase.

Joanna ran back into the house to where her boss kept his wallet in a box in the kitchen. Earlier that day, she had noticed that the wallet was full of cash – she estimated over a thousand dollars. Now the wallet was empty.

Joanna called the police, who attended and took a report. A fingerprint expert, Sergeant Peter Townsend, came to the house and dusted for fingerprints in Sandra's bedroom. He found a latent fingerprint on a drinking glass that Sandra had used. The fingerprint remained on file but it wasn't of sufficient standard to match with any on the new computer system at the Fingerprint Branch.

When Joanna's employer was questioned by police, he told them he had taken out his wallet to give Sandra money for the errand earlier that day. She must have seen then that it was bulging with cash.

Despite an investigation into the incident, detectives at the Richmond CIB drew a blank. Joanna worked with police to provide an identikit photo of the thief that remained on file with the detectives, but despite extensive inquiries, the case remained unsolved.

James was a housekeeper at the Victoria Hotel in Little Collins Street in Melbourne. On Saturday 15 August 1987, he was working a morning shift when one of the cleaning staff called him up to room 338 at around 8.15 am. She had tried to open the door to clean the room, and while the door could be unlocked and opened a few centimetres, something was blocking it on the inside. James helped her push the door open a fraction more and looked through the gap to find out what was in the way. Through the narrow opening, he could see that there was a man lying on the floor in front of the door. James and the cleaner gently pushed until they could move him enough to get inside the room.

James knelt down beside the prone figure and could see that the man was elderly. He gently shook him and the old man groaned. Until James heard the groan, he hadn't been certain that the man was still alive.

'What happened? What's wrong?' James asked.

But the old man could only groan. It was then James noticed that the man had vomited nearby. He ignored the pungent odour and manoeuvred his arms under the old man's shoulders and knees and lifted him up onto the bed, which, James observed, hadn't been slept in and was still made up.

James looked around the room for clues as to the guest's condition. He saw a bottle of port on a nearby bench. Perhaps the man had drunk too much, but there wasn't much missing from the bottle. He washed out one of the glasses that the hotel provided and filled it full of water to try to get the man to drink, but it was no use; the water spilt over his face.

James alerted senior management of the situation. People from the hotel crowded into the room, and then another guest, who said she was a nurse, came in and made a cursory examination of the elderly man. She told hotel staff to call an ambulance immediately. Just to be on the safe side, they also called the police.

By the time the doctor examined the elderly man in the emergency department of the Royal Melbourne Hospital around midday, he had started to come around and was able to give an account of what had happened to him. He told the doctor that his name was Joseph and that he had been drugged by a woman he had picked up in the city. He said that she had given him a glass of port and that was the last thing he remembered. Even several hours after being found, Joseph was very drowsy and difficult to rouse. The doctor found it impossible to get anything but the bare facts from the man, and decided to keep him in hospital for observation.

When Detective Sergeant Alex Robertson and Detective Senior Constable Peter Wheeler from the Russell Street CIB were alerted by staff at the Royal Melbourne Hospital to the possible drugging of the elderly man, the case was deemed something out of the ordinary. Wheeler, at 26 years of age, had two years' experience as a detective in the CIB, but this type of offence was unknown to him and his colleagues. More typical CIB work consisted of common burglaries, thefts, deception, dud cheques, armed robberies, drug matters and assaults. Sergeant Robertson was ten years older than his partner, and although he had seen a lot of things in his time as a detective, he too had never had a case like it.

After meeting Joseph in the hospital, the detectives were left in no doubt that the woman had lured him to the hotel room with the promise of a sexual encounter that she had no intention of keeping, but rather to drug and rob him. It was callous, considering the state the detectives found Joseph in at the hospital, and it struck Peter Wheeler how vulnerable the elderly could be. Here was a 72-year-old man who had gone willingly to a hotel room with a strange woman, ending up at the mercy of someone who had none.

Hospital tests failed to identify the drug that Joseph had ingested. Alcohol analysis was nil, and the hospital analysis, while failing to identify the drug, did rule out the hundred most common drugs and poisons.

Local uniform cops had examined Joseph's hotel room for clues. They collected samples from the glasses that Joseph and the woman had used, and then sealed off the room for forensics. An expert from the Fingerprint Branch, Sergeant Stuart Thompson, dusted the room for prints. He developed latent fingerprints on the bottle of Penfold's Royal Reserve Port. Thompson took a telephone information booklet from the room along with the paper bag that the port had come in. He was able to develop latent fingerprints on both. What remained in the glass that Joseph had used to drink his port from was collected and taken to the Victoria Police State Forensic Science Laboratory for analysis. Despite the examination of samples taken from both Joseph and his room, forensic scientists failed to determine which substance had been used to drug him. A 'basic drug' – according to the medical report – was detected in his system; however, it could not be identified further.

❖ ❖ ❖

Joseph was still in hospital the following Tuesday when Wheeler and Robertson visited him again. He lay in his hospital bed looking frail after his ordeal, but by then, he had recovered sufficiently to tell his story and give a proper statement to the police officers. He told the detectives that he was a 72-year-old pensioner, and the previous Friday, he had caught the train into the city, getting off at Flinders Street station. He had gone to a cafe near the famous Young and Jackson's pub, where he'd had a meal of bacon and eggs. He'd then wandered around the city and ended up having a few beers at the Victoria Hotel. The elderly man explained to the detective that after he'd had a few drinks, he had decided to treat himself to a call girl. He had obviously done this before because he had then tried to telephone a girl he knew but there was no answer. He then noticed a woman standing near the public phones and he approached her.

'How do you do?' Joseph had asked politely.

'I'm fine,' the woman replied. 'You feeling lonely, are you?'

The woman wasn't especially young, but Joseph thought she was quite pretty. She had told Joseph that if he bought them both a bottle of drink, she would 'look after him'. Having established the terms, he then booked a room at the Victoria Hotel while the woman waited over by the elevators. Once in the hotel room, the woman insisted on making Joseph a cup of coffee which she then urged him to drink. He had taken a couple of sips but it tasted peculiar and he tipped it down the sink. The two then left the room to visit a nearby bottle shop. Joseph bought a bottle of port and the woman bought a packet of Peter Jackson cigarettes. Back in the hotel room, the woman poured them both a drink of port. Again, she urged Joseph to drink up. It was the last thing he remembered.

Joseph told Wheeler that before he had met the woman, he had about $900 in his wallet. The money was now gone. He described the woman as being around 35 years old, about 163 centimetres tall, with black hair. She had a slightly Asian appearance, but he thought she could have been Caucasian. She had been wearing a light blue silk dress and a knee-length fox fur coat.

The detectives found the actions of the offender calculated and cunning. It was obvious that she had put some thought into committing the crime, and what was equally obvious, not to mention chilling, was that she had a total disregard for her elderly victim. Had Joseph had a heart condition, or other medical complications, whatever drug she had given him might have killed him. Added to the drugging was the fact that he had obviously tried to get up in his delirious state, and suffered a fall. At some stage, he had also vomited – luckily on the floor – but the detectives both knew how easy it was for an unconscious person to choke on their own vomit. As it was, Joseph would spend the best part of a week in hospital recovering from his ordeal.

Joseph was drugged by the mystery woman on the Friday night, and by the following Monday, she had claimed her next victim.

Kyle was a company director who lived in a small country town in western Victoria. On Monday 17 August, he came to Melbourne on business and had several meetings in the afternoon. In the evening, he checked in to the Park Avenue Motel on Royal Parade and was given the keys to room 17. After checking in around 9 pm, he decided to head back into the city and make the most of his time in the big smoke. Driving in a 1979 Ford LTD that he'd borrowed from his brother-in-law, Kyle parked in Lonsdale Street. He had in mind to try to see a show at the Comedy Theatre, but it turned out that the tickets were a bit expensive and the show had already started so he decided to come back another time with his wife and make a night of it.

He walked back down Lonsdale Street and went into the upstairs bar at the Zanies Hotel where, for entertainment, a piano player provided background music and sang for the patrons. Kyle ordered a Scotch and water and sat down at the bar. He had a chat with the bartender, noticed a couple of Asian men sitting nearby, and after that, to the best of his memory, he collected his car and returned to his motel room alone. He remembers making himself a cup of coffee, having a shower, watching a show on TV about Elvis Presley, and after that ... nothing. Until he woke up in hospital.

The bartender, Bettina, told a similar story, with one important addition. She remembered the two Asian men. She remembered Kyle coming in and she remembered him telling her he was from the country. But she also remembered seeing a woman standing alone at the other end of the bar. The mystery woman hadn't ordered a drink and had kept her back turned so the bartender hadn't seen what she looked like. Bettina continued with her work, and when she next took any notice, Kyle and the woman had both gone.

Robert worked at the Park Avenue Motel where Kyle had checked in earlier. He started his shift at 11 pm, and one of his jobs was to cross-check the car registrations that the visitors had given when they checked in with the cars in the car park. He noted that the car belonging to the guest in room 17 was not in the car park.

Just after midnight, a brown car drove into the car park and then at around 12.30 am, Robert received a phone call from room 17. The guest asked Robert if he could purchase a bottle of port from the motel. He replied that the restaurant was closed and he couldn't help him. About five minutes later, he noticed the brown car drive out of the car park.

Some time around 4 am, Robert heard a car driving into the car park. It was the brown car again. This time, he could see there were two people in it. The car was gone early the next morning. He was taking some rubbish to the dumpster and saw one of the hotel staff holding a breakfast tray and knocking on the door of room 17.

'I think he's gone already,' Robert called out.

'No, he's not – I can see him lying on the bed,' replied the staffer, who could see the prone man through the open curtains. Opening the door with the key, the staffer saw Kyle lying unconscious with his face at the foot of the bed. He wasn't wearing any clothes.

Martin was an accountant, and he had a business appointment with Kyle on Tuesday 18 August at 8 am, but Kyle didn't show up. Martin knew Kyle to be punctual and was surprised when he failed to arrive at the appointed time.

At around 11 am, Martin received a phone call from the staff at the Park Avenue Motel. They explained that they had a guest who was ill and that they'd found Martin's contact details among his personal effects. Martin immediately drove to the motel. Staff took the accountant to Kyle's room, where he found his client to be barely coherent, and having trouble standing up and keeping his balance. It was as if he was drunk but there was no smell of alcohol on his breath. The motel staff suggested a local doctor, and Martin helped Kyle to the car and took him to a clinic.

The attending physician suggested that it would be in Kyle's best interest to go to hospital, and Martin took him to the Royal Melbourne Hospital, where he was admitted. There was a graze on his forehead, bruises on his knees, and grazes to his left shin and right arm. The hospital doctor found him to be in a state of decreased consciousness with a slight slurring of speech and slow coordination. He was kept in for observation. Both the car Kyle had borrowed from his brother-in-law and $180 from his wallet were missing. It was then up to Martin to report the matter to the local police and ring Kyle's family.

By coincidence, detectives Robertson and Wheeler had come back to the Royal Melbourne Hospital again to interview Joseph, when they heard of another man who had been admitted under similar circumstances. The two detectives made their way over to his ward and introduced themselves. Even though Kyle said that he couldn't remember being with any woman, his symptoms were so similar to those of Joseph that the detectives suspected the cases were connected. Kyle's urine had been tested for traces of drugs or poison. Some type of amphetamine was detected. Here were two men staying at city hotels within days of each other, robbed, drugged and hospitalised. To the policemen, it didn't seem like a coincidence.

By then, police had spoken to staff at the motel and they knew that during the night, Kyle's missing car was seen driving into the motel with a man and a woman inside. Unfortunately, by the time police were notified of Kyle's drugging, his motel room had been rented to another tenant and was therefore cleaned and stripped of any potential forensic evidence.

Back at the Russell Street CIB offices, Wheeler and Robertson discussed the two druggings. Neither they, nor their colleagues, had ever had a case like it. The detectives needed to do some research to determine the most appropriate charges to lay against the woman when she was eventually arrested. After consultation with lecturers at the Victoria Police Detective Training School and lawyers at the Department of Public Prosecutions, they finally determined that 'administering a substance to interfere with bodily functions' was the closest thing to describing what the woman had done to her two victims.

Wheeler and Robertson also agreed that all metropolitan hospitals needed to be notified and told to keep a lookout for any men with suspected drugging symptoms. Consulting the list of major hospitals on display in their office, Robertson and Wheeler rang each one and outlined the case for them. If any male presented with symptoms of being drugged after drinking with a woman in a hotel room or a bar, the detectives wanted to be alerted immediately.

When Joseph was released from hospital, Wheeler organised for him to come to the Russell Street police headquarters to do an identikit photo. The resulting picture of a young woman with short dark hair seemed incongruous with the callousness of one who had drugged the two men, leaving the older one to lie in a pool of his own vomit.

Nineteen-year-old bank officer Adam came to Melbourne from Mildura for a bank tellers' course. He checked in to the Victoria Hotel in Little Collins Street – the same hotel where Joseph had been drugged.

On Tuesday 1 September, Adam had dinner at a restaurant next to his hotel, drinking four wines with his meal. Then he went out to meet up with a mate to go drinking. He and his friend hit several bars and drank either beer or black Russians. At the end of their evening of drinking, Adam walked his mate to the tram stop to catch a tram home, and then he went to the Swanston Street McDonald's. He bought a takeaway coffee, which he drank on the way back to his room. And that was all he remembered.

Malcolm was in charge of the bank tellers' course that Adam was supposed to attend and when he didn't show up on Wednesday 2 September, he tried to ring Adam's hotel room around 9.30 am but there was no answer. He tried again at 9.50 am. Still no answer. Finally, when Malcolm tried again, Adam answered the phone at 11.15 am. He apologised for oversleeping and promised to leave shortly. At 12.10 pm, Malcolm tried again, and again Adam apologised and promised to leave within fifteen minutes. At 1 pm, Adam still hadn't arrived and during this third conversation, he said he was leaving then. Adam checked out of the hotel and arrived at the course 40 minutes later.

When Malcolm finally caught up with his wayward trainee, he could see straightaway that something was wrong. Adam's speech was slow and incoherent, and he couldn't maintain any kind of train of thought, nor could he offer any explanation for his condition. Malcolm decided that it was useless for Adam to attend the course in the state he was in and told him to book an earlier flight back to Mildura. Malcolm watched Adam try and fail to dial the phone number. One of the conference centre staff dialled for him, and then Adam fell asleep during the conversation. There were no earlier flights, and by this time, Malcolm was concerned enough to call a doctor. Initially, he had suspected that Adams condition was probably caused by a hangover, but he could smell no alcohol on the young man's breath.

One of his co-workers took Adam to the doctor, who pronounced him well enough for the flight home. Colleagues then took him out to the airport and escorted him to his flight.

He was met in Mildura by his mother, who drove him straight to the Mildura Base Hospital. The attending physician tested him for any drugs that he could think of that would bring on the symptoms with which the young man presented. They were so severe that the doctor informed Adam and his worried family that he suspected they might be early signs of multiple sclerosis.

Albert was 57 years old, and he had just been to Adelaide to attend his mother's funeral. Before returning to his home in Sydney, he decided to spend a week in Melbourne to catch up with some friends. He booked himself in to the Great Southern Hotel in Spencer Street in Melbourne. He checked in to room 4 and spent several days staying mostly in his room listening to the races on the radio. Around 6.30 am on Wednesday 2 September, Albert left his room and walked down the hotel hallway to go to the toilet. Halfway along the corridor, he saw an attractive woman walking down the stairs from the floor above.

'I can't sleep,' she told him. 'Would you mind if I came into your room and kept you company?'

'Yes,' Albert replied, 'but you'll have to wait until I come back from the toilet.' Albert was flattered that the woman whom he would later describe as 'beautiful' wanted to come into his room.

She waited in the hallway until Albert returned and followed him into his room. Inside the room, the woman sat on the bed and looked at the mug of tea Albert had just made himself. She asked him if he could make her a cup of coffee. Albert turned away and made her a cup of coffee and placed it on the table next to the bed. The woman then told Albert that she was going to go upstairs and get her handbag. A minute later, she was back with her bag and resumed her position on the bed. While they were on the bed talking, Albert drank his cup of tea ...

Albert opened his eyes and tried to move. He was on the floor wearing his pyjamas. He tried to lift himself to a sitting position but kept falling back onto the floor. Eventually, he made it back up onto the bed. He looked groggily around the room and could see his wallet sitting open on the end of his bed. He fumbled for it and found the $350 that he'd had was missing. The aerial on his portable radio had been snapped off, and he could see blood on two of the walls and on the sheets of the bed. He struggled to his feet and got some underwear from the wardrobe, wet it under the tap, and tried to wipe the blood off the walls. When he lifted his arms, he noticed that his arms were scraped and bleeding. He checked the rest of his body and found lacerations on his legs, head, knees, and lower back. He was aching all over.

Albert later told police that he had made his way down the corridor to the bathroom and had a shower to clean himself. He said that he got dressed as best he could and went down to the motel foyer and called the police.

Janine, the hotel manager, had a different story. She was on duty at the reception area and at around 3.45 pm on Thursday 3 September, she saw Albert coming down the stairs in his pyjamas. Standing at the base of the stairs, he tried to tell her something but she couldn't understand him. His head was covered in cuts and he pulled up his sleeves and she saw that both arms were cut and covered in dried blood. Even though he was mostly incoherent, she could see that he was holding his empty wallet and he kept pointing to it. She suspected that he was either drunk or drugged but she couldn't smell any alcohol on his breath. It was she who had told him to call the police.

And Wheeler and Robertson attended yet another male drugging victim.

According to their respective statements, more than 33 hours had passed since Albert drank his cup of tea in the company of the woman he'd met in the corridor. His injuries were an added distress. At some point after being drugged, he had obviously fallen several times and cut and grazed himself. The female offender might have simply thought she was sending her victims to sleep, but the injured, bloodied victim in this case was proof of the dangers of her methods. Both police officers had attended cases where men in fistfights had died simply by falling over and hitting their heads on pavements. Albert was lucky that cuts and bruises were all he'd suffered when he'd fallen.

Police made a check of the hotel register, but as was the case in most hotels, there were hundreds of people registered at any given time and it was impossible to interview every one of them. In addition to this, there was only the word of the woman to say that she was even staying at the hotel when she had met Albert in the hallway.

On Friday 4 September, Detective Sergeant Robertson received a phone call from the doctor in charge of Casualty at St Vincent's Hospital. The doctor told the detective that he had a male patient who was suffering an apparent poisoning and was complaining of being robbed of his money.

Robertson and Wheeler drove to St Vincent's and got an update from staff before approaching 68-year-old Arnold, who told an increasingly familiar story. He had been in his rented room at a boarding house in Fitzroy the previous day, Thursday 3 September, when a woman knocked on his door and asked if she could come into his room and watch television. She introduced herself as Sandra. After a short time, she had offered to make him a cup of coffee, which he drank. He remembered nothing until the next morning when he woke up to find both the woman and the $400 he had in his wallet missing.

When Arnold gave a description of the woman who had come into his room to the detectives, it was no surprise that it closely matched that given by the first victim, Joseph, and the woman seen by the bartender at the same bar Kyle had a drink at. When Arnold left the hospital and had recovered from the ordeal, he was able to help police make an identikit photo of the woman. The resulting identikit was very similar to the one made by Joseph.

By now, similar facts were emerging. When Joseph took the woman to the bottle shop, she bought Peter Jackson cigarettes. When Kyle's abandoned car was found on the Western Highway near Ballarat the day after his drugging, there were Peter Jackson cigarette butts with pink lipstick on them in the ashtray. None of Kyle's family smoked. The identikit photos were similar, as was the woman's modus operandi.

Paul finished work as a clerk around 4.30 pm on Friday 4 September and headed into the city with a mate from work. The two men made their way to the Royal Arcade Hotel in Little Collins Street to play some pool and have a few drinks. After a couple of games of pool and a few beers, they were standing at the bar when a woman approached them and began talking. She told them that she was new in Melbourne and that she wanted some company and conversation.

After some general chatter, the woman made it clear that she only had designs on one of the men, and it was Paul who thought his luck had changed when the woman talked about going to a hotel. Soon after, the couple left. They went first to a bottle shop, where she bought a bottle of McWilliam's port and he bought half a dozen stubbies. The two caught a taxi to Spencer Street and Paul booked a room on the second floor of the Spencer Private Motel.

Once inside, the woman complained about being cold and Paul rang reception and got them to bring up an oil heater. He stripped off his clothes and hopped into bed. The woman asked him if he wanted a port or a coffee. He said he didn't like port and that he'd rather have another stubbie. She told him that it would be better to have a coffee rather than more alcohol. He didn't want to argue with the woman he thought was about to get into bed with him, so she made them both a cup of coffee and sat on top of the covers while they each drank them. Several times, the woman said she wanted to have a shower before going to bed. Paul finished his coffee and that's all he remembered until a wake-up call roused him the next morning.

The woman was gone and so was the $200 that Paul had in his wallet the night before. The only thing left behind was an empty packet of Peter Jackson cigarettes and the bottle of port. When Paul climbed out of bed and stood up, he felt disoriented and it took a while for him to regain his senses. He knew that whatever it was that he was feeling, it wasn't a hangover. He simply hadn't had that much to drink the night before and, because he was a seasoned drinker, he knew that he only got hangovers after marathon drinking sessions. The previous night wasn't one of them.

Paul showered and dressed and later, at home, he contacted Peter Wheeler at the Russell Street CIB and told the detective what had happened.

On Saturday 5 September Patrick watched a game of footy at VFL Park (now Waverley Park) and then caught public transport into the city. He went to the Young and Jackson's Hotel and drank eight or nine beers over several hours in the front bar. At 8.15 pm, he made his way to the saloon bar that used to be called Chloe's in honour of Jules Lefebvre's famous painting, which had graced the hotel walls since 1908.

After half an hour and a few more beers, Patrick noticed a woman enter the bar. She began talking to two men drinking at the bar and Patrick assumed that she was with them. A minute later, the woman came up and stood by his side.

'Would you like to get out of here?' she asked Patrick.

'Why? What's up?' he replied.

The woman said something about some blokes that were going to grab her, and Patrick assumed she was talking about the two men she'd just been talking to. He told her that if she stayed where she was, she'd be all right. Any mention of anyone grabbing her was forgotten, and instead the woman began asking Patrick about himself. Did he live alone? Was there anyone else back at his place? He told her that he was single and lived alone. When he finished his beer, the woman asked him to take her back to his place.

'Yeah, no sweat,' said Patrick casually, thinking that he might be in with a chance with this woman. The two walked to a bottle shop where the woman bought a packet of Peter Jackson cigarettes and a bottle of McWilliam's port and Patrick bought himself half a dozen cans of beer. In the taxi on the way to his flat the two chatted and the woman was friendly and affectionate, and when they reached his flat, she was quite insistent that he have a glass of port with her. He poured two glasses. She offered to make them both a cup of tea, and while she was doing that, Patrick left the room to go to the toilet.

When the tea was ready, Patrick settled himself in his armchair and the woman turned all the lights off, leaving only a lamp to illuminate the room. She sat on the floor at his feet. He sipped his tea and told her it tasted funny but she insisted that he drink it all. When he finished, she handed him the port, which he also drank. He finally thought to ask the woman her name and she told him it was Sandra. The two talked for a while and then Sandra told him to turn off the lamp. The room was lit only by the faint glow of the TV show they were watching. Sandra kissed Patrick on the neck and undid the top button of his shirt. That was the last thing he remembered ...

The next thing Patrick knew, it was around 5 am the following day and he was still sitting in his armchair. The woman had gone and he felt really sick. He went straight to his bedroom and crawled into bed.

He woke again soon after 9 am, still feeling sick. He fought the urge to fall asleep again and checked his wallet. The $80 in cash that he'd had the night before was gone. He had a shower to try to revive himself, but it didn't help. The only feeling that he could equate this to was being drunk, but he knew that he hadn't drunk enough the night before to feel like he did.

Around lunchtime, Patrick decided to return to Young and Jackson's to try to find the woman who had stolen his money.

When he got there, she was nowhere to be found, and people at the pub told him to go and see a doctor. Instead, he returned home and went to bed. By the Monday, he really felt as if something was wrong with him. Luckily, he had a rostered day off work. On Tuesday he returned to work but didn't really feel better till the following Friday. By then, he had already spoken to Peter Wheeler at the Russell Street CIB and told the detective his story.

Because of the escalating attacks and the very real possibility that the mystery woman could kill her next victim, Wheeler and Robertson made the decision to involve the media. Peter Wheeler was nominated to address the media in the St Kilda Road Police Complex in a televised press conference. As the journalists gathered, Alex Robertson heard one of the journalists refer to their offender as 'Poison Ivy'. The press loved a good nickname.

Wheeler told the gathered journalists that the State Forensic Science Laboratory had unsuccessfully attempted to identify the substance the woman had used to drug the unsuspecting victims.

'Whatever it is, it appears to produce an almost instant reaction. The victims have all received bruising when they've collapsed and fallen over,' Wheeler told the press. 'We want to warn people, especially men who might be drinking or living alone, that this woman is active around the city area. Her activities are potentially very dangerous. If she was to administer too much of this substance or spike the drink of someone who was already in poor health, the consequences could be extremely serious.'

On Monday 7 September, articles and a copy of the identikit photo compiled by Joseph, the first victim, appeared in local and national newspapers. The press picked up the nickname bandied around at the press conference, and quickly dubbed the mystery woman 'Poison Ivy'. The police were inundated with calls claiming 'Ivy' was everyone from a single mother in Chelsea to a chemist in Endeavour Hills who resembled the identikit. One journalist described her as a 'latter-day Lucrezia Borgia'.

While the media gave the case exposure and hopefully made men drinking in the city more cautious, Wheeler and Robertson knew that their offender was growing more confident daily. She had perfected an easy means of committing her crimes. Both detectives knew that if she continued to offend, the likelihood of her getting caught increased, but so did the possibility that the next person she drugged could die. The detectives were putting in long working hours to try to solve the crime. They started work each morning at 7 am, often continuing till 10 pm. The druggings were all so similar, but the evidence collected from the scenes wasn't really getting them anywhere. Latent fingerprints had been found and photographed at a number of the crime scenes, but they weren't of sufficient quality to register on the newly installed computer matching system. If the police had solid suspects who had prints on file, they could have directed fingerprint experts to manually compare file prints with the ones lifted from scenes of the spate of druggings. But there were no solid suspects.

Not only did the media attention encourage people to phone in and report women they thought might be Poison Ivy, but it also brought other victims to light. Joseph, her first victim, who confessed to using call girls, described her as having the 'demeanour of a prostitute'. That meant that the men whom she targeted had a pretty good idea that, when they were taking her back to their rooms or homes, money would change hands. Because some of the men were married or in relationships, they didn't report their experiences to police initially, because they didn't want their wives or girlfriends to know. Obviously, the men suffering the dangerous drugging symptoms had little choice in the matter, but the detectives working on the Poison Ivy case knew that her victim count could be much higher.

The day after the story hit the press, another man was out on the town. He too would have a chat to a woman who had been standing alone at a bar. On Tuesday 8 September, New Zealander

Phil left the ship on which he worked as a cook, and hit the streets of Melbourne after berthing at Victoria Dock. Phil was in the company of a fellow ship worker and two female friends. The four went to the movies to see the newly released *The Witches of Eastwick*, and then went to Isabella's Hotel, which was a favourite with the ship's crew when they were in Melbourne.

Around midnight, Phil went to the bar to buy some drinks, leaving his friends and some fellow sailors from his ship enjoying themselves. There was a woman standing alone at the bar and he made casual conversation with her. When he returned to the bar a little later, the woman was still there. For the next half an hour, Phil chatted to the woman, eventually inviting her back to his ship.

'Will there be many people around?' the woman asked him.

'Most of them will be in bed,' he replied.

The two caught a taxi down to the docks and during the ride the woman asked several times if there was anywhere on the ship she could get a cup of coffee. At the docks, Phil escorted her up the gangway of his ship. Once onboard, he took the woman to the mess room and made two coffees. He then took her into the stewards' bar, where he grabbed some beer. He couldn't carry both the beer and the coffees, so the woman offered to carry the coffees. She walked behind him and followed him to his cabin. Phil put the beer down in his cabin and left the woman in his room while he went to find a tape deck so he could play some music. Finally alone together in his room, Phil sat on his bunk drinking his coffee while the woman sat in a chair. She poured herself a beer and offered him one, but Phil had to work at 5.30 the next morning and decided against drinking any more. He finished his coffee and the next thing he knew, it was after 7 am the next morning and someone was banging on his door.

Phil felt terrible. He was dazed and confused. And his wallet, when he thought to check it later, was empty of the $200 that he'd had the night before. When he saw that his money had been taken, he realised what must have happened. He knew he hadn't been drunk the previous night and that the woman must have put something in his coffee.

Phil went straight to the ship's captain and explained what had happened. His captain told him to ring the police. Around 3 pm, detectives arrived at the ship and Phil showed them to his cabin, telling them that he was still feeling light-headed. Sitting on a counter were the two coffee cups and the glass from which the woman had drunk her beer. One police officer searched the contents of the rubbish bin in the small cabin and located a cigarette butt with lipstick on the filter. He bagged it for evidence. Sergeant Richard Harnwell from the Fingerprint Branch examined the coffee cups and the glass for prints. He found a clear fingerprint on the glass the woman had used. He photographed the fingerprint. The police officers took the cups and glass as evidence, and Phil provided a urine sample for analysis.

In response to the media attention surrounding the Poison Ivy druggings, bank clerk Adam and his family contacted detectives from their Mildura home to report their suspicions that his condition was similar to that of the drugging victims reported in the media, and that they felt he might have been a victim of Poison Ivy.

He gave a statement to police; what happened to him when he came to Melbourne for the bank tellers' course certainly fitted Ivy's modus operandi. Adam's doctor in Mildura also read the media reports of a woman spiking drinks and robbing men in Melbourne. He contacted police and gave a statement to the effect that since Adam was in Melbourne during the spate of poisonings, then perhaps he too could have been a victim. He sent Adam's specimens to a lab in Melbourne to be screened.

And then finally, Ivy's moment came. Fingerprint expert Sergeant Richard Harnwell took the prints he'd lifted from the glass found in the ship's cabin back to the offices of the Fingerprint Branch at the St Kilda Road Police Complex. The print he had was clear and of a good quality. He placed the latent fingerprint on a photographic enlarger called a crimcon machine and printed out an image five times larger than the original. Harnwell attached a transparent film over the enlargement and carefully traced the characteristics of the fingerprint image. When the tracing was complete, he separated it from the enlargement and placed the tracing on a piece of white A4 paper. The print was then photocopied and reduced to its original size. The hand-drawn replica of the fingerprint was then attached to a computer search card so that it could be searched on the national database. Harnwell added the unique identifying details of the job to the card and began the task of loading the image onto the system.

The computer began the scan of the image and once completed, began the task of matching. Before long, the computer matching system returned ten candidates whose fingerprints most closely resembled the latent print taken from the cabin.

Harnwell looked at the candidates to make a visual comparison and cross-checked print characteristics against them. His task was to find at least eight characteristic matches. And as he scanned the ten possible candidates, he soon saw that one was a definite match. The name of the candidate was Robyn Bennison.

Harnwell got Bennison's fingerprint card, which was stored with thousands of others in the Fingerprint Branch's files. He cross-checked her print card with the latent print from the cabin. When he had matched eight characteristics from the inked impressions, he was satisfied that the fingerprints did indeed belong to Bennison and signed his name to the identification. As per protocol, Harnwell had another two fingerprint experts check his results. They confirmed his findings, and he rang his results through to Wheeler and Robertson at the Russell Street CIB. At last, they had Poison Ivy's real name.

As soon as the fingerprint from the glass from Phil's cabin came back matched to Robyn Bennison, Wheeler and Robertson raced against the clock to locate her. She was drugging men almost daily now, despite the media coverage featuring her identikit photo. Finally, they tracked down her last known address and sent a couple of detectives to see if she was indeed still living there.

When the detectives got to the address of the hostel in Nicholson Street, Fitzroy, they knocked on her door, but there was no answer. They had someone from management open the door for them. There was no-one in the room, and after looking around, the detectives were just about to leave when a woman and a man arrived at the door. Poison Ivy had been located at last.

The police officers introduced themselves to Bennison and showed her their search warrant. She and her male companion were separated. The companion told police that he'd just met her and she'd invited him to her room for coffee.

Meanwhile, the suspect was taken inside her room and searched by a female police officer. The police officer found nothing incriminating during the body search, but as Robyn Bennison was putting her clothes back on, the policewoman saw her tuck a packet of Peter Jackson cigarettes under her pillow. The police officer retrieved the packet and inspected the contents. Inside, she found a silver foil wrapper at the bottom of the packet.

By the time she was dressed again, Wheeler and Robertson had arrived. They had been contacted by their colleagues as soon as Bennison had made an appearance back at her room.

Peter Wheeler introduced himself and then read the suspect her rights. To the detective, she looked like a typical drug addict – frail, thin and generally unhealthy. He could also see that she clearly matched the descriptions that witnesses had given. Wheeler said later, 'When you're looking for the first time at someone you've known for a month through identikit photos and statements, it completes the puzzle.'

Inside her room, Wheeler partially unwrapped the silver foil that Robyn Bennison had tucked into her cigarette packet.

'What's this?' he asked her.

'Heroin,' she replied.

'Does this heroin belong to you?'

'It's mine,' said Bennison resignedly. 'It's no use lying to you, I'm in enough trouble.'

Sometimes a suspect is resistant to being interviewed. Robyn Bennison wasn't. Wheeler and Robertson prided themselves on being able to read the play when it came to dealing with people in their line of work. Both detectives had a gut instinct that Bennison would respond to a sympathetic approach – even though they felt none for her.

A thorough search of her room turned up a number of items of interest: a syringe containing a liquid solution, a silver spoon lined with residue, and two ampoules of a liquid solution.

'What's the situation concerning the syringe and spoon?' Wheeler asked when an officer found them in a drawer.

'They're mine,' Bennison said. 'I have a heroin habit.'

'I see you're also prescribed Valium tablets,' said Wheeler, inspecting a bottle of tablets. 'What are they for?'

'Nerves,' Bennison explained. 'I'm a nice person. I don't know what's wrong with me. I've had a nervous breakdown. I've got an appointment to see a psychiatrist.'

When Wheeler asked what she was seeing a psychiatrist for, she told him, 'Because I think there's something wrong with my head.'

'What makes you say that?' asked Wheeler gently. He was a quietly spoken man by nature, and he knew from experience that if he treated suspects with respect, they would often open up to him.

'I don't know. I mean, I'm a nice person, you know what I mean. I'm normally a nice person. Um ... it's just that something's wrong with my head. I don't know what.'

'What makes you think that you've got something wrong with your head?'

'Just the way I've been acting.'

'What have you been doing for the past few weeks?' Wheeler asked, knowing full well what the true answer should be.

'I've spent most of my time down at St Kilda doing a few jobs.'

'What sort of jobs?'

'I'm a prostitute.'

'How much money have you got during the past few weeks?'

'Just a couple of hundred dollars, that's all.' Bennison started to get upset. 'Look, I'm trying my hardest to give it up. I really am. I've got no support from my family at all.'

Then the woman they'd been searching for over the past month began to cry.

Peter Wheeler told her to calm down and to take a seat. 'There's no need to get upset,' he said soothingly. He then informed her she was under arrest for the possession of heroin. But Bennison had enough street smarts to know that five police officers don't come knocking for a single foil of heroin. She had to know the game was up.

The detectives drove their suspect back to the Russell Street police headquarters. On the way, she opened up a bit more. She talked about her hard life. Robertson had no sympathy. He'd had a hard life too and he'd turned out okay. To him, there were choices in life to be made regardless of where and what you came from. As far as he was concerned, nobody had held Robyn Bennison down and forced her to take drugs. She had chosen her path, and couldn't have cared less about anyone but herself. She had showed absolutely no regard for the men she had drugged. No matter what her story was or what excuses she gave, he thought that she could have at least called an ambulance anonymously after she was finished with her victims, yet she didn't do that.

Back at Russell Street, it was time to confront the woman who had in all likelihood drugged and robbed at least eight men and left them for dead.

Several times in the car on the way to police headquarters, Bennison had asked if they could stop at a shop and buy some Peter Jackson cigarettes – the same brand that had been found at most of the crime scenes. The detectives refused, but a police officer was sent out to get them for her once they had arrived. When she was settled in the interview room with her cigarettes, Wheeler warned her again that she was not obliged to say anything, but anything she said could be used in evidence.

'Do you realise why we have come to your room today?' Wheeler began the interview.

'No,' said Bennison, lighting a cigarette. She exhaled smoke, and the smell filled the small interview room.

'You think about it. Why do you think we came there today?' Wheeler prodded.

'I know. I want to tell you but I'm scared.'

'What are you scared about?'

'Just the whole thing. I'm glad you caught me, I really am.' Bennison again began to cry.

'There's no need to get upset,' said Wheeler quietly. 'All we want to know is what's been going on.'

'I'm a nice person really. I'm glad you caught up with me before I really hurt someone.'

'Well, what's been going on then?'

'You know what I've been doing,' she replied.

'Well, you tell me. I'd prefer you tell me in your own words what's been going on.' Wheeler knew that it was always better in court if the accused admitted to their crimes independent of any prompting by the interviewing officers.

Still tearful, Bennison finally confessed: 'I've been putting tablets in men's drinks and stealing their money.'

Wheeler asked the big question that had been plaguing detectives since the druggings began: 'What tablets have you been putting in the men's drinks?'

'Normison,' she told him.

'What's Normison?' asked Wheeler, none the wiser.

'They're sleeping tablets,' Bennison explained.

That mystery cleared up, Wheeler then moved the questions around to the actual victims. He knew from Bennison's demeanour that she would be reasonably candid in her responses. Her body language was open, and she almost seemed relieved to be getting it off her chest.

'Do you recall an incident at the Victoria Hotel recently?'

'Yes, which one do you mean – the old chap or the young one?'

'The elderly gentleman,' said Wheeler knowing that both Joseph and Andrew had stayed at the Victoria Hotel. 'What do you recall happening?'

'I met an elderly chap down in the foyer of the Victoria Hotel. He had been using the phones. He wanted to know where he could get an escort girl at that time of the night and I said if he liked, he could invite me up to his room. He then booked into the room and we both went up. We talked and I made him a cup of coffee.'

'What happened then?'

'After I made the coffee, I put two Normison tablets in the elderly chap's drink.'

'Why did you do that?'

'To make him go to sleep so I could take his money,' she replied without hesitation.

Bennison explained that the first two tablets hadn't worked so she had suggested a trip to the bottle shop for port and cigarettes. 'We went back to his room. I poured out two glasses of the port and when he wasn't looking, I put two more Normison tablets in his drink. A short time later, he was snoring his head off. I then took his money from his wallet and left the room.'

'What did you do with the money you took?'

'Used it to buy heroin and food.'

'Did you have permission from the elderly male to administer to him any drug or to take his money?'

'No.'

'Did you realise that what you were doing was wrong and that you were in fact stealing the money?'

'Yes.'

These questions were vital and were repeated after the recount of each of the victims. In court, Bennison might have claimed that the men gave her their money, or perhaps claimed that she was high on heroin and didn't know what she was doing.

Peter Wheeler then asked her, in turn, about the other seven victims. She confessed to drugging six of them and taking their money. Strangely, with regard to Andrew, she admitted stealing his money, but said that he was so drunk she didn't have to drug him. Wheeler knew that Andrew had spent days in hospital after his ordeal and suffered exactly the same symptoms as his fellow victims, so he doubted her recollection.

During a dinner break, Bennison ordered chicken and chips, and a police officer was dispatched to a local takeaway store. She ate alone in the interview room while detectives monitored her through the open door.

After dinner, Wheeler and Robertson asked her about each of the other victims. Bennison admitted to drugging and robbing all eight of them. At the end of the interview, Wheeler said, 'In relation to all of these matters, you are going to be charged with administering a drug to interfere with bodily functions, recklessly causing serious injury, theft, theft of a motor car, and possession of heroin. Is there anything you wish to say in relation to these charges?'

'I didn't want to hurt anyone. I want help for my heroin problem and I only did what I did to get money for drugs and food.'

The two detectives walked their quarry over the road from the Russell Street headquarters to the city watch house. Gathering media snapped shots of Bennison flanked by Wheeler and Robertson. She had placed a coat over her head.

The confession of a suspect is not the end of the story. Suspects have been known to retract their statements and plead not guilty in court. A smart defence lawyer can make it seem to the jury that the poor defendant was bullied into a confession, and without backup evidence, cases can be lost. As soon as Robyn Bennison was arrested, forensic evidence was necessary to make sure the case against her stood up in court.

Although many of the early victims had samples taken, tests had failed to identify the Normison that Bennison had used to drug her victims. The final victim, Phil, gave a urine sample, and a scientist at the Forensic Science Laboratory found the chemical temazepam, which was a benzodiazepine derivative used to induce sleep. Tests couldn't tell how much of the chemical Phil had ingested, but it was present nonetheless.

Meanwhile, alert detectives at the Richmond CIB couldn't help noticing the similarities between the Poison Ivy druggings and their unsolved housekeeper case from back in July. When Bennison was arrested, it was apparent that she also bore a strong resemblance to their identikit photo provided by the incumbent housekeeper. A fingerprint had been lifted at the scene, and now detectives from Richmond asked that their print be compared with Bennison's arrest set. Sergeant Peter Townsend, the fingerprint expert who had attended the housekeeper robbery seven months earlier, was given the set of Bennison's prints. He manually compared them with the prints he had lifted from the glass at the house. They were a match.

Sergeant Stuart Thompson from the Fingerprint Branch, who had examined the room of the first victim, Joseph, and lifted prints from the bottle of Penfolds Royal Reserve port and its paper bag, as well as a telephone information booklet from the hotel room, compared the prints he had with those of Robyn Bennison. Again, a match.

On 17 September, Janine, the hotel manager from the Great Southern Hotel where Albert had been drugged, checked back through the hotel register and found the name Robyn Bennison listed as a guest on the night of Albert's attack.

Bennison had been referred to their establishment by the Epistle Centre in Fitzroy, who sent her with a cheque for $18 to cover a night's accommodation. On the same day, the manager at the accommodation house where Arnold lived checked his register at the request of police. Bennison had booked in on 2 September for two weeks.

Although initially denied bail, Bennison was released from the remand centre so that she could participate in a detoxification program for her drug habit.

Over a year after her arrest for the Poison Ivy druggings, and facing additional charges relating to drugging the housekeeper and taking the money from the elderly vision-impaired man's wallet, she finally fronted court in December 1988.

After some pre-hearing wrangling, the charge of recklessly causing serious injury was dropped for the lesser charge of recklessly causing injury. Bennison pleaded guilty to all charges and was given a 30-month sentence with a minimum of 21 months to be served. She was out in fifteen months.

In 1992, Robyn Bennison was featured in a three-page article in *New Idea* under the bold headline 'Poison Ivy'. The article claimed that Bennison 'is determined to reveal, for the first time, the story of her broken life, her "possession" by Poison Ivy and her high hopes for future happiness'.

She explained to the journalist that she was now married to a man whom she met while she was vacuuming the corridors of Pentridge Prison. Her new husband was serving a life sentence for murder. But Bennison had found God as well as a husband in jail and declared herself to now be both drug-free and a high-church Anglican.

Describing a childhood marred by alcohol and violence, Bennison said she was raped by four men when she was thirteen years old, and at sixteen, she married a sailor who left her with their son while he travelled overseas with the navy. Detailing her post-natal depression after the birth of her second child, she remembered feeling lonely and unloved. She and her first husband agreed to separate, giving him custody of the children.

Bennison's next relationship produced a daughter, but left her 'on the verge of a breakdown'. Then came a second marriage, another child, and more severe post-natal depression. After a stay in a psychiatric ward, she was discharged, but she then became reliant on Valium and Serepax. Taking a night job as a waitress, Bennison fell in with the wrong crowd and had her first taste of heroin. She said that it made her 'feel relaxed and gave [her] the missing confidence'.

Within weeks of her first hit, Bennison was working as a sex worker to support her habit. And it wasn't long before she began her first stint in Fairlea women's prison. Back on the streets of

St Kilda, she claimed she was 'raped, bashed and robbed over and over again'. She said she tried to kill herself several times.

Describing her emergence as Poison Ivy, Bennison said that 'all the hurt I had suffered for years at the hands of men came out and combined with my drug addiction. I simply hated prostituting myself. Then one night, this man came along wanting sex with me and we went to a hotel room. I had sleeping tablets and I just slipped them into his cup of coffee, and robbed him when he dropped off to sleep. It was really a payback. I didn't want to hurt him, but I did feel all this hate and anger towards men. I became Poison Ivy.'

By the time of the interview in 1992, Robyn Bennison said she had a job in a plastics factory, and prayed every day. Of Poison Ivy, she said, 'Now she is dead. She can never come back.'

Detective Peter Wheeler cut out the article and added it to his bulging file on Robyn Bennison. It was ironic that five years later, in March 1997, she appeared in court charged with three counts of administering a substance to interfere with bodily functions, three counts of theft, as well as other charges. She was found guilty on all charges and given a three-year sentence with a non-parole period of fifteen months.

It seemed that Poison Ivy wasn't in fact dead, but merely sleeping – perhaps she had taken a couple of her own Normison tablets.

Chapter Two

THE CRIME SCENE EXAMINER

In 2006, Sergeant Trevor Evans had been in the police force for 27 years, and a crime scene examiner for the past seventeen of those. When he was 19 years old, Evans decided he wanted a career that offered different experiences every day. He'd tried working as a clerk, and some part-time study, but those weren't for him. As a teenager, he'd met a couple of cops and their work sounded interesting. Evans applied to become a police officer, and was accepted to train at the Victoria Police Academy.

On 7 November 1977, Trevor Evans arrived at the imposing police academy in Glen Waverley with his packed suitcase and his regulation short-back-and-sides haircut. In those days, many of the classes were run by senior constables who fashioned themselves after army drill sergeants. On the very first day, Evans recalls one such man standing in front of the new recruits screaming so loudly that his face glowed red and spittle flew from his mouth as he yelled. He finished his baptism of fire with a directive – they all had to go home and get their hair cut even shorter. It would be the last chance they would get to leave the academy during the week. Their 20 weeks of training was akin to being in prison with weekend leave.

That night at home, Evans's mum took one look at her son and knew that if she had told him he didn't have to go back to the academy, he wouldn't have. Luckily, she had the sense to keep her own counsel and her son returned the following day.

This old-style training for police recruits was raw and regimented. There was a definite pecking order, and the juniors did as they were told. Trevor Evans enjoyed his training but really didn't like the academy, and each Sunday, after a weekend's respite, he drove up Waverley Road, saw the huge imposing police academy looming on top of the hill, and shuddered inwardly.

Despite not enjoying the place, graduation happened soon enough. When the day of the ceremony rolled around, so did the dark thunder clouds, literally raining on their parade. Evans and his squad ended up graduating in the academy's beautiful chapel.

After graduation, Trevor Evans had a slow start in the real world of policing at Ringwood police station. There was much patrolling in the van, and lots of foot patrols through the Eastland Shopping Centre. After his three-month probation period was over, Evans was sent to the Information Bureau of Records (IBR).

In those days, information on criminals was stored on cards not unlike the old library cataloguing systems. When police officers rang through for information on someone, IBR personnel would locate the alphabetised drawer, pluck out the appropriate card and read out the information over the phone.

During the twelve-month secondment, Evans learnt the importance of writing as much information about people as you could for future reference – tattoos, distinguishing features, known associates – information that could prove vital for future investigations.

Next posting for the young recruit was at the Richmond police station. Here, Evans really started his policing education. The good Catholic boy from the eastern suburbs was about to learn that inner-city Richmond, with its clusters of monolithic housing commission towers, high unemployment and 37 pubs for its hard-drinking locals to choose from, would certainly provide him with an interesting work environment. Nothing in Richmond was mundane.

He remembers domestic violence as being particularly prevalent in the Richmond housing commission flats. Neighbours would call and report screaming matches from nearby flats, and Evans, then aged just 20, would find himself mediating between warring couples old enough to be his parents. As a young man, he found it hard to understand why a man would raise his fists to the woman he loved. He found it equally hard to understand the conditioning and coercion at play when women often said: *I love him. He only bashes me when he drinks.*

Trouble was, a lot of the husbands drank all the time.

Another thing the young constable learnt early on in Richmond was that you never park a police car near the housing commission high-rises. When he'd been there a while, he was driving a fellow officer to a domestic dispute at one of the towering buildings. His colleague had recently transferred to Richmond, and Evans told him about the parking rule. Another backup police car from a nearby policing district had arrived ahead of them. Those cops had already raced into the building, leaving their car parked too close to the towers. As Evans and his partner walked past the police car, pausing only to take in its smashed windscreen and fresh dents from bottles pelted from upstairs windows, Evans said laconically, 'That's why you never park near the buildings.'

The high-rise flats also came with their own sets of rules. If cops were called to a disturbance they would catch the lifts, which always smelled pungently of urine, to a floor above or below the floor they'd been called to – just in case the call was a set-up and people were waiting outside the lifts to jump the cops. And some of the Richmond youths started their apprenticeships early. Evans remembers being called regularly to the local primary school to disarm a nine-year-old boy who had a habit of coming to school armed with a knife.

As a uniformed constable, Trevor Evans didn't really come across any of the hardened criminals, although he was well aware of the presence of the notorious Pettingill family in the area. Mostly, the uniform cops were kept busy enough patrolling the streets and dealing with the local drunks and street offences like assaults, offensive behaviour and thefts. Richmond had a host of old drunks who were real characters. On a cold winter's night, they would parade into the Richmond police station and say, 'It's cold out tonight, sir.' Evans recalled this with a shrug. 'We'd give them a bed for the night. They were harmless. Mostly you'd lock them up for their own safety. If we didn't, they'd be staggering around the street.' His father had worked closely with the St Vincent de Paul Society, and helping people was a family trait.

After two years in Richmond, Evans, who was by now married with a baby, decided that a move to the country would be a refreshing change from the excitement of inner-city policing. He applied for a position in Camperdown – a small town halfway between Colac and Warrnambool. Camperdown was farming country where it was said that it rained for nine months of the year and dripped off the trees for the other three months.

Richmond cops had patrolled two-up so there was always someone to back you up; in Camperdown, police officers often rode solo, so you were on your own. Evans enjoyed the self-reliance. Country policing also meant that you were never really off duty. He remembers a time when he was driving home after visiting his wife in hospital after she had delivered their second child. On the way home, he saw a police colleague parked on the side of the road having trouble with a gang of youths. And so the new dad pulled over and helped his colleague with the arrests, then took them back to the police lock-up.

In the country, everyone knew everyone, and it was important to integrate into the community; Evans joined the local footy club, the local church and a couple of the services clubs. He stayed in Camperdown for four years and loved the community, but with a wife and two young children, he decided to try for a position closer to home and the support of his extended family.

During his policing years in Camperdown, Trevor Evans had come into contact with a couple of crime scene examiners. Having observed the work they did, he started to think about applying for a position himself. He was a keen amateur photographer and after spending seven years in general policing, he decided that he'd like to specialise, perhaps starting with crime scene photography. One particular case influenced the decision.

In Camperdown, Evans was called out when a car was reported stolen from a car yard. When it was finally located, he noticed a shoe impression on the rubber floor of the car, and carefully sketched its pattern in his notebook. When a suspect came to light shortly after, Evans asked the suspect to take off his shoes. The soles had the same patterns that he had sketched earlier. Being able to link evidence to an offender in this case was a defining moment in his decision to work crime scenes.

After a couple of applications to the sought-after positions at crime scene photographics, Evans was finally accepted in May 1988. The Victoria Police State Forensic Science Laboratory by then had moved to the large complex in Macleod, and training for the first three months involved buddying up with an experienced crime scene photographer and working alongside them. After that, he was on his own.

One of the first valuable lessons he learned was that you should never answer the phone at the scene of a homicide. While he was training, he and his photographic mentor attended a case where a woman had been murdered and lay dead on her bed with a Wiltshire knife sticking out of her neck. The phone rang and, without thinking, Evans picked it up.

'Who are you?' demanded a female voice.

'Er ... I'm from the police ...' Evans stammered, '... and who are you?'

'I'm her mother!' came the reply.

Not knowing even where to begin, Evans quickly handed the phone over to an experienced homicide detective to explain to the woman that her daughter had been murdered.

In those days, a crime scene photographer photographed a diverse range of things: collisions, stolen property, suspicious deaths, bank robbery scenes, and of course murder scenes. Photographers also spent time at the old city morgue and took photos of post-mortem examinations. The morgue is remembered fondly by few – Trevor Evans thought it had all the atmosphere of a B-grade horror movie. Luckily, he only had to work there a few times before the new state-of the-art complex opened in Kavanagh Street in Southbank.

In his work in photography, Evans soon got used to bodies in various states of damage and decay. He says bodies that aren't found for a while are the worst. Once an old lady had died in her home and had not been found until weeks after her death. The partially decomposed corpse was covered in maggots and the stench was overwhelming. Sights like these became part of the rich tapestry of crime scene examination.

In those days, at every murder or suspicious death, Forensics sent two crime scene examiners, one crime scene photographer, and two video operators. More recently, they only send one of each.

In the year and a half that he was a police photographer, Evans worked closely with crime scene examiners. He was a keen assistant and followed their directives on what to photograph at the scenes he attended until the work became intuitive. A crime scene examiner's role was to attend and make a search of the crime scene, then record the scene using notes, photographs and sketches, and finally to collect and record evidence in such a way that it can be used in court to give a picture of what may or may not have happened. Crime scene examiners were the central figures in the work done to process a murder scene – which also put them in the front line of every major crime committed in Victoria. Evans knew that one day, he would like to be in that position.

In September 1989, a vacancy came up for a crime scene examiner and Evans applied for and was accepted to the position.

The first homicide in which Evans acted as the main crime scene examiner took place in 1990. A woman of Asian background had found out her husband was having an affair with another woman. She went around to her rival's house armed with acid and a knife. When the other woman opened her front door, the wife had thrown the acid in her face and then stabbed her. By the time Evans arrived, the wife was in custody, the victim was dead and the house was a bloodbath.

One of the worst cases in terms of what Evans describes as 'sheer nastiness' was when he was called to a double murder at a massage parlour in a lovely old Victorian house in Fitzroy. The massage parlour had a number of bedrooms and three were set up with massage tables; the fourth bedroom was rented to a male Chinese student. In the living room, a deceased Filipino woman was slumped handcuffed on the couch. She had suffered so many stab wounds in her chest, it was difficult to count.

In the kitchen, the Chinese student lay face down on the floor, dead. He too had been handcuffed and unable to defend himself. Investigators were shocked to find that he'd been stabbed many times in his back – all along his spinal column, as if the killer had tried to sever his spinal cord in as many places as possible. When the body was rolled over, investigators saw that he had also been stabbed once in the abdomen. The perpetrators for this double homicide were never caught.

While some homicides are open and shut, some are not. The aspect Evans most enjoys about his job is searching for clues and being able to link physical evidence to an offender. And when an offender is caught, the evidence he collects can either challenge or corroborate their account.

In his seventeen years examining crime scenes, Evans has worked on some high-profile cases such as Jaidyn Leskie and Jane Thurgood-Dove.

In Moe, on the night of 14 June 1997, Greg Domaszewicz was minding the son of his girlfriend, Bilynda Murphy. Little Jaidyn Leskie was just thirteen and a half months old. In the early hours of the next morning, Jaidyn vanished, a severed pig's head was thrown at Domaszewicz's house, and a mystery began that would get much of Australia pontificating on the state of small-town poverty, unemployment and single mothers.

When Trevor Evans was called in to examine the crime scene, he, the photographer and two video operators met first at the Moe police station for a briefing. Domaszewicz had told police that he had gone to pick up Bilynda Murphy from a night out and left the sleeping baby home alone in the early hours of 15 June.

When the two had returned to Domaszewicz's house, the infant was gone.

Evans examined the pig's head that was lying outside a broken window at Domaszewicz's house in Moe. The crime scene examiner could see that the object had been thrown at least twice at the house. On the eave above the window was evidence of blood and pig's hair, where the head had obviously struck at least once before it was thrown again, this time at the window. Although the pig's head had smashed the window, it had bounced back and landed on the ground outside the house. Inside the house, there was no sign of the missing little boy. Evans did find some hair on the heater, and blood on tissues in the rubbish bin that would later be found to belong to Jaidyn. But that was about it.

When a child vanishes, it is always the collective hope of the community that perhaps some childless couple has taken him to bring him up as their own, showering him with love and joy. To entertain any less-positive thoughts is to invite the unspeakable. For months after his examination of the toddler's disappearance, Evans would sometimes wake in the middle of the night and wonder, *What did I miss?* But he knew that he and his colleagues had got everything they could get out of the crime scene. It just wasn't enough to indicate where the missing boy might be, or to definitively prove who was responsible for his disappearance.

Part of the mystery was solved on New Year's Day 1998, when Jaidyn Leskie's body was recovered from Blue Rock Dam, near Moe. Greg Domaszewicz was charged, tried, and found not guilty of Jaidyn's murder.

Five months after Jaidyn Leskie went missing from Moe, another case would capture intense public interest. On 6 November 1997, Jane Thurgood-Dove, a 35-year-old mother of three young children, was gunned down in the driveway of her home in Muriel Street, Niddrie. When crime scene examiners get called out to murder scenes, they never know how big a case will be – although they get pretty good at guessing. This case would end up being front-page news for weeks. When Evans stared down at the dead woman, a suburban mother, who had been shot three times in the head, he certainly knew that the case had the potential to attract a lot of public attention.

Here was a mother who had picked up her kids from school one afternoon, driven them home, pulled into her driveway and then been chased around her car by a pot-bellied gunman before tripping over and being shot dead in front of her children.

In Evans's experience, some homicides that happen in Victoria each year attract the media, but most don't. Crime scene examiners never let that fact get in the way of their work. By the time he arrived at the Thurgood-Dove murder scene, the children of course had been taken away, but the body still lay where it had fallen. The immediate site had been screened off from the eyes of the neighbours, and Muriel Street had been cordoned off. Residents had to be escorted in and out on foot by uniformed police.

Together with a video operator and a photographer, Evans and his colleagues examined the scene. Ballistics was also called in because Jane Thurgood-Dove had been shot. This was one of those crime scenes where there wasn't much to go on and there was little in the way of evidence to link this shooting to an offender. The shooter and an accomplice had driven a stolen Holden Commodore, which was found burnt out in nearby Farrell Street. They would have swapped the Commodore for a second getaway car after torching the first car in case it contained any evidence.

Evans spent many hours working on the burnt-out Commodore. The plastic mouldings on the dash had melted and collapsed onto the floor in the front of the car. One of his tasks was to extract anything that had been in this area that could have melted into the plastic. Incongruously, there was a large piece of floral fabric in the burnt wreck that Evans spent a lot of time trying to isolate. But despite the investigative hours, the fabric – like much of the other evidence – could never be connected to anything and the case remained unsolved. Two suspects emerged, but because both men have died since 1997, they can never be brought to justice.

Rumour has it that the Thurgood-Dove killing was a case of mistaken identity.

Evans cites one of the cases he worked on in September 1997 when he gives lectures to crime scene students. In some ways, the case was open and shut, but good crime scene work gives investigators the evidence to make charges stick in court. His involvement began when he was paged at 2 am on 16 September. He rang D24 to get the details and was told that they had a job in St Albans, and they'd just got a second job in Footscray. The choice was his. Evans chose the one in St Albans, in Melbourne's western suburbs. A body had been found in an empty house in Main Road West.

Before Evans left home, he organised a second on-call crew to attend the Footscray crime scene. Around 3.50 am, wearing blue overalls and carrying only a torch, Evans walked up the front path of the triple-fronted cream brick veneer suburban house. The garden looked neglected and overgrown, and the letterbox was crammed with unclaimed junk mail. The crime scene examiner met the investigating officers out the front and they briefed him on all the details they had to date.

During the briefing, Evans was told that an anonymous call had come through to the Keilor Downs police station at 12.01 am. The caller had said, 'Now listen to this; I'm only going to tell you this once. There's a body in the front room of a house in Main Road West in St Albans.' The police station at Keilor Downs had recently received some threatening phone calls and the station had installed a call tracing device. The police officer who took the call left the line open after the caller had disconnected. The call was quickly traced to a woman's mobile phone.

Shortly after the tip-off, police had gone to the address the caller had given and found what they thought to be a man's body in an empty lounge room, lying in front of a heater. The first police on the scene were uniform officers. Once they ascertained that the body was in fact deceased, they then left the scene so as not to contaminate any possible evidence. They called the local Criminal Investigation Unit detectives, who went to the house in Main Road West.

When the detectives confirmed the case looked like murder, they in turn notified the Divisional Detective Inspector, who then called in the Homicide Squad. Once the Homicide Squad was called, D24 paged all on-call crime scene members who were required – in this case, a video operator, a crime scene photographer, and Trevor Evans as the crime scene examiner.

Meanwhile, other police had gone straight to the home of the woman who was listed as owning the mobile phone used for the anonymous call. She told the police that she had lent the phone to her brother, Theo. The police took down Theo's address and paid him a visit. Shocked to find the cops on his doorstep so soon after his anonymous tip-off, he quickly began to 'assist police with their inquiries'.

At the house in Main Road West, the first police on the scene had also notified the SEC and instructed them to reconnect the power to the empty house. A technician arrived and duly did this. Having the lights on in the house made it easier for the investigators to see what they were dealing with.

Evans took charge of the crime scene. The uniformed sergeant indicated where the body was and told him where he had walked when he'd entered the house. It was vital that Evans knew who had been inside the house so that he could tell what evidence could be attributed to the homicide and what evidence might have been generated by the police themselves. It was crucial that the least amount of people possible enter a crime scene for fear of contamination.

The sergeant went back outside and left Evans to do his job. He began with a visual examination. In the lounge room at the front of the house, he could see the body lying in front of a gas heater set into a fireplace with a tiled hearth. The body lay parallel to the hearth. Contrary to what Evans had been told about the body being male, he could see, on closer examination, that it was a woman's body. She had suffered massive head injuries and the dried blood on her face almost made her look like a burn victim. Evans could see that the woman's throat had been cut and she had been stabbed a number of times in the throat and chest. A pool of blood next to her head indicated to Evans that the woman had received the head injuries while she had been lying on her side. After these injuries had been inflicted, she had been rolled onto her back, leaving a pool of congealed blood adjacent to where her head was now positioned.

The woman was wearing a blue tracksuit and a white T-shirt. A pair of white socks lay on the blood-splattered hearth. At her feet were a jacket, a pair of boots and a toilet roll. Her feet were bare, and the boots and jacket probably belonged to her. Evans noted that the boots were Blundstones. In the event that he discovered any shoe impressions, he would know which ones were hers.

Evans studied the blood splash patterns on the wall and on the tiled hearth adjacent to the body. He knew from experience that splash patterns only occur with repeated injuries. It made sense that this woman must have been hit several times to bleed enough for the weapon to then spray the blood on subsequent strikes, making the pattern he could see on the wall. To the untrained eye, splash patterns don't mean much, but the expert knows that the tail patterns of the splash droplets always point away from the point of the blows. To Evans, the tails also indicated that she was hit in the vicinity of where she lay.

On the dusty polished boards of the dining room floor of the empty house were a number of distinct shoe impressions. Lucky for this job, Evans was in charge of the shoe file database at Forensics and he had a very good knowledge of shoe impressions. There were Doc Martens shoe impressions in blood on the hearth, which meant that the Doc Martens wearer was involved or very close by when the woman was bludgeoned to death. Not only that, but there were a full set of right/left, right/left bloodied shoe impressions showing the exact path the Doc Martens wearer had walked away from the room where the body lay.

After his visual examination of the surroundings where the body had been found, Evans went outside and told the investigators that the victim was in fact a female, and that she had sustained severe trauma to the head. He told them that her throat had been cut and she had been stabbed in the throat and chest. The police photographer and the video operator recorded the scene as it was found. Evans was able to tell the investigators that three people had recently walked in the vicinity of where the body lay. One was wearing Blundstones – probably the victim, since the Blundstones were found near her body. The other shoe impressions belonged to someone wearing a pair of Doc Martens boots, and someone wearing Converse skate star runners.

Evans retrieved his crime scene kit from his car and began the formal examination. The kit contained a myriad of tools that could be needed on a job: swab sticks, casting materials, plastic bags, labels, tweezers, scalpels, Hemastix for presumptive blood tests, a torch, gloves, rulers, scales, distilled water, a tool kit, a magnifying glass, scissors and writing materials. He wrote his notes and sketched his diagrams on a foolscap pad fixed onto a clipboard.

On the floor near the dead woman's head was a small piece of mortar that looked out of place. Evans instructed the photographer to take a picture of it, and then he collected it as evidence. There were also a number of cigarette butts in the house, and Evans had these photographed and then collected them for evidence. Because a smoker leaves saliva residue on a cigarette butt, these would later be examined for DNA that could potentially be matched to an offender.

By the time he began his examination of the wider scene, both inside and outside the house, the sun was coming up, turning the sky a pale shade of pink. Around the back of the house, he saw a table underneath a rear window. There were several shoe impressions on the table and a partial one on the windowsill.

Evans used powder to dust the shoe impressions; it was obvious to the trained eye that one set of shoe impressions had been made when the shoes were wet because of indications of moisture and residue in the impression, while another set was made when the shoes were dry.

The difference between the two types of impressions was quite marked. A print made on a dusty table with a dry shoe simply picks up the dust and leaves a negative impression. A shoe that has moisture on it leaves the moisture residue behind and leaves a positive impression. When dusted, the shoe impressions with moisture show up much darker than the ones left by a dry shoe.

As well as the shoe impression evidence, Evans found something else that could prove important. At the side of the house, on a concrete path, there was a row of square concrete bricks. One of the bricks was missing and had recently been removed from where it had lain, leaving the concrete underneath looking cleaner and less discoloured.

Considering the piece of mortar that Evans had found next to the body inside the house, he thought there was a reasonable possibility that the missing concrete brick could have been the weapon used to repeatedly smash the victim's head.

Evans sketched the lined pattern of the Doc Martens shoe impression and gave the sketch to local detectives. Other uniformed police had been used to make a search of the local area, and they were all given copies of the sketch. During the course of the day, Evans left the crime scene examination at the house in Main Road West, when he was called to a park in St Albans. An astute police officer involved in the foot search of the local area had noticed Doc Martens shoe impressions leading into and out of the park.

A shallow concrete drain that marked the end of Jones Creek ran through the park and disappeared under a nearby road. Police searchers had located a burnt backpack-type handbag on the muddy bottom of the drain. They fished it out and left it on the bank. It was Evans's job to examine the bag to see if it was connected to the murder. While he examined the handbag where it lay on the ground, he noticed a concrete brick in the creek. It looked similar to the ones at the house. It was too much of a coincidence for the seasoned crime scene examiner. He had the brick photographed and then retrieved it from the creek. His hunch proved correct; a biologist would later find blood, hair and material fibres on the brick matching the victim.

According to identification found in the backpack handbag, the victim was a 20-year-old woman called Corie. It turned out that she was a local drug addict and was known to police. She stole to support her drug habit and stayed wherever she could find a bed for the night.

By this time, the anonymous caller, Theo, had told the police that he had gone to the local pub for a drink when he'd met up with a man called Joseph Defalco, aged 30, and his eighteen-year-old girlfriend, Pamela. According to Theo, the conversation, over several beers, went something like this:

> *Defalco: Hey, you know Corie, the druggie?*
> *Theo: Yeah.*
> *Defalco: Well, we killed her.*
> *Theo: Bullshit!*
> *Defalco: Come on, we'll show you.*
> *Theo: Orright.*

And that's how Theo – who had the sense not to go alone, and picked up his brother Con on the way, came to be at the house in Main Road West. When they got there, Defalco had jumped up onto the table at the back of the house in order to climb through the window. Once he was inside, he had unlocked the door for his girlfriend, Con and Theo to enter. Theo told the investigators that he and Con hadn't wanted to get too close to the body and that Defalco had gone right up to it and illuminated her face with his cigarette lighter while they had stayed as far back as they could.

And the motive? Apparently Defalco thought that Corie had broken into his parents' house a year before the murder. A ring of sentimental value had been stolen in the burglary. Defalco had given Corie's name to the police as a suspect and they had interviewed her, but she denied stealing the ring. Joseph Defalco didn't believe her.

On the night of the murder, Defalco and his girlfriend Pamela had met Corie at the St Albans railway station and they had again argued about the ring. Then, Defalco told Corie about an abandoned house that he sometimes used and invited her over. Corie was perhaps persuaded with the promise of somewhere undercover to spend the night. At the house on Main Road West, the three unlikely companions drank a cask of wine, and Corie soon fell asleep on the floor in front of the hearth.

It was then that Joseph Defalco told Pamela that he was going to kill Corie. He got a brick from outside and dropped it onto her head a number of times, crushing her skull. When he was done, he could hear her making gurgling sounds, so he rolled her over and slashed her throat with a knife. Mistaking the sound of air escaping through her severed trachea for breathing, Defalco thought she must still be alive, so he stabbed her in the chest and neck.

All the evidence that Trevor Evans found at the crime scene corroborated the stories of those involved. The brick taken from the scene, found in the creek with blood, hair and fibres matching the body, the shoe impressions that were later matched with Joseph Defalco's Doc Martens boots, and some of the cigarette butts found in the house with Defalco's DNA on them. Blood from the victim was also found in the ridges of the soles of his boots. Pamela's Converse skate star runners matched the other shoe impressions found at the house. Defalco was charged with murder and got seventeen years with a fourteen-year minimum. Pamela was charged with being an accessory after the fact and served fifteen months in remand, eventually released with time already served. She gave evidence against Defalco.

An increasingly important aspect of crime scene examination is Disaster Victim Identification (DVI). Wherever there are two or more bodies whose identities might be difficult to ascertain – like in an air crash, bombing, or widespread disaster like the Boxing Day tsunami – DVI-trained officers are called in to manage the situation. It is a vital legal requirement that bodies are identified, and it is a vital emotional requirement that relatives are able to bury their loved ones. In a disaster like the World Trade Center terrorist attack in New York on 11 September 2001, many of the victims were never found and their remains were lost when the north and south towers collapsed after they were struck by hijacked planes. In cases like this, sometimes families do not get a body to bury.

DVI training involves police officers being put in simulated scenarios that might befall a modern society: gas attacks, terrorist situations, large-scale collisions, and bombings. DVI units comprise crime scene investigators, photographers, missing persons experts, fingerprint experts, medical and dental experts, victim support groups, and sometimes other personnel like the SES, the Red Cross or the Salvation Army. These DVI teams work together, arriving at a disaster scene with the bodies, where possible, having been left in situ (meaning in the place in which they had been found) so that they can be photographed, tagged and recorded before being transported to the mortuary. Any property located at the scene is also labelled and its location recorded.

At the mortuary, bodies are logged and placed in cold storage before being examined. Fingerprints and photographs are taken. Dental records are recorded, post-mortem examinations are performed, and any personal effects on the bodies like clothing and jewellery are photographed and logged. While this phase of the DVI process is happening, relatives ring hotlines that are quickly set up and they give details of their loved ones in the form of missing persons reports. Relatives are asked to provide information about identifying details such as tattoos, jewellery, clothing and dental records, medical histories, X-rays, photographs and a DNA sample, which can be obtained from hair from a hairbrush that the deceased has used, or from relatives. This is known as the ante-mortem phase.

The next phase in the process is known as reconciliation, where the post-mortem details are matched with the ante-mortem information provided by the relatives. Problems with positive identification arise when, like in the 2004 Boxing Day tsunami, whole extended families and their homes were wiped out. There were often no loved ones left to report people missing, and no homes in which to find medical records or even photographs.

On 12 October 2002, an explosives-packed van detonated outside the Sari nightclub at the Balinese beachside resort of Kuta, killing 202 people, including 88 Australians. Within days, a joint Indonesian–Australian taskforce was established, and Australian personnel were sent to Bali to assist in the investigation and body identification.

Trevor Evans was keen to use his training to assist on such a large-scale disaster and volunteered to be a part of the DVI team. He described the experience as 'the most surreal ten days of my life'.

When Evans and a team of DVI experts travelled by bus to the bomb site, suddenly the images he had seen on the TV became real – the damage, the devastation, the wreaths and public appeals for missing loved ones were all right in front of him. At the hospital, the scene was the same. Makeshift coffins, grief-stricken relatives and armed guards made the situation very real indeed.

As a crime scene examiner, Evans, along with other Australian experts, had the responsibility of body identification. Each bombing victim was examined, and their friends and relatives were asked to provide details of anything that might assist in identification. Experts then examined the remains, and their findings were matched with information from relatives. The two lots of evidence were then compared and matches found. Evans worked in the reconciliation stage. He was part of the team that matched victims with information and then presented the information to a coroner. This was done at chaired hearings when the experts presented evidence to give the anonymous remains a name.

What made the time in Bali more stressful was that the crime scene examiners worked under constant armed guard; they had been told that a further attack on Westerners was a strong possibility.

While the crews were working to identify the remains of the 202 people killed during the bombings, they didn't have time to rest and reflect on what they were seeing and experiencing. One moment stands out in Evans's mind. He was standing among a sea of bodies, laid out and covered in plastic. A wall of plywood had been erected to shield the scene from the public. On the wall, someone had drawn a rough outline of a map of Australia. Inside the map, they had written, 'There's no place like home'. Seeing the map made Evans stop in his tracks. Home for him was a place of safety: a refuge from the madness that had been unleashed the moment the bomb detonated.

By the time Evans finished his ten-day tour of duty, the count of bodies positively identified by the DVI team working in conjunction with the Indonesians had risen from 36 when he arrived to 88 when he left. Fifty-two more families had been given the remains of loved ones to bury.

When Evans arrived home in Australia, he got off the plane in Melbourne and caught a taxi to the Victoria Forensic Science Centre to collect his car. At work, he checked the roster. At the time, his division was short on crime scene examiners, and he was rostered on for the following day. Having worked twelve days straight before he left for Bali, and the ten days there, Evans had worked 22 days in a row. He was beyond exhaustion and told his colleagues he wouldn't be in the next day.

In 2004, Sergeant Trevor Evans and Acting Sergeant Shaune Ward were made responsible for the curriculum at the four-week training program at Project Clarendon at the Victoria Police Academy. Evans and Ward trained recruits in an innovative program that set up divisions called Crime Desks at major police stations around Victoria.

The program aimed to send trained crime scene officers to every house break-in and car theft in the state. During the four-week course, Evans taught trainees crime scene techniques including how to take crime scene photographs, how to search a crime scene, and how to take comprehensive notes. Fingerprint expert Shaune Ward instructed students on fingerprinting techniques including the theories of fingerprints, and how to identify and lift them from crime scenes.

The impetus for the need for this new service came from changing patterns in crime deterrence. Where once armed robberies on banks were common, the advent of security measures like surveillance cameras and pop-up screens sealing the robbers on the wrong side of the counters meant that robbers then chose softer targets like convenience stores. When the convenience stores upped their security with timed safes and cameras, homes became the next target of choice. Governments had recognised this change in burglary patterns, and legislation changed to accommodate this. The term 'aggravated burglary' had been previously used to describe violent attacks on people in their homes perpetrated by burglars. This was changed to describe a burglary where the occupant was at home when it happened, whether injured or not. Victoria Police set up Project Clarendon for the purpose of training uniformed police officers to become proficient in lifting fingerprints and collecting evidence.

Before Crime Desks were implemented, the Fingerprint Branch was called to attend only 23 per cent of burglaries. Now, crime scene officers attend all such crimes and any prints lifted are sent to the Fingerprint Branch for examination.

The public's fascination with television programs like *CSI* means that the public also has a higher expectation of police who attend their own house break-ins.

'People expect to see examiners arriving with crime scene kits,' said Ward. 'They get that from TV.' And the reality is that when the crime scene officer in his or her examiner's uniform arrives at the door with a kit filled with powders and brushes and an impressively large digital camera, victims know their burglary is being taken seriously. On a practical level, because the response is usually on the same day, victims are then able to get their doors or windows fixed and clean up the mess – rather than waiting days for fingerprint experts or detectives to arrive. This minimises victim impact and maximises customer service.

To give their trainees realistic experience, Evans and Ward set up practice sessions in the Operational Safety Tactics Training village (OSTT village). It cost over $8 million to build the mock suburban street complete with pub, petrol station, bank, and houses of various sizes. Trainees from different courses run at the academy can use the OSTT village to simulate raids, sieges, and almost any policing situation. Evans uses the village to show his students how to make the most of light when taking photographs at dusk, and Ward uses the mock pub to set up the simulated aftermath of a pub brawl. He uses pig's blood from a vial to drip onto the floor, and pours out pieces of broken beer bottle from a brown paper bag. As the trainees come into his 'crime scene' he tells them that in a situation like this, they are collecting evidence merely of an assault at the pub, but, he explains, if the victim dies, their evidence could be presented at the Supreme Court at a murder trial. It's a sobering thought.

These days, the question most frequently asked of a crime scene examiner is: 'Is it like *CSI* on TV?' The answer is a definite and resounding no. Indeed, crime scene examiners tend to avoid watching TV shows that deal with their line of work because the errors are too annoying. Flashy, good-looking crime scene photographers snap pictures of crime scenes without ever placing a scale or ruler next to items like shoe impressions – which would in fact render the picture useless in court. They never take notes to indicate which picture was taken where – again, a big no-no.

On TV, crime scene examiners like Gil Grissom on *CSI* run the investigation and catch the bad guys. In reality, crime scene examiners gather the evidence and present it to the investigating detectives who catch the bad guys.

Another favourite of crime scene shows is the chemical luminal, which is a spray that can indicate the presence of blood. A room must be completely dark to detect the bluish glow that results when the luminol mixes with the iron in haemoglobin. TV crime scene examiners regularly spray luminol in dimly lit rooms or even in daylight. In reality, luminol, which has the potential to contaminate or destroy existing evidence, is only used after other tests have been completed, and only in complete darkness.

Time of death cannot accurately be predicted to the minute; the margin of error can range from hours to days. Factors include body temperature prior to death, ambient temperature of the surroundings where the body was found, levels of alcohol in the bloodstream and obesity. On TV, medical examiners are usually very specific and pinpoint times of death to within very narrow margins.

Forensics does not have a computer that superimposes suspect shoe impressions over known patterns and then matches them. It is also very difficult to give an accurate assessment of a shoe size. Computers also do not read a fingerprint and spit out a match. When an expert feeds a print into a fingerprint database, the computer will return up to a hundred matches and then the fingerprint expert examines the first matches manually until he finds eight points of similarity between his print and the ones the computer has matched. Two other experts must then agree to his findings before a fingerprint is deemed to be a correct match. On television, the computer usually matches a print in seconds, and then, helpfully, it usually provides a name, address, and photo of the suspect or victim.

On *CSI*, they can turn blurred and pixilated images into sharp, clear images by zeroing in on a part of the picture. The more a TV image is blown up, the clearer it becomes. In reality, the more you zero in on an image, the more pixelated it looks.

DNA evidence on TV is the doyen of the investigators' tools. In real life, DNA evidence is not processed in minutes and can only be matched to a suspect if their DNA is on file or available for comparison.

And finally, TV murders are solved in hour-long programs because crime scene examiners and detectives use state-of-the-art – often fictional – tools to catch their killers. The reality is that some cases can take years to solve and others can remain on file with the Cold Case Squad indefinitely.

Trevor Evans has come full circle from the young recruit who disliked the imposing Victoria Police Academy in 1977. Now, he enjoys his role as crime scene instructor at the academy, and has branched out to lecture at Swinburne and LaTrobe universities and does the occasional lecture for budding crime writers at the Council for Adult Education. Evans knows that the future of crime scene examination continues to develop with technological advances, meaning it will become easier to link offenders with their crimes.

An old saying among crime scene examiners is that forensic evidence is the 'silent witness'. As long as Trevor Evans and his colleagues maintain their commitment to its gathering and analysis, they will continue to make the silent witness speak.

Chapter Three

✦

WHERE IS
PAUL SNABEL?

About halfway between Melbourne and Sale lies the small
town of Mirboo North. It is south of the town of Moe, which
became infamous in 1997 with the disappearance of toddler Jaidyn
Leskie. But eight years before the Leskie case hit the headlines,
the area hosted a different kind of tragedy. It was from here that
28-year-old Paul Joseph Snabel suddenly vanished.

Around 9 pm on Saturday 18 November 1989, Detective Senior
Constable Michael Grunwald was on call at the Morwell Criminal
Investigation Branch and was informed that Moe resident Paul
Snabel had been reported missing by his housemate Paul Friend.
No-one had seen Paul since Sunday 5 November.

Early on Sunday morning, Detective Michael Grunwald paid a
visit to a 26-year-old woman called Karen Randall. Police had been
told that the missing Paul Snabel and Karen Randall had been in
a relationship that had turned violent. In April, Paul had pleaded
guilty in the Moe Magistrates' Court to assaulting Karen. Grunwald
wanted to see if Karen could shed any light on Paul's disappearance.
He also rang Karen's sister, Donna, to see if she could help. Later,
the detective met up with both sisters at a house in Mirboo North
belonging to a friend of theirs, Rhona Heaney.

According to Karen and Donna, Paul had been at a party at
Donna's on the night of Saturday 4 November. Both women had
seen him on the Sunday at Rhona Heaney's house, where Karen
had been staying. Paul had left on his red and white Yamaha

motorbike around 5 pm. The Randall sisters said that they had no idea where he could be.

Early police inquiries could not find anyone who had seen Paul Snabel after he left Rhona Heaney's house. Local detectives organised a search of surrounding areas in case Paul had had an accident on his motorbike or had met with foul play of some kind. Within days, Paul's disappearance had become local news and a lot of people were keeping an eye out for the missing man and his red and white Yamaha motorbike. If Paul had in fact come off his motorbike, he could be lying in a ditch somewhere. Searches of the area by the police helicopter failed to find any trace of him.

Michael Grunwald also made inquiries at the local railway stations to see if anyone matching Paul's description might have caught a train out of town. The inquiries led nowhere.

On Wednesday 22 November, Detective Grunwald went to visit a teenager called Peter who had reported finding some motorcycle parts at the local Boolarra tip. Peter had made several trips to the tip looking for parts and among other things, he had found a motorcycle windshield, a rear wheel mudflap and mudguard, a black plastic chain cover, a set of rear indicator lamps on a bracket, a white plastic oil tank, a rear tail-light unit, a black plastic grill, a front headlight, a disc brake, left- and right-hand foot rests, a front brake lever, wiring, a rear wheel and tyre, and a sprocket and chain cover.

Grunwald went with Peter to the tip and the teenager showed the detective where he had found all the parts. Grunwald had a look around and then helped organise a line search of the surrounding area, which located more of what appeared to be parts of a dismantled motorbike similar to the one belonging to Paul.

Some of the wiring was found in plastic bags marked with 'SEC' from the State Electricity Commission. The wiring had been removed from the motorbike and tied neatly in left-handed knots.

When it began to look like something untoward had happened to Paul, Detective Sergeant Shane Downie was called in to assist

Michael Grunwald. Downie had worked at the local District Support Group (DSG), which dealt mainly with drug-related crimes. Prior to that, he had spent six years as a detective at the Morwell CIB and had experience working on cases from armed robbery to murder.

Downie organised a coordinated search of a number of tips in the local area and released information to the media about the missing motorbike, appealing for members of the public to come forward if they had recently found any bike parts.

In response to the public appeal, Michael Grunwald spoke to a man who had also found some motorbike parts at the tip. He handed over to the detective a mudguard and some red and white fairing marked with 'RZ250'. Most importantly, the man said he had found the pieces of motorbike on Monday 6 November – the day after Paul had last been seen.

The following day, another man contacted police and handed over a motorbike seat that had been found by his thirteen-year-old son while he was treasure-hunting at the local tip. A fourth man volunteered that he'd found a red and white–coloured motorcycle fuel tank. The police took it with them and, bit by bit, the red and white Yamaha was coming together.

Back at the CIB offices, detectives rang Paul's housemate, Paul Friend, who had initially reported him missing. Friend came to the CIB offices and the detectives showed him the motorbike parts that they had located so far. He recognised one of the parts from the bike because it had the same scratch on it that he'd remembered from Paul's motorbike. He also recognised one of the levers; it was brand new and he had bought it himself for the bike.

Detective Sergeant Downie asked a local motor mechanic called Glenn to come to the CIB office. Glenn had worked on Paul's motorbike and replaced parts when they needed replacing. A month earlier, Paul had ordered a sprocket set and an accelerator cable. Glenn had also fitted a Perrelli MT 28 Phantom front tyre. Glenn could say with certainty that the tyre now in the CIB office was the same brand he had fitted to Paul's motorbike. More importantly, Downie gleaned from Glenn that Paul loved his motorbike. What possible reason – even if Paul had wanted to disappear voluntarily – would he have for dismantling his motorbike and scattering it around local tips?

A little after 4 pm on Thursday 23 November, detectives Downie and Grunwald, together with two of their colleagues and some uniformed police, drove out to Rhona Heaney's house in Mirboo North. Downie had organised a search warrant, figuring that if this was the last place that Paul had been seen, it was the first place to start looking for him. Rhona wasn't home when the police arrived, but shortly after, she drove into her driveway with a number of children in the car and a male friend.

Rhona Heaney spoke to one of the detectives. She told him that on 5 November, Paul had been at her house with both Donna and Karen Randall. Karen and her six-year-old son had been living at Rhona's Nicholls Road house but were in the process of packing and moving into her new Housing Commission house that day.

Rhona, who was helping Karen pack, explained that 22-year-old Donna wasn't much help because she had recently moved in to a new house in Moe, and had had a house-warming party the night before. She had a bad hangover. Paul had been at her party. Rhona told the police officers that Paul had been drinking all that Sunday and wanted to party on. She said that when no-one wanted to join him, he had left on his motorbike.

After an hour and a half of searching her house, police failed to find anything of evidentiary value. Leaving Rhona Heaney's house empty-handed made Detective Shane Downie wonder what to do next. The leads were drying up. It was time to call in the Homicide Squad.

Three detectives arrived the following day from the Homicide Squad in Melbourne. Detective Senior Constable Peter Wheeler was working with a senior sergeant and a detective from another crew because his regular crew was on leave. The three Homicide detectives went with some local cops to the Boolarra tip and had a look around. After that, Michael Grunwald took the three detectives to visit Karen Randall at her house in Mirboo North. Karen's sister, Donna, was there too.

The detectives asked Karen for a statement of her account of the disappearance of Paul Snabel. Karen said she had known Paul for five or six years but they had become close about eighteen months earlier and for a while she had lived with him, but they had broken up when he assaulted her and she had him charged.

Karen said she had last seen Paul when he and Donna had woken her up at Rhona Heaney's house early on the morning of Sunday 5 November. They had all had coffee in the kitchen and Karen noticed that Paul had been 'speeding' – he had a way of grinding his jaw when he had taken speed and he was doing that at Rhona's house. A couple of hours later, Paul said he was going to drive home and swap his car for his motorbike and then come back later. Karen said that while he was gone, she, Rhona and Donna continued to pack up her things in preparation for her move into her new house.

Paul had come back later on his bike and asked Rhona to go and get him a bottle of whisky. He had given her $50. While Karen needed to pack, Paul had wanted to party. Finally, Karen said she had told him that if he didn't want to help with the packing, he could leave. Around 5 pm, Paul had ridden off on his motorbike after drinking a bottle of whisky. She had been concerned at the time about how much he had drunk. She could hear his bike being accelerated hard up Nicholls Road.

Karen said that she hadn't seen or heard from Paul since he left Rhona Heaney's house that day.

Back at the Morwell CIB offices, the detectives discussed the case. At this stage, it could be a voluntary disappearance, or something more sinister, but the dismantled motorbike scattered around various locations certainly suggested something was amiss. More parts had surfaced at another local tip. Someone had obviously gone to a lot of trouble to take the bike apart and scatter its parts. The question was, why?

On Friday 24 November, Homicide detective Peter Wheeler took a statement from Donna Randall. Donna said she regarded Paul as a good friend who she would see around once a week.

'Paul was going out with my sister, Karen Randall,' she said in her statement. 'Approximately four months ago, Paul and my sister broke up. I think this break was instigated by my sister because recently Paul had been getting a bit rough with her. Karen actually had him charged with assault on her, but I can't remember when this was. The break-up between them hasn't resulted in any problems or hassles as far as I know,' said Donna.

'The last time that I saw Paul was on Sunday 5 November 1989 at Rhona Heaney's place in Nicholls Road, Mirboo North. On the previous night, Saturday 4 November, I had a party at my house.'

Donna said that Karen hadn't come to her house-warming party, but that she had called while the party was on and had spoken to Paul on the phone. After the phone call, Paul had asked Donna if she had wanted to leave the party and go to Rhona Heaney's house where Karen was. Donna said she had put off leaving her house while there were so many guests still there.

It wasn't until around 5 am, according to Donna, that she and Paul had finally left to go to Mirboo North. Donna said that she had driven him in his car. According to Donna, the two had woken Rhona up when they arrived and then Karen had joined them in the kitchen drinking cups of coffee. Donna said that she lay down and slept on the couch.

After Donna had slept off some of the effects from the previous night's party, she woke up and joined Rhona, Karen and Paul in the kitchen again. She said that she wasn't sure what time Paul had left but when he went, he promised to come back later.

Paul had come back on his red and white Yamaha motorbike around lunchtime and Donna said that he was still a bit drunk and delirious from not having slept the night before. She said that she spent much of the day dozing on the couch. At one point, she had woken up and seen Paul drinking from a bottle of Johnnie Walker Black Label whisky.

'While myself, Rhona and Karen were packing, Paul kept on saying, "Come on, let's party", and wanted us to have a drink with him. Karen ended up saying to him that if he wasn't going to help that he'd better leave. He just said, "All right then, no worries, see you later". He put his helmet on, went and started his motorcycle and left ... that was the last time I saw him. He didn't appear too upset when he left. He probably was a bit irritated about what Karen said to him but appeared all right.' The time, according to Donna, that Paul left Rhona's house was around 4.15 pm. 'That was the last time I saw him.'

Donna concluded her statement to police by adding that when Paul had arrived at her party the night before he disappeared, he had told her that he had been taking speed. She said that she had known that Paul had been using speed for about three or four months. She also said that he was a regular marijuana user.

Talking down at the local pub after taking statements from Rhona Heaney and the Randall sisters, detectives Peter Wheeler and Shane Downie agreed that it looked like something had happened to Paul Snabel. Wheeler found it suspicious that the statements from Donna, Karen and Rhona were all so similar. Usually statements, unless they had been rehearsed, emphasised different things even when people were talking about the same event. There was something not quite right about the accounts of the three women who were the last people to see Paul. Downie agreed and the two detectives talked strategy. The Homicide detectives would have to return to Melbourne in the absence of any hard evidence that a murder had taken place. Wheeler told Downie to keep digging.

On the same day that Peter Wheeler spoke to Donna Randall, another detective took a statement from Paul Friend, who shared a house with Paul. Friend said that he had known Paul for about six years and had lived with him for the past six months. Friend detailed the relationship between Paul Snabel and Karen Randall as he saw it.

'For the past two and a half years, Paul has had an on-and-off relationship with a girl I know as Karen Randall. I suppose I could describe their relationship as stormy. Karen sometimes would want to piss off Paul and then she would want him back. This sort of pissed me off recently. Whenever I would come home, Paul would be on the phone to Karen and would be arguing with her over something. When he'd hang up, he would come into my room and say things like, "Fuckin' bitch" and would carry on about her, but I guess he was just as bad because he would get back on the phone to her and it would start over again. I don't know how many times I told him it wasn't worth it but he kept on trying with her.'

Friend went on to describe how in the past couple of months, Paul had lost a lot of weight.

'A while ago, I saw Paul use some speed. By speed, I mean amphetamine. When I saw him use it, he snorted it. I've seen him snort it and I think he also put it in a drink and took it that way. I have a fair idea that he used to use it fairly regularly. When he started to lose all that weight, I put that down, subconsciously I suppose, to him using speed. When he took speed, it changed his moods. It was like he became schizophrenic. If something annoyed him ... he would get an aggressive tone about him. Normally he's a very placid and bouncy sort of bloke that makes friends easily. He had heaps of friends around and a lot of people knew him.

'Generally people knew him by his nickname "Rat" but he was well liked. He never did anyone any harm – apart from him and Karen and their situation, but he'd never harm anybody.'

Friend speculated on Paul's disappearance. He said that Paul was a happy person and apart from his fights with Karen, he was generally in a good mood. 'I don't think he was a suicidal type, although you never know, I suppose.'

According to Paul Friend, a couple of months earlier, something strange had occurred at their house. Friend said that he had seen the barrel of a gun sticking out from under the coffee table. He had asked his housemate why they had a gun in their house. Paul had replied that there were some guys after him. He hadn't said who they were and at the time, Paul Friend thought that Paul was fantasising. He had even joked to Paul later that perhaps the Mafia were coming after him. Paul had gotten rid of the gun soon after and the subject was never raised again between the two men.

The last time Friend had seen Paul was on Saturday 4 November. They had watched *Hey, Hey it's Saturday* on the television and then Paul had gone out with some friends. They had met up in the small hours of the morning at Donna Randall's house-warming party. Friend admitted being quite drunk at the party and didn't remember talking to Paul. The next day, Friend had gone out with mates and then stayed at his girlfriend's house. He didn't go home until Tuesday and by that time Paul had vanished.

'I remember Paul's work rang for him and said that he hadn't turned up. I started to ring around to see where he was, but no-one knew. Paul's mum rang on the Friday and I thought that I'd let it ride through to the following Monday because I thought that maybe he'd just gone for a ride or something. When I hadn't seen him on the Monday, I got really worried and went to the Moe police and reported him missing.'

On Saturday 25 November, Detective Michael Grunwald went back to Rhona Heaney's house in Nicholls Road and took a formal statement. Rhona said that she had known Karen Randall since August when they had both enrolled to do a modern office skills course at the Traralgon TAFE. The course was 20 weeks and would run until December. Rhona said that Karen had pulled out of the course in September, but by then the two women had become friends. Occasionally during the course, Rhona had picked Karen up because she had to drop her own two children at a babysitter near where Karen was living at the time.

In early September, Karen had moved into Rhona's house. Rhona said that she had met Karen's boyfriend Paul about four times. In her statement, Rhona Heaney stated: 'I knew from Karen that Paul used to get violent with her at times, and I think that's why Karen moved away from Moe. I recall Karen coming to the office skills course one day with a black eye.

'On one occasion when Paul was here, he said to Karen words to the effect, "I'd be nice to me today if I were you", after having a minor argument with Karen, but after that exchange, he came in for a cup of coffee and everything seemed all right again.'

Rhona said that she had only met Karen's sister, Donna, about four times as well. According to Rhona, Donna Randall had hosted a house-warming party on the night of Saturday 4 November at her house in Moe. Rhona had been invited, but she said that she had stayed home with her boyfriend and watched videos. Some other friends had also visited. Karen was there as well.

The week before, Karen had been allocated a house of her own through the Ministry of Housing and had been packing and moving some of her things into the new house.

On Sunday 5 November – the last day that anyone had seen Paul Snabel – Rhona said in her statement that she had woken up at 6 am when Donna and Paul had come in her back door. Both were 'pretty boisterous and sounded pretty drunk'. The two had woken Karen up and they had all sat around the kitchen table drinking coffee.

Soon after, Donna had curled up on the couch and fallen asleep and Paul had left. Rhona said that she thought the only reason Paul had been there was to drop Donna off. At that stage, Paul had been driving his Holden but returned around 11 am on his motorbike.

According to Rhona Heaney, Paul had been in a good mood. He had played outside with her two children and Karen's son. While the women were helping to pack, they would occasionally stop and join in the games with him and the kids.

After they'd stopped for a lunch break, Rhona took the children to the house of a friend, Irene Maslin. Karen, Donna and Paul stayed at her house. On the way, she had stopped at the local hotel and bought a bottle of Johnnie Walker whisky and two bottles of Pepsi. Rhona said that Paul had given her $50 for the whisky.

After she got home, Rhona continued to help Karen pack while Paul drank the whisky. He had helped the women load up some of the heavier things.

'I have found out since,' said Rhona in her statement, 'that Paul was using speed whilst he was here but I didn't know it then. I think he drinks it with his whisky and Coke.'

When the women had finished packing, Rhona said that they had told Paul they had to take some of Karen's things to her new house. She said that he was keen to continue 'partying' but the women weren't interested.

'When Karen told Paul that we had to go, Paul sort of shrugged it off that nobody wanted to party on with him. I think that Paul decided that he would go for a ride by himself. I think that Paul left my address at around 5 pm. At around that time, I saw Paul get on his motorcycle, put his crash helmet on and drive down the driveway. At the end of the driveway, he turned left and headed south down Nicholls Road.

'At the time, Paul was wearing blue jeans, denim, his red and white helmet. I think he may have had a windcheater on. I think the windcheater was a blue one with a hood. This is the last time that I have heard from or seen Paul Snabel.'

Rhona finished her statement by saying that Paul appeared to be in a good mood when he'd left and she could see no reason why any person would want to harm him.

After speaking to Rhona Heaney, Detective Michael Grunwald went to the Mirboo North Hotel and spoke to an employee there called Shirley. She told him that she remembered Rhona Heaney coming into the bar sometime between 3 and 4 pm on Sunday 5 November. 'She came up to the bar and purchased a 750 ml bottle of Johnnie Walker Black Label whisky and two bottles of

Pepsi Cola. I remember what she purchased because we never sell any Black Label because it is expensive, and I know that Rhona is a single mum, and at the time I wondered how she could afford the Black Label. This is why I remember it.'

The bar attendant also remembered that Rhona had paid with a 50-dollar note and when she'd handed the money over, Rhona had said, 'I hope he's given me enough money.'

At 9 am on Saturday 2 December, Senior Constable Michael Grunwald and Detective Sergeant Shane Downie drove out to a property in Darlimurla. A local resident had found a motorcycle engine in a dam on the edge of a pine forest. Grunwald removed the engine from the water and inspected it. The engine was new, but the engine number had been filed off. The engine was photographed and then taken back to the Morwell CIB to be added to the other recovered motorbike parts.

By mid-afternoon, the detectives had organised for a police diver to come up from Melbourne to search the dam. The diver found a piece of cloth with grease marks on it. Nothing else turned up, but there was another similar dam about a kilometre away and the detectives thought it was worth the diver taking a look. Within minutes of beginning the second dive, the diver found a motorcycle muffler, a red-coloured motorcycle frame and a front fork shock absorber.

On Monday 4 December, the two detectives and seven other police officers arrived at the home of Irene Maslin and her husband, Jano, with a search warrant. Rhona Heaney and the Randall sisters were friends of the Maslins and Rhona had admitted visiting their home on the day Paul went missing. Indeed, all of the people who had last seen Paul regularly frequented the Maslins' house. Also of interest to police was the fact that the house had a garage large enough to dismantle a motorbike away from prying eyes. None of the other homes had a garage.

At the front door, Detective Sergeant Downie explained to Irene Maslin that the search of her house was in relation to the disappearance of Paul. Irene said she'd never heard of Paul until she had seen reports of his disappearance on the news. When asked for her whereabouts on Sunday 5 November, she said that she was at home all day with her husband, Jano, two male friends, and Rhona Heaney's two children, who she'd minded from 1 pm till 7 pm. According to Irene, no-one else had come and no-one left. The men had worked on a pool they were putting in. During the exchange, Irene looked nervous and at one point, she started crying.

When Downie spoke to Jano, he was told that Jano had met Paul a couple of times at Rhona Heaney's house, but didn't really know him to talk to. Jano Maslin's story matched his wife's. He said he had spent Sunday 5 November digging his pool all day with two friends. He remembered the date specifically because, he explained, he was originally from England and 5 November was Guy Fawkes Day. If his wife was nervous when talking to police, Jano Maslin, with his long hair pulled back into a ponytail and sporting a bushy beard, was as cool as a cucumber.

Shane Downie was particularly interested in the Maslins' garage. Could this have been the place where the motorbike had been dismantled? Entering the garage, Downie could tell that Jano was fastidious about his workspace. The place was immaculately clean and everything was stored neatly. Of particular interest were coils of wires and cords – each was tied in left-handed knots in exactly the same way the coils of wires from the dumped motorbike had been tied. Some of the dumped parts had been put into plastic SEC bags. The fact that Jano Maslin also worked for the SEC could be a further link.

The floor of the garage had been neatly swept, but a closer examination revealed tiny red paint flakes in some cracks in the concrete floor. Among other items of interest located at the Maslins' house were a file in the garage with obvious red paint flakes on it, and a knife with red flakes on it. Police collected any tools that could have been used to assist in taking apart Paul's motorbike.

In a jewellery box in the Maslins' bedroom, police found a green key ring with a tag for a Yamaha motorbike.

After the Maslin search, the police officers drove straight to Karen Randall's house, five minutes away. She wasn't home so an officer entered through an unlocked window and let the others in. The police found nothing of evidentiary value and left a copy of their search warrant on Karen's dining-room table.

With the suspicion that Paul's motorbike had been dismantled in the Maslins' garage, police needed a motive – what reason could the Maslins have for dismantling the bike? Was it possible that Paul had enlisted their help because he wanted to voluntarily disappear? Or could they have been involved in something more sinister? Shane Downie and the local detectives worked long hours to try to establish a connection between the Maslins and Paul. Rumours spread around the local community – one of them was that Irene Maslin was into drugs and that Paul had threatened to 'lag' on her. Another rumour was that Paul might have been 'taken care of' because he had bashed Karen.

On 17 December, Downie and another detective went back to the Maslins' house, where they spoke to Jano outside the house. Downie asked Jano to come to the police station to give a statement in relation to Paul Snabel. Jano asked the officers to wait a moment while he spoke to his wife in the house. Minutes later, he came back out and told Downie that he would not make a statement until he had seen his solicitor. His wife would refuse to speak to them as well. This time, Jano Maslin wasn't calm; he was in fact very nervous.

The next day, Jano didn't turn up for work, Irene's child had been removed from the local primary school, and there was no sign of any of the Maslins at their house. They too had disappeared.

Two days after the Maslins had vanished, detective Shane Downie pulled over a car being driven by Rhona Heaney. Two fellow officers searched the car while Downie talked to Rhona. Asked if she knew where the Maslins were, she said that they had gone on holidays but she didn't know where. Downie asked her if she had heard from Paul. She hadn't. She said that there were some people who would have some trouble over Paul, but not her. When Downie asked her what she meant by that, she refused to elaborate.

On 21 December, Shane Downie went to the Frankston Peninsula Private Hospital with three other detectives. Karen Randall was being treated in hospital for alcoholism and drug abuse and the police wanted to talk to her.

During the initial conversation, Karen broke down and began crying. Karen explained that her earlier statement was not correct and that she felt that something might have happened to Paul. Downie stopped Karen and set up a tape recorder. This was what he had been waiting for – one of the people connected with Paul to finally start talking.

Downie began reading through Karen's original statement. When he got to the part about Paul leaving the Nicholls Road house to get his motorbike, Karen told him that Rhona had gone with him. She also said that Irene Maslin had been at the house.

'What time did Irene get there?' asked Downie. This was the first time anyone had said that Irene Maslin had been at the Nicholls Road house on Sunday 5 November.

'I don't know what time she got there,' said Karen.

Karen explained that when Paul came back on his motorbike with Rhona, she had continued packing.

'I got upset with Paul because he was ... he was starting to touch me and stuff like that and I just didn't like it.' Karen said that soon after, she and Donna had left to go to Irene's house. Irene, Rhona and Paul had stayed at the Nicholls Road house. That was the last time Karen had seen Paul.

Karen said that Jano Maslin and Rhona's partner, Steve, and the kids were at the Maslins' house when she and Donna got there.

'Was there anyone else there?' asked Downie.

Karen said that she hadn't seen anyone else at the Maslins' house and no one else had come while she was there. Karen said that Jano Maslin had driven her and her son and Donna home later on that evening.

The following day, Karen had taken her son to an eye specialist in Melbourne and had gone to the Maslins' later in the afternoon when she'd returned from the city. According to Karen, Irene Maslin had taken her into the bedroom and told her that Paul wouldn't hurt her again. Karen said that she had burst out crying. She explained to the detectives that Irene had previously told her that Paul would kill her one day, but now she was saying that he would never bother her again.

Downie asked Karen what she thought that comment had meant.

'Well, I thought then that something terrible had happened.' After that, Karen said that Irene told her to watch herself and that she would have to do what they told her to do.

Downie asked if anything was said about Paul's motorbike. According to Karen, Irene had said that it hadn't taken long for them to take it apart.

'Was there anything else that she indicated to you?' asked Downie.

'Um, just that my life was gunna be in um ... in danger if I ... if I said anything or if I um ... because I was the weakest one. They felt that I was the weakest one, so therefore ... um ... I'd cop it. And there's people watching me. Um, there's people in Melbourne that have got my address ... ah ... know where I live, know where my parents live. Um and then even two years down the track, if I slip up, they know where I am.'

Karen said that later she had told Rhona that Irene had threatened her, and Rhona repeated the threats.

After this, Karen had gone to stay with her mother in Moe, having become a nervous wreck with the police investigations and the interviews and the search helicopter flying overhead. It had all been too much for her and she had checked in to the hospital.

Downie asked why they had concocted their statements.

'Because um ... we were told to do exactly what they said to do, what ... Irene made it quite clear that if we didn't do what she said for us to do, that we would have our heads blown off.'

Karen said that three weeks earlier, Donna had telephoned from Rhona's house and Irene had been there too. Irene had told Donna to tell Karen she was 'polishing the barrels'.

After speaking to Karen Randall, Downie drove straight to her sister Donna's house and asked her to come to the Morwell CIB. Downie explained what Karen had told them about Paul being murdered. He asked her if her original statement had been correct.

'Um, most of it,' she replied.

Downie started reading her original statement back to her. When he got to the part about Donna driving Paul in his car to Rhona Heaney's house at 5 am on the Sunday morning, Donna interrupted him.

'Paul drove,' she said. 'We had a few near misses on the way because Paul was pretty drunk.'

Downie read the part of the statement about Donna and Paul arriving at Rhona's house and waking her up.

'That's wrong,' said Donna. 'She was already up.'

'Who else was at the house?' asked Downie.

'Irene, Karen and Rhona.'

'Irene was at the house?'

Donna said she was and that she presumed that Irene had stayed there the night.

The detective asked who had gone on the motorbike ride. Donna said that she thought Rhona went on the back of Paul's bike and that Karen and Irene shared a bike.

Downie kept reading from the statement. Donna agreed that she had fallen asleep on the couch but when the detective got to the part about Paul leaving, she said, 'That's when they went – like Irene got onto some other bike too and they all went for a drive on the bikes ... um, I think Rhona was on the back of Paul's bike.' Donna said that they had come back about an hour and a half later. Downie asked how was it that Paul had his motorbike, since he had arrived at Rhona's house in his car.

'Yeah, he must have gone with Rhona before that into Moe in his car and come back on the bike.'

'How do you know Rhona was with him?'

'I think I saw her get in the car ... or she said she was going to.' Donna said that she had been inside when Paul had come back with the motorbike so she hadn't seen him and Rhona return.

According to Donna, it was when they came back that Paul had started drinking the whisky.

Donna recalled that Karen had gone to bed for a lie down, and then she had heard Irene and Rhona talking while Paul was outside. She said that Irene had joked that they should get a baseball bat and use that, and Rhona had giggled.

'Were they talking about doing something to Snabel?' asked Downie.

'Um ... someone mentioned ... about breaking his legs or something ... tying him to a tree.'

Donna said she wasn't sure who was saying what, but that the conversation was between Rhona and Irene. Karen had woken up and they all went outside to join Paul, who was playing with the kids. Donna said that Rhona had then taken the children somewhere and when she returned, Irene suggested that Paul and Rhona go for a walk with her.

The three had gone up the paddocks and into an old shed. They had been gone for a while and when they returned, Karen had told Donna they were leaving. The two sisters had headed out to Rhona's car. They were just about to drive off when they heard Paul calling out from one of the paddocks. He had been riding a motorbike that had become stuck in a ditch. He called for the two to help him, but Karen had told Donna to get in the car. Then the sisters drove off to the Maslins' house.

Some time later, according to Donna, Irene Maslin had called Karen on the phone and told her to pull herself together and stop crying and carrying on. Later, Jano Maslin and a friend, Ian Gillin, had driven Karen and Donna back home to Moe.

Detective Sergeant Downie asked Donna about the rest of her statement.

'Load of rubbish, really.'

'Three statements were made,' said Downie, 'one by yourself, one by your sister, Karen, and one by Rhona Heaney. Each of those statements are very similar. Can you tell me why they're very similar?'

''Cause they told us what to say.'

'When you say "they" …?'

'Oh, Irene and Rhona discussed with Karen and I what to say to police if something happened, like when they started asking questions.'

Downie sought to clarify the point at which the stories had been concocted. Donna said that after 5 November, she had gone to Lakes Entrance for a week and when she came back, she had been at Irene's house when Detective Grunwald had telephoned and wanted to speak to her.

'I got off the phone and I was upset, crying … Irene took me into her bedroom, sat me down and said, "They're gunna start asking questions … you know what you have to say … that he left on his motorbike".'

Donna recalled that Karen had turned up and she thought Rhona was also there.

'So it was prior to the police interviewing you that the three of you discussed it in the presence of Irene?'

'Yeah.'

Downie asked, 'Why did you get there and concoct a story because Irene told you to?'

'Because,' replied Donna, 'I was scared if I said anything – I got the impression I wasn't gunna live long.'

'And what gave you that impression?'

'Irene made comments like, "I'm polishing my barrels – if one of us is gunna go down, we're all gunna go. If this gets out of hand, the big boys are gunna have to deal with it" and—'

Downie interrupted to ask who the 'big boys' might be.

Donna didn't know but the threat had scared her. She had only decided to tell the truth now because Karen had phoned her earlier that day and said that she had told the police everything and that Donna should do the same. Donna said that she was still scared of Irene's threats.

Donna said that in early December, Irene had been busted for drugs and that afterwards, she had told Donna she was glad that it was drugs she was busted for and 'not the Paul incident'.

When news of Paul's disappearance had become public knowledge through the media, Donna said Rhona had assured her that they would never find the motorbike because it was scattered in a thousand different places 'from here to Melbourne'. Donna had taken that literally and was surprised when, after the police's public appeal, the bike parts had started turning up at the local tips.

Donna told the detectives that she believed Irene and Rhona had done something to Paul but she could shed no light on what that might have been.

On Christmas Eve morning at 7.30 am, Shane Downie arrived at Donna Randall's house in Moe for yet another interview. This time, Shane Downie was interested in what had happened in the three days since Donna's last interview. He knew that because the police were putting pressure on all the key players in Paul Snabel's disappearance, they were all getting jumpy.

According to Donna, around 3 am on 23 December someone had knocked on her window. Irene Maslin's Subaru was parked outside. A male friend of Irene's was outside, and told her to pack some things. The friend said he would take Donna to Irene, who was staying with him at his house in Corio because she was being hassled by police. Donna had obeyed and met up with Irene, who told her that she was leaving for Shepparton. Rhona had turned up later on and she said that she was going to Shepparton too.

The three women had discussed what had happened and Irene Maslin had said that the police knew a lot about what had happened to Paul. According to Donna, Irene had suggested that it was strange that the police knew things that only the people involved could have known.

'She said ... it sounds like someone's been talking.'

Later that day when Donna was alone with Rhona, the two had got talking about where Paul's body was. Rhona talked about a bush location near a hidden drug crop.

'Rhona said that ... they grew the crop, the crop had been there for five years and no-one's been in there yet so no-one will find it ... and that he'd be rotten there, rotting away, that's if the animals and things hadn't dragged him off.'

Downie asked if Rhona had talked about burying Paul or if his body had been left on top of the ground.

'It was on top of the ground – that's what she was talking about.'

Downie asked Donna if the women had discussed changing their story in light of the police suspicions. Donna said that Rhona had a story to cover if anyone had seen her during the motorbike ride she had taken with Paul on 5 November to Leongatha. She said she would tell people that she had to visit someone at the hospital there.

Donna said Rhona had told Irene that the police knew she had been at her (Rhona's) house on 5 November. 'Irene said they're just guessing here because if they knew all these things ... we'd all be behind bars.'

Rhona had told Donna to tell Karen the right things to say. She asked Donna if she thought it was Karen who had spoken to the police. Donna lied and said she hadn't. Rhona and Irene had no idea that both Karen and Donna had spoken at length to detectives investigating the case.

Then, chillingly, Rhona had added, 'Well, someone obviously has and I think Karen's the weak link. But we'll find out on Wednesday.'

'Do you know what she meant by that?' asked Downie.

Donna said that she had the definite impression that they would approach Karen.

Two days after Christmas, Peter Ross, a scientist at the Victoria Police forensic science laboratory, examined the evidence that had been taken from the Maslins' home during the police search.

Some of the items were Jano Maslin's tools from his garage, but other items included paint flakes and metallic shavings. Ross was able to report that there was no difference in the paint flakes taken from the painted red and white motorcycle fairing and the particles of paint flakes found in Jano Maslin's file, and also in some of the flakes taken from the garage floor. Ross also found some dark red paint flakes from where the fuel tank had been damaged and touched up with a darker red paint.

He found similar darker red flakes in the file and on the floor of Jano Maslin's garage. Forensic evidence backed up what police had already suspected – Paul's motorbike had been dismantled in Jano's garage. It was the first solid link between the Maslins and Paul Snabel.

On 28 December 1989, Homicide detective Peter Wheeler went to the Peninsula Private Hospital in Frankston to speak to Karen Randall. Wheeler had spent some time up at the Morwell CIB at the beginning of the investigation before returning to Melbourne. He and his sergeant, John Robertson, who had come back from leave, assisted the investigation by offering any guidance they could. They spoke to their country colleagues daily for updates on the case. By now, a pattern was emerging. One person would give a statement and then someone else would add something to their statement, and then the police would go back to the first person who would in turn add something else. It was a frustrating and time-consuming way to get information.

Wheeler figured it was time to give the main players a bit of a push. He believed that they all knew more than what they were saying, and that perhaps one of them could have been responsible for Paul's disappearance. The investigation was six weeks old and only now was it coming together.

Karen said that her last statement was correct but that she had some things to add to it. On the night of Donna's house-warming party, Irene and Jano Maslin had been at Rhona's house, as well as Rhona and all of their children. The adults had all sat around smoking bongs of marijuana. Karen said that she had gone to bed and that when she had been woken up by the arrival of Paul and Donna early in the morning, all the people from the night before were still there because they had stayed the night. After a while, Jano had taken Irene's and Karen's sons back to his house when Rhona had gone off with Paul to get his motorbike.

Karen said that Irene and Paul discussed going for a ride and asked her to go along with them. Karen rode on the back of Irene's bike and Rhona rode on the back of Paul's bike. They had all gone to Leongatha.

When they arrived back at the Nicholls Road house, they had all sat around drinking coffee and Paul had rubbed his hand up and down Karen's back. She moved over so that he would get the message not to touch her. A little later, when she passed Irene on her way to her bedroom, Karen said, 'God I hate it when he touches me.'

Karen said that she had slept for a couple of hours and when she woke up, Paul was on Irene's bike in the paddock spinning it around and getting it bogged. She overheard a muffled conversation between Rhona and Irene. Irene had said, 'Bastard! He's got mud all over my bike. He can't ride.'

When she'd heard this, Karen had an uncomfortable feeling and asked Rhona if she could borrow her car to go to the Maslins' house to check on her son. She said that as she and Donna left, they heard Paul yelling something to them from the paddock. She didn't know what it was. The two sisters had driven away.

Karen said that she and Donna had gone to the Maslins' and then home. The following day, as in her previous statement, Karen repeated that she had gone to Rhona's house and that Jano and Irene were there. Irene had taken her into the bedroom.

'Irene said that Paul would no longer bother me. Then she started with the threats. When she said that he would no longer bother me, the way that she said it, with evil eyes and an aggressive look on her face, it really scared me and I could tell that Paul was no longer with us. By that I mean that I believed that he was dead. I started shaking and was distraught and was crying. It was at this stage that Irene started with the threats. She said, "Pull yourself together".' Karen said that Irene had told her that she was an accessory and if they went down, she would go down with them. Then according to Karen, Irene told her that if she said anything to the police, her head would be blown off.

Karen added that when Irene spoke of what had happened, she referred to 'we' and Karen had assumed that she meant herself, Rhona and Jano Maslin because he had left the house for some time before returning to drive Karen and Donna home. Afterwards, when Rhona had repeated Irene's threats, she told Karen that she could be killed and it would be made to look like a suicide, and if she dared leave a note about what had happened, her family would be in danger.

Karen said that she had got paranoid and panicky after these two conversations, but nonetheless had asked Irene what had really happened on that night. She was told that a baseball bat had been used. Karen had seen one at Rhona's house. Irene also said that there was a lot of blood and that things had gone terribly wrong. Karen hadn't wanted to know any further details.

Karen said that once the media started showing pictures of Paul and the bike parts that had been found, Irene had become angry at her and very controlling. Irene had told both Karen and Donna what to say to the police.

At the end of her statement, Karen denied any involvement in Paul Snabel's death.

On Friday 29 December 1989, Ian Gillin was brought in for questioning at the Shepparton CIB offices. Donna Randall had mentioned in her statement on 21 December that Jano Maslin and Ian Gillin had both driven her and Karen home on Sunday 5 November. Nobody else had mentioned Ian Gillin's presence at the Maslin house but it was worth looking into what he was doing there. Detective Senior Constable Andrew McLoughlin took Ian's statement. Of all the people on the periphery of Paul's disappearance, Ian, at 22 years of age, was different; he seemed more honest and simple than the others.

Ian told the detective that he worked as an electrical fitter and had started his apprenticeship back in 1985 at the State Electricity Commission at Morwell. In 1986, he had begun working at the SEC electrical workshops and had been there for about a month when Jano Maslin started working there. Ian and Jano worked in the same sections and over the following months had become friends. At that time, Ian explained, he still lived at home with his parents, and Jano began inviting him over for dinner to his house in Shady Creek. It was at the house that Ian met Jano's wife, Irene. Visits to the Maslins' house became more frequent. Ian enjoyed the company of the couple even though, in their early thirties, they were a decade older than him.

One thing that Ian admired about his new friends was their love of motorbikes. Ian recalled that in early 1988, the Maslins had moved to their current house in Mirboo North and Jano had put up a garage to house his collection. Between them, the couple had five motorbikes as well as their brown Subaru station wagon, which was their family car.

After they moved to Mirboo North, Ian would often help Jano with home improvements. The Maslins put a fence around their one-acre property, and built a shed and a hothouse, which Ian described in his statement as having 'black mesh stuff on top'. And when Jano told him that he was putting in a swimming pool, the young man agreed to help him dig the foundations.

Ian estimated that he visited the Maslins at least once a week and regarded them as good friends. He would come for tea and help Jano around the place. Ian said that he also met some of the Maslins' friends. A man called Steve was boarding with the Maslins for a couple of months, but he moved out with another friend of theirs, Rhona Heaney. Around the same time Ian had met Rhona, he also met Karen Randall, who lived at Rhona's house. Ian had gone with the Maslins to Rhona's house. He saw Steve there and remembered him from when he was boarding with Jano and Irene. Even though they occasionally socialised, Ian regarded them in his statement to police as 'not real good friends'.

Ian had met Karen Randall a couple of times and as far as the young man could tell, she had a boyfriend who he'd heard referred to as 'Paul' but he had never met the boyfriend. Ian knew that Paul came from Moe and Karen had told him that Paul had bashed her and that she had a rough life with him. She had only mentioned this to Ian once, but he had heard general discussion between Irene, Jano and Karen about the way Paul treated Karen. Ian made it clear in his statement that he hadn't participated in this talk, but rather just kept in the background and listened.

Ian said that on a Sunday at the start of November – he couldn't remember if it was the fifth or the twelfth – he had gone to the Maslins' house after lunch to help Jano dig the swimming pool foundations. As soon as he and another friend got there, they had headed straight outside and started digging. Ian said that the only other people at the house were Irene and her young son. At some point, the men had gone inside for a cuppa and, while the Maslin boy was inside, there was no sign of Irene.

Late in the afternoon, Karen had arrived with a young woman who she introduced to Ian as her sister Donna. This was the first time Ian had met Karen's sister. He wrote in his statement that while Karen was talking to him, he could smell spirits on her breath and while he said she wasn't drunk, she was well on the way to being drunk because she was starting to slur her words. Ian couldn't tell if Donna had been drinking because he had just met her and didn't know what she was normally like.

The women sat on chairs in the backyard. Karen's young son played with the Maslin boy. Afterwards, according to Ian, he and his friend finished their digging and left around 8 or 9 pm. Karen and Donna were still there, but Irene had left.

Ian visited the Maslins again sometime in the middle of the following week and had spent some time in the garage with Jano, who was fixing one of Irene's motorbikes. He hadn't noticed anything unusual about the garage. A week after that, he went with the Maslins to a house-warming party at Karen Randall's. Rhona and Steve were there, and so was Donna. Ian wrote in his statement that a couple of weeks before Christmas he had gone to the Maslins' house to celebrate the birthday of their son. Jano told him that the police had been around to take statements from him and Irene but they had refused to talk. He had assumed Jano was referring to a statement about stolen motorbike parts – and nothing more serious.

According to Ian, the week before Christmas, Jano had come to his home and left one of his motorbikes in Ian's shed. Ian asked why and Jano told him that he was getting hassled by the police too much and that his house had been turned upside down. Jano told Ian that he and Irene were going away for a while and that the couple would catch up with Ian at Ian's mum's house in Shepparton at Christmas. Jano and Irene and their son had left the following day.

On Christmas Day, Ian had seen Jano and Irene at his mum's house. Rhona Heaney had arrived in Shepparton on Boxing Day. The next day, the police had turned up and Ian had been asked to give his statement.

On 3 January 1990, detectives tracked down a man called Michael, who had been Rhona Heaney's de facto partner and was the father of her two children. Michael had since moved to America to work. He told the police how he had sent one of his sons an aluminium baseball bat for his birthday in June 1987. He recalled that his son had been disappointed with the baseball bat at the time, saying he would have preferred a cricket bat.

The detectives investigating the murder of Paul Snabel were by now getting used to the drip-feed way in which the story was coming together. Key players were being interviewed over and over and each time, a little bit more would be added to their stories. As a result, they then had to go back to the other key players to confirm or deny new information and then in turn, they would be told something else. But piece by piece, the picture of what had happened to Paul was becoming clearer.

When Donna Randall walked into the Moe police station on 5 January 1990, Peter Wheeler wondered what new information she would disclose. Donna began by saying that her previous statements and interviews had not been correct and hadn't contained her full knowledge regarding the matter. She stated again that the reason that she had not made full disclosures was because she was scared. She said that Rhona Heaney and Irene Maslin had told her what to say, and that Irene had threatened her by saying that if anyone let the cat out of the bag, the 'big fish' would have to step in. Despite the slightly skewed metaphor, the threat had been taken seriously.

Donna's subtle additions made a lot more sense as she launched into her story. Karen hadn't wanted to come to Donna's house-warming party on Saturday 4 November because she was scared of getting into an argument with Paul. Karen, however, had telephoned and invited him over to Rhona's house. Throughout the evening and into the early hours of the morning, Paul had kept asking Donna to come with him. Finally she had agreed. On the way, with Paul driving badly, he had stopped off at the Gunn's Gully Service Station, where he worked. Paul had chatted to another man who worked there. A couple of times along the journey, Paul ran the car off onto the gravel at the side of the road.

Irene, Karen and Rhona had been in the kitchen when the pair arrived at Nicholls Road. They had sat around and talked and then Donna had fallen asleep on the couch. When she had woken up, she saw that Paul's motorbike was there and his car was gone. It had been afterwards that Rhona told her that she had in fact accompanied Paul back to his house to swap the car for the bike. Rhona had said that she had checked out Paul's place while she was there and that he had a really good stereo, and that she should go back and rob his place and take the stereo.

On the way back, Paul had pulled into the Gunn's Gully Service Station again to fill his tank with petrol. Irene had asked Rhona if anyone had seen her, to which she replied that she had kept her helmet on so no one would recognise her. On another occasion, Rhona had said that she made a point of going back to the Gunn's Gully Service Station to see if anyone recognised her or said anything to her about being with Paul on that day. They hadn't.

After the motorbike ride, Irene and Rhona had asked Paul how much speed he was using and how he used it. Paul said that he either snorted it or drank it. Donna said she had overheard Rhona telling Paul that he should inject it because it gave you a better buzz. Initially, Paul had said no way, but the two women had worked on him for a long while as Donna lay on the couch pretending to be asleep. According to Donna, Rhona had told Paul that she had three years of practice and that she would inject him and get the vein straightaway. He finally agreed to it. Donna said that she had dozed off again and the next time she saw the three of them was when they all came out of the bathroom and Paul was rubbing his arm. Donna watched them and Irene saw her.

'She then came over to the end of the couch with her back facing the kitchen and whispered to me that if I didn't want to see this, that I'd better take off because he's going to fall any minute and it wouldn't be nice.'

Donna had been too scared to move. She said that Irene asked Paul if he wanted to go for a walk and they had headed up to the paddocks. Soon after, Karen – who had also been asleep – came out of the bedroom and asked where everyone was. Donna said that she and Karen waited for nearly an hour for Paul, Irene and Rhona to return from their walk.

When they came back, Donna said she had overheard Irene tell Rhona that Paul was getting on her nerves and that she had to do something about it. It was then that Irene had asked Rhona about the baseball bat. The women had giggled about the suggestion. Irene also asked if Rhona had any rope that they could use to tie him to a tree. The women had again laughed at the suggestion. Finally, they had whispered something to Karen that Donna couldn't hear, and then Karen told Donna they were leaving. Meanwhile, Paul had gone out to ride on one of the motorbikes and called out to the sisters as they were leaving. Karen was shaken and upset and had said as they drove off, 'I don't believe this'.

Donna and Karen had gone to the Maslins' and stayed there. Irene rang and spoke to Karen, then spoke to Jano, who left shortly after with Ian. When the two men returned an hour or so later, they drove Donna and Karen home.

On Saturday 18 November, Karen had a house-warming party. Irene, Jano, Rhona and Ian had attended. Donna said that Karen had got really drunk and Irene wasn't happy about the way she was behaving.

The following day, Donna's mother had rung Donna at Irene's house and said that she had given the police Irene's number because they wanted to talk to Donna. About ten minutes later, Detective Michael Grunwald had rung.

Karen arrived at Irene's soon after and she said that she had police at her place that morning too, asking questions about Paul. Irene told Donna that if the police asked, she had not been at Rhona's house on the day Paul vanished. Irene instructed Donna to say that Karen and Paul had had an argument and Paul had left. And that was the story that Donna had told the police in her early statements.

When Jano had driven Donna and Karen home, Grunwald was waiting for them. Considering the two quiet weeks that had elapsed since Sunday 5 November, the people who knew what had really happened to Paul could be forgiven for thinking that they'd gotten away with murder. But they hadn't.

When the search for the missing man started, Donna remembered police helicopters flying overhead and people out searching for him. She also remembered Paul's sister visiting to make sure that Karen was all right. In the following days, Donna said, the police had search warrants and had searched Irene's and Rhona's houses, and then Karen's.

In this latest statement, Donna said that when they all went to stay at Irene's friend's house in Corio, she presumed Jano, Irene and Rhona had gone there 'to do their drug dealing'. She said that Irene had wanted her to go to Corio to get her away from the police, whose visits were becoming more frequent.

Donna said that while Jano, Irene and Rhona were away over the Christmas–New Year period, Rhona had telephoned her to check that she and Karen were sticking to their stories. Donna assured her that they were.

At the end of her latest statement, Donna had two new pieces of information to add to her story. Firstly, she remembered that on 18 November, she had been with Rhona when she dropped off her lounge suite; she was giving it to a friend. Donna couldn't understand why Rhona would be getting rid of the lounge suite since it was comfortable. Karen had later told her it was because they couldn't get the stains off it.

Donna inferred that Karen was talking about bloodstains and that it was connected with what had happened to Paul. The second new piece of information was that when Irene and Rhona had taken Paul into the bathroom to inject him with speed, they had added battery acid to the syringe.

While Peter Wheeler was interviewing Donna, Detective Downie was taking a statement from a man whose girlfriend was a friend of Rhona Heaney's. The man recalled that around mid-November, Rhona and another man had come to their house in Morwell and had dropped off a couch, which the man's girlfriend had bought from Rhona. The couch was at his house now. Police collected it and took it to the Morwell CIB office to add to their growing list of pieces of evidence.

Karen Randall also wanted to add a couple of things to her account and she gave her third statement to Detective John Robertson on 7 January 1990. She told Robertson that since she had been in hospital, she had more time to think things through and wanted to add a couple of points that she thought might be significant.

Karen said that when she had gone for a nap on the Sunday afternoon of Paul's disappearance, Rhona had come into the room and told her something like, 'We've just given him a dirty shot but he is still standing.' Irene had later told her that they had to kill Paul because 'he knew too much'. Karen said she didn't know what that was in reference to but she surmised that Irene had talked to Paul about her drug taking or drug dealing.

'On another occasion, I was with Rhona and Irene, and Irene said that Paul had been hit over the head with a baseball bat and that then they had tried to inject Paul with battery acid, but that it didn't work. She said that they put a plastic bag over his head. Irene said that she saw Paul take his last breath. Irene said that they took Paul's body away in the Subaru ... I don't know where Paul's body was dumped but I can recall Irene saying a few times that she knows a place in the Baw Baw, Shady Creek, Warragul area where she is considering putting in a crop. She has also mentioned that Paul's body is in a place where it will never be found.'

A couple of weeks after his original statement to the detectives at Shepparton, Ian Gillin stood outside Jano and Irene Maslin's house in Mirboo North. With him were the two Homicide detectives, Peter Wheeler and John Robertson, and Shane Downie from the Morwell CIB.

The interview was being videotaped and Ian was advised of his rights in front of the camera. He repeated how he and a friend had come over to help Jano Maslin on Sunday 5 November and that Donna and Karen had visited. Then he told the detectives that Jano Maslin had said that he 'was going down the street to get some stuff' and had been gone for several hours.

'Did he say why he was leaving?' asked Detective Wheeler.

'No, he didn't,' replied Ian. 'He's just said he was going down the shop.'

When Jano returned some hours later with some shopping, he asked Donna and Karen if they wanted to go back to Moe. Ian drove the girls to Moe and then returned to the Maslins' house. Interestingly, although Jano had driven off in his Subaru, Ian had not heard the car when he returned, and it wasn't in the driveway when he left to take Karen and Donna home.

Ian had stayed over at the house and around midnight, Jano announced he was going out again and later had returned towing a motorbike on a trailer behind his Subaru.

'You mentioned that when he returned from the shop, he didn't have the Subaru?' said Wheeler.

'Later on that night, the Subaru was back there.'

'Did he say where the Subaru was when he came back from the shops and you didn't hear the Subaru?'

'Yes, he said Irene and Rhona had the Subaru – they had to go and see someone.'

'Did he elaborate on where they'd taken the Subaru?'

'No.'

When Ian returned from Moe, the Subaru was back and Irene and Rhona were inside the Maslin house. Ian said that the second time Jano had left the house, he had been gone for around three-quarters of an hour and when he returned, the Subaru had the trailer with the motorbike on it.

'What happened when he returned with the motorcycle and the trailer?' asked Wheeler.

'We were told that we had to strip it down,' replied Ian.

'Who said that?'

'Irene.'

Standing outside the Maslin house, Ian indicated the Maslins' shed. He said that he and Jano had unloaded the motorbike from the trailer.

'And who was involved in stripping the bike down?' asked Wheeler.

'Jano, Irene, Rhona and I.'

Ian showed the detectives the place where the foursome had disassembled the bike.

'Was anything said to you about where the motorcycle had come from or the reason for the motorcycle being there?' asked Wheeler.

Considering that stripping a motorbike after midnight on a Sunday night was a tad unusual, Ian said that he had just been told that the bike had to be stripped down and gotten rid of.

Ian said that he had taken off the back wheel, the springs, the exhaust, the seat, the pack-rack and the lights and guards. He remembered the bike was an RZ250 and that it was red in colour. Ian said that Jano had used some of his tools to file off the engine number. When the four had finished stripping the bike, they put all the parts in bags and the two men loaded the dismantled bike into the back of the Subaru.

'Was there any discussion between anyone during the dismantling of the bike?'

'No, there wasn't,' replied Ian. 'We just hooked in and helped to strip the bike down.'

'When that was all finished and the Subaru's been loaded up, what happened then?'

'Then Jano and I've taken off in the Subaru.'

'For what reason?'

'To get rid of the parts.'

'Had there been any discussion between anyone as to where you were going to go with the parts?'

'Irene asked where's a good place to put 'em and I said I know where there's a couple of dams. And Jano's said, "What about the tip?"'

Wheeler asked what they finally decided on and Ian said that they had decided on the dams and two local tips – which was exactly where the parts had later turned up. Ian described how he and Jano had driven around to the dams and the tips depositing parts of the bike. Irene and Rhona had stayed back at the house.

When Ian came to the end of his story, Wheeler asked him if he had anything else to add that might be relevant.

'On Sunday when I got there, I asked Jano where Irene was and he said that she was out riding with Paul.'

'Right,' said Wheeler. 'Do you know Paul's surname at all?'

'Snabel, I think it is.'

Wheeler asked Ian whether there had been any mention of Paul when they were all dismantling the motorbike. Ian said there hadn't.

Wandering around the Maslins' property, Ian showed the detectives the swimming pool that they had been digging out on the day Paul vanished. He also pointed out the trailer that had been used to bring the red motorbike to the Maslins' home later that night.

After the walk around the Maslins' property, the videotaped interview continued at the site of the first of the dams where Ian and Jano had dumped motorbike parts in the early hours of Monday 6 November. He said he knew about the dams because he used to swim in them when he was a child. With the detectives, he then visited the other dam and the tips and explained how he and Jano Maslin had scattered the remaining motorbike parts.

At the end of the interview, Wheeler asked Ian if he had any idea that the motorbike had belonged to Paul. He said he didn't know whose bike it was.

Back at the Morwell CIB offices, Ian made another statement for the police after the videotaped interview was over. He admitted that some parts of his earlier statement that he'd made just after Christmas weren't true. 'I now want to tell the truth,' he said.

Ian explained that when he'd gone to the Maslins' on Sunday 5 November, Jano had told him that Irene was out riding with Paul. When asked who Paul was, Jano told him that Paul was Karen's boyfriend. This time, he said that when Karen and Donna were taken back to Moe after dinner, Jano had driven them in his (Ian's) car, and he had gone along for the ride. When the two men had arrived back at the Maslins' house, the Subaru was there and Irene and Rhona were inside. Jano had then gone off in the Subaru and returned with the red RZ250 motorbike on the trailer. Ian had helped him unload it off the trailer and take it into the garage. In this statement, he admitted that when Jano had told him that the motorbike needed to be stripped down, he thought that the bike might have been stolen. For the first time, there was a hint of fear in his recollections. Describing Jano filing the identifying numbers off the motorbike frame, Ian said, 'I didn't know why he was doing this. I didn't want to ask any questions.'

He again described how the two had dumped the motorbike at the dams and the tip and how they had returned home around 4.30 am. Jano Maslin had driven Ian home in the early afternoon of the next day.

'On the way home, I didn't ask any questions. I was too scared to ask. About two weeks later, I heard in the papers that a bloke had gone missing. Then I heard that the motorbike parts were found and I thought that the bike must have belonged to him. Today I have told police the truth and I went and showed them where the parts were dumped. I was put on video. I agreed to this because I was telling the truth, and I didn't want it pinned on me.'

And Ian *was* telling the truth – just not the whole truth.

The next day, Ian Gillin was taken to the Homicide Squad at the St Kilda Road police complex in Melbourne. After he'd been read his rights, he was told for the record that the police wanted to talk to him about the murder of Paul Snabel. The interview was conducted by Detective Andrew McLoughlin, who had spoken to Ian in his earlier interviews. Sergeant John Robertson sat in on the interview.

Ian explained that he'd met Jano Maslin when both of them had worked at the SEC and through Jano, he'd met Irene Maslin and the Randall sisters.

'I met Karen about three or four months ago. Irene went down to Moe to pick her up ... to bring her to Rhona's place because she had been bashed. She had a black eye.' Ian said that he had gone with Irene to collect Karen.

'And how did you meet Donna Randall?'

'I met her on Sunday 5 November when Karen came around ... she brought Donna.'

McLoughlin asked Ian if he knew Paul. Up until now, Ian had denied ever meeting Paul although he had admitted hearing about him.

'I met him on the fifth of November, round at Rhona's place.'

'Is that the first time you've met him?'

'Yes.'

'And who's Paul Snabel? How does he fit with everybody?'

'He's meant to be Karen's boyfriend.'

'Why do you say "meant to be" Karen's boyfriend?'

'Well, I think they were split up at the time.'

Step by step, Mcloughlin had Ian go over his movements on the weekend that Paul had vanished. He said that when he'd gone to the Maslins' house on the Sunday to dig the swimming pool, Karen's son had been there playing with Irene's son. Karen and Donna had arrived in the afternoon. Ian said he thought that they might have been driving Rhona's car, and that the sisters smelt as if they'd been drinking whisky.

This time, when Ian talked about Jano's announcement that he had to go out in the early evening, he said, 'And he asked me if I wanted to go with him, so I went with him.'

The two men had driven in the Subaru to the shops for smokes and Coke in the main street of Mirboo North.

'Then we went back to the car and he said, "I've got to take the smokes to Irene and Rhona", so I thought, all right.'

McLoughlin asked if Ian remembered the phone ringing at the Maslins' house before the two left to go to the shops. He didn't remember if it had or not. He said that after the shops, Jano had driven him to Rhona's and parked the car next to a shed beside the house.

'We hopped out of the car. We started walking inside and ... Irene was in the shed ... We walked in and said hello and she said hello and she had something in her hand. It looked like a syringe and she was fillin' it up with some stuff. I asked what the stuff was and she said, "It's battery acid ... There's a guy in there that has to go. If someone doesn't do somethin' about him, he's gunna end up killin' Karen.'"

'Did you ask who that was?' asked McLoughlin.

'No, she said, "It's Paul. He used to be Karen's boyfriend. He used to always bash Karen all the time. Karen was too scared to do anythin'." And after she filled [the syringe] up, we walked inside. I got introduced to him.'

Inside, Rhona was sitting in the lounge room with Paul. She introduced Ian and Paul to each other. She and Paul sat at either end of a three-seater couch and the others took an armchair each. Rhona offered to make cuppas for the men and left the room, closing the door behind her. Irene was in the kitchen with Rhona.

'How did Paul seem to you when you spoke to him?'

'Well, he looked ... he was a pretty mess.'

'Why?'

'Well, he was drinkin' ... I think it was Jim Beam ... he was drinkin' a big bottle of that.'

'And what do you mean he looked a mess? What does that mean?'

'Oh, well, just by lookin' at him, lookin' at his eyes, he was sort of swayin' a bit.'

Ian then left the room to go to the toilet and stopped in the kitchen on the way back.

'I walked up to 'em to see if the cuppas were ready and Irene turned around and said to me, "I want you to knock this guy over the head."' Ian told the detectives that Irene had suggested using a baseball bat as the weapon and pointed to a bat leaning next to the kitchen door. McLoughlin asked if Irene had spoken in a normal voice, but Ian said that she looked pretty drunk herself. He hadn't known what to do so he had simply grabbed his cuppa and gone back into the lounge room.

Rhona and Irene came back into the room and Ian finished his cuppa and took the empty cup out to the kitchen. He told the detectives that by that time he was shaking. Irene followed him into the kitchen and according to Ian, she'd asked him, 'Now do you wanna hurry up and do it 'cause he just has to go.''

'And what did you do then?'

'I just ... I didn't know what to do. I was sort of shakin' and she ... she went out of the room and then ... um ... I picked up the baseball bat.' Ian had opened the door to the lounge room. Jano Maslin and Paul Snabel were in there but neither could see him because both were facing the television.

'And what happened then?' asked McLoughlin.

'Um,' said Ian quietly, 'as I opened up the door I looked ... I sort of started shakin' a bit. I thought, I can't do it. Then, I didn't know what to do so I just walked in and knocked him over the head and he fell.'

McLoughlin asked Ian to show them how he had held the bat, and the young man stood up. Captured on the police video that was taping the interview, Ian Gillin was nearly as tall as the doorway. He showed how he had swung the bat.

'Where did you strike him?'

'In his head,' said Ian describing that since he was left-handed, the blow from behind had been to the left side of Paul's head.

'And what did you see after you hit Paul with the baseball bat?'

'I saw blood drippin' onto the carpet.'

'Where was the blood coming from?'

'From his head.'

'What did Paul do immediately after you hit him?'

'He just ... he just fell unconscious straightaway.' Ian described how Paul had fallen sideways in the armchair in which he was sitting. While all this was going on, Jano had stood up, and Irene and Rhona had come back into the room.

Ian said that Rhona was holding a syringe – the same syringe that Ian had seen earlier in the garage, which Irene had been filling up with battery acid. According to Ian, Rhona had bent over the unconscious man and tried to inject him with the syringe. First she had tried his arms and then when that didn't work, she tried injecting it into one of his ankles. Irene had helped her. Ian said that while the two women were trying to inject Paul with acid, he stood back out of the way.

Paul had remained unconscious while the women struggled to inject him.

'Was he still bleeding?' asked McLoughlin.

'Yes, he was still bleeding ... it was drippin' onto the floor ... onto the carpet.' Ian indicated an amount the size of a saucer with his big hands. While this was going on, Jano Maslin had stood silently watching the two women.

'And what happened after Rhona couldn't put the needle into Paul's ankle?'

'Well, she discovered the needle was buggered.'

'And she said that?'

'Yeah.'

Ian told how Irene and Rhona had gone into the kitchen and Jano Maslin had followed them. Rhona had snapped the end off the syringe and had then thrown it in the bin.

'And what did you do?' asked McLoughlin.

'And then Paul started wakin' up so I gave him one more hit.'

'How did you know he was starting to wake up? What did he do?'

"Cause he was startin' to moan a bit.'

'Did he move at all?'

'Yes, he started movin, moanin',' said Ian in a quiet voice.

One more hit with the baseball bat had sent Paul back into unconsciousness. Ian said that Paul hadn't really moved from his original position of being slumped over in the armchair. He said that all he could see on the side of Paul's head was blood – and that made him feel like being sick. After he had hit Paul for a second time, he noticed Jano by his side. He passed the bat to Jano and walked outside.

McLoughlin asked why Ian felt sick and the young man confessed that he didn't like the sight of blood.

'Why did you strike Paul with the baseball bat if you don't like the sight of blood?' asked the detective.

'Well, I ... I knew if I didn't do what Irene said ... what could've happened to me.'

'Why do you think that?'

"Cause I was ... I get scared of her.'

'Why?'

'It's just the way she talks and treats people.'

McLoughlin asked him to explain what he meant by that.

'Well, her and Jano, they always argue all the time. Jano's gotta do everything around the house – if he doesn't, he really gets told off real bad. And I sort of just ... well ... whatever she said, I more or less just done. I didn't backchat or nothin'.'

Pressed for further details, Ian remembered that before he hit him a second time, Irene had heard Paul moaning from where she was in the kitchen and yelled out for Ian to hit him again. McLoughlin tried to make sense of how Ian could have hit someone over the head with a baseball bat simply because they were told to by their mate's wife. Ian was a strapping lad of 22. Could he really have been as scared of Irene Maslin as he said he was?

'It's a pretty strange thing to do, if somebody asked you to do that to somebody.'

'Yes, I know. I know it was,' agreed Ian.

'What made you do it?'

'Well I was just scared. I just thought if I didn't do it, it might happen to me.'

'Why did you do it a second time? You hit him once, why did you hit him twice?'

'Because he started wakin' up and Irene said, "Just hit him again."'

After Ian had gone outside feeling sick, Rhona had joined him in the backyard and asked him how he was feeling. He stayed outside for a while alone and when he went back inside, Jano held the baseball bat and Paul was slumped in the chair.

Ian could see from the movement of his chest that Paul was still breathing. He began to rouse from unconsciousness again. Ian said that Jano swung the bat and whacked Paul in the head twice in rapid succession. Paul went quiet again.

Ian said that minutes after Jano had hit Paul, Irene and Rhona came back into the room. Irene carried a clear plastic bag. Ian described how Irene had gone over to Paul and put the plastic bag over his head and then fixed it in place with an elastic band around his neck. She told the others that the bag should make him die.

McLoughlin asked Ian to repeat Irene's exact words.

'She said, "That should make him die; he should suffocate".'

Ian said that before Irene put the bag over his head, Paul had still been breathing because he could see the movement of his stomach going in and out. He added that while Irene was putting the bag over Paul's head, Rhona got a towel from the laundry and laid it over the blood. After the plastic bag was secured, Ian could see that Paul was still breathing because the bag moved in and out. While he didn't want to look too closely, he could also hear the bag being sucked in and out by the dying man.

McLoughlin asked what Jano Maslin had been doing while Irene put the bag over Paul's head.

'Jano was just standing there.'

'Did he say anything?'

'No, he did not. I could tell that Jano looked pretty scared himself too.'

'How could you tell that?'

'Just by looking at him.'

According to Ian, Irene had then told her husband to get a tarpaulin off the back of their trailer. Jano had fetched the tarp. Twenty minutes later, Paul Snabel had stopped breathing.

'Hang on,' said McLoughlin when Ian skipped over Paul's eventual death. He had to get the facts straight in this statement. He also had to elicit Ian's motivations. 'Before you go any further, why didn't you try and take the bag off Paul's head?'

"Cause I didn't ... I was that scared, I didn't want to really get involved with it.'

'What did you think was going to happen to Paul with the bag over his head?'

'He was gunna die.'

'And you didn't do anything about it?'

'No, 'cause I reckon if I stepped in and done something about it, it could've happened to me. I might've been the next one.'

The scene that Ian described sounded macabre to say the least: Rhona Heaney kneeling by the dying man rubbing the carpet back and forth with a bath towel; Irene Maslin standing over Paul Snabel watching the plastic bag puff out and suck in over and over; Ian Gillin too scared to do anything; Jano Maslin fetching a tarp for the body.

After a while, the movement of the plastic bag slowed down. Jano laid out the large green tarp next to where Paul lay slumped in the armchair. Irene and Jano lifted Paul out of the chair and laid him on the tarp. They folded the tarp over his body and tied the ends up with rope that Jano had also brought in when he fetched the tarp. When Jano had finished tying the ropes around the body, he asked Ian to help him carry it out to the car. The two men put the body in the back of the Subaru station wagon. Back inside, Rhona had got a bucket from the laundry and was cleaning the blood off her carpet. She also wiped the baseball bat clean.

Ian told the detectives that he didn't remember any conversation taking place during the clean-up. After the house was put back in order, Rhona locked it up and the four of them hopped into the car. He noticed the red motorbike parked under the carport; it had been there when he'd arrived with Jano, but he hadn't paid much attention to it. Irene sat in the driver's seat with Rhona in the front while the two men sat in the back seat.

The parking lights had been left on, Ian thought since they'd arrived, and when Irene tried to start the car, with the dead man in the back, the battery was flat and it wouldn't start. After some discussion, the four decided to roll-start the car by pushing it down the driveway until the motor kicked over. Finally, they got it going. Irene took the back roads, avoiding the main streets of Mirboo North, and arrived at the Maslins' house. When she dropped Jano and Ian off, she told the two men that she and Rhona would be back later.

Ian said that when they entered the house, Karen was crying in Irene's bedroom. The rest of the people at the house, including Donna, sat watching television. Jano and Ian had a cup of tea in the kitchen, then Jano asked Donna and Karen if they wanted a lift home. They dropped Karen and her son back to her house in Mirboo North. She didn't have her keys so Jano and Ian climbed through a window and opened the door to let her in. She packed some clothes for herself and her son and then hopped back in the car. Jano and Ian drove their passengers to Donna's house in Moe.

When the two men were finally alone in the car, Ian said to Jano, 'What have we done?' Jano told him that if he didn't talk about it, they would all be fine. Ian hadn't said another word about it.

By the time the two returned to the Maslins' house, Rhona and Irene had also returned. It was then that Jano told Ian that they needed to go and get Paul's motorbike, which was still at Rhona's house.

The next part of the interview retraced Ian's original story but this time, he admitted that he'd helped Jano get the motorbike and bring it back to Jano's garage. He told again how he, Jano, Irene and Rhona had all stripped the bike and put the parts into plastic bags.

McLoughlin asked Ian why they had all stripped the bike. In hindsight, the fact that the parts had begun surfacing at the tips had been the first clue that something sinister had happened to Paul. He said it was Irene and Jano who had decided that the bike had to be stripped and its parts hidden. Ian described tossing many of the bigger bike parts into the two dams and then told the detectives how he and Jano had driven to the tip and how Jano had told him to take the parts out of the plastic bags and scatter them around. Fortuitously for the two men, the tip gates were open when they got there in the small hours of the morning. The two then drove to a second tip and scattered the contents of the remaining bags.

In the car on the way back to Mirboo North, Ian had said, 'Those tips should be getting dozed in the next week 'cause they're pretty full.' Jano had agreed and then said nothing else. If the rubbish in the tips was crushed or moved by bulldozers, then the evidence of their crime could lay buried forever under tonnes of rubbish. The two conspirators remained silent for the rest of the trip home.

After a break in the interview, during which Ian had a coffee and a cigarette, he continued his story from the point of returning from scattering the motorbike parts. The two had gone to bed. Ian didn't remember if anyone else was up when they had arrived back at the house, but he thought not. The next morning, everyone had slept late and it was around 11 am when he woke up. Jano made him a coffee and then told him that there had been a bit of blood in the back of the Subaru and he had cleaned it up.

Ian said he hadn't seen the Maslins again until the Wednesday, when he went around to their house for dinner. Rhona was there as well. According to Ian, Rhona said she had a set of car keys that they could use to break into a house in Moe. Ian told her he wasn't interested. Homicide detective John Robertson asked whose keys Rhona was talking about. Ian said that the keys belonged to Paul and that they would open his Commodore. It was Ian's impression that Rhona intended to steal Paul's car.

At the end of the interview, McLoughlin asked Ian why he hadn't been up-front about his involvement in his two earlier interviews with police.

'Because I was scared; scared to say anything.' Ian explained that a while earlier, he had been at the Maslins' house when two big guys had come looking for Irene. When they went off with her, Ian had asked Jano Maslin who they were. He told Ian that they were hit men. 'I ... got a bit scared. If I started sayin' anythin', I'd probably be a goner.'

Detective McLoughlin told Ian he would be charged with causing the death of Paul Snabel. He also asked Ian if he agreed to be filmed in a re-enactment video. Ian agreed and the re-enactment was set for the following day.

On 9 January, the day after Ian Gillin told his story to the detectives, Jano Maslin was interviewed at the Homicide Squad offices at the St Kilda Road police complex. Detective Sergeant Shane Downie conducted the interview. Jano Maslin wore his brown hair long and tied back into a scraggly ponytail, and a faded dark blue T-shirt with a small tear in the front. Maslin gave his name and address for the record and listed his occupation as an electrical fitter. He said he was 30 years old. Downie advised him of his rights and Maslin said that he wished to phone his parents. The interview was suspended to allow Jano to make his call.

When the interview resumed, Jano said in a quiet measured voice that he used to work in Melbourne before he met his wife. Then he'd moved from Dandenong to Shady Creek, which he said was just out of Yarragon near Warragul. The conversation was chatty enough when Jano said, 'Hang on a minute. Er, when you said before about caution ... directly after that I was going to say I'll decline to say anything.'

Downie explained that he still had to put the allegations to Jano and told him that he could say 'no comment' or answer questions if he wished. Downie told Maslin that all he wanted to begin with was a bit of his history. Maslin was happy enough to oblige. He said that he'd moved to Mirboo North two years earlier with Irene and her eight-year-old son to another man. Maslin detailed the improvements that he had made to his property, with new fencing and a concrete slab that had been poured for the new garage. He had concreted a driveway and insulated the house.

Downie moved the questioning to 5 November 1989. Jano said that he especially remembered 5 November because it was Guy Fawkes Day. He recalled Ian and another man coming around to his house on 4 November to help dig the swimming pool. Irene's and Karen's sons were playing in the backyard while the men worked on the pool.

'Where was Karen?'

'As far as I remember, she was back at Rhona's house packing furniture,' said Jano before explaining that Karen was moving out of Rhona's house and into a place of her own. Rhona had come around later that day to collect Karen's son. Jano denied that Karen or Donna had come around to his house, but said that Rhona had returned later to watch some videos.

Next, Downie asked Maslin about his garage. He listed all the motorbikes he and Irene owned and described how he fixed them himself if he could to save money on maintenance and repairs. Downie asked Maslin to describe his garage on 5 November. He said that his normal tools were in the garage, along with his caravan and a couple of motorbikes.

'Did you leave those premises at any time during the day?'

'No.' Maslin rubbed his bushy dark beard.

'That being daytime and night-time? Did you leave ...?'

'I'm fairly certain that we didn't ...' He went on to say that he didn't remember, but he might have left to get a trailer of sand for his swimming pool base.

'Well, I put it to you,' said Downie, 'that on the day of the fifth of November you in fact didn't sleep at your premises in the morning. What do you say to that?'

'I can't remember,' he replied, crossing his muscly arms firmly across his chest, where they would remain as the questions probed the murder of Paul Snabel.

Downie pressed on. He asked Maslin whether he had brought Irene's and Karen's sons to the house that morning from somewhere else. Jano said he couldn't remember. Then the detective asked about Paul's motorbike and whether it could have been in his garage. Jano said, 'No comment.'

'I also put it to you that you brought that motorcycle to your premises with your Subaru station wagon, in a trailer ... what do you say to that?'

'No.'

'I also put it to you that after the bike was dismantled, that you and Ian Gillin decided to take that in the back of the Subaru and place it in the two ... dams, the Boolarra tip and the Yinnar tip. What do you say to that?'

'I'll deny that.'

'I also put it to you that during the course of the afternoon, you left your premises in your Subaru and went to Nicholls Road where you assisted in the removal of a human body from those premises. What do you say to that?'

'I deny that,' said Jano, who went on to deny all involvement in the activities surrounding the murder.

'Do you know a person by the name of Paul Snabel?'

'Yes. We ... well no – I met him once. Very briefly.' He said that he had met Paul a couple of months earlier at Rhona Heaney's house.

Downie paused the interview to offer Jano a cup of tea. After the break, the detective asked if he had anything to say about the allegations.

'Only other than the things I've said earlier are the things that actually took place as far as I can remember,' he replied.

Downie told him that he didn't believe that he was telling the whole truth and asked him if he had any reason to lie.

'No,' Jano said, 'no reason to lie.'

Downie informed him that he would be charged with the murder of Paul Snabel.

While her husband was being interviewed by Shane Downie in a nearby interview room, Irene Maslin walked into another interview room and sat opposite Andrew McLoughlin. She was wearing a navy blazer and a bright yellow dress underneath stretched tight across her frame. McLoughlin established her name and address. Irene lit a cigarette and dragged deeply on it. She gave her age as 32 and gave her occupation as 'home body, home duties care giver' in a monotone voice that sounded annoyed and perhaps angry.

Andrew McLoughlin advised Irene of her rights. She asked for a phone book.

'Who do you wish to contact?' McLoughlin asked.

'Anyone that's a solicitor,' Irene snapped at him.

Irene and the detectives left the room after the interview was suspended. About fifteen minutes later, the trio returned and took their seats again. Irene lit another cigarette and sat side-on to the detectives and stared at the wall.

McLoughlin started the interview again but Irene continued staring at the wall and gave no response to his questions. Occasionally, she dragged on her cigarette. This behaviour continued for the entire interview. Irene Maslin said nothing. At the end, McLoughlin told her that she was going to be charged with murdering Paul Snabel. She didn't react at all, but her body language and the way she stabbed her cigarettes into the ashtray suggested that Irene Maslin was angry. Very angry.

With all detectives on deck to interview all of the suspects in the death of Paul Snabel, Peter Wheeler interviewed Rhona Heaney. The interview began at 1.45 pm. Wheeler read Rhona her rights and told her that he wanted to talk about the events of Sunday 5 November.

Rhona admitted knowing Paul and told Wheeler that she had met him through Karen Randall. Rhona said that not long after she had met Karen, her new young friend was going through a hard time. Rhona had asked Karen to stay at her house in Nicholls Road.

'What was the "hard time"?' asked Wheeler.

'Oh, just everything in general was going wrong for her, so she said, the usual – money, boyfriends – things like that.'

Rhona said that after Karen had come to live with her, Paul had visited a few times.

On the night of Saturday 4 November, Rhona said that she and her friend Steve and Karen were home with the children. The visitors that she had mentioned in her earlier statement, she said, had actually visited the week before that. She had made a mistake. She didn't think anyone was at her house on the fourth.

'Think carefully,' said Wheeler, 'because I put it to you that Irene and Jano Maslin were also at your premises on that evening of the fourth.'

'They might have been,' she replied. 'I couldn't really confirm it.'

When Rhona saw that Peter Wheeler had her previous statement on the desk in front of him, she asked why it was there. Wheeler told her that he would refer to it in the interview.

'Is that a true and correct statement?' he asked her.

'I have no comments to make on that,' she replied.

'Is there any reason why you don't want to comment on the truthfulness of the statements that you've made to the police?'

'No, not really. No reason,' said Rhona, who added shortly afterwards that her solicitor had told her to make no comments to any of the questions police asked her.

During the interview, Rhona seemed happy to answer some of the questions but was pointed in the ones she wouldn't answer. She refused to comment on questions that were about who else was at her house on Sunday 5 November or the night before. She refused to comment about her accompanying Paul to get his motorbike from his house on the Sunday. She wouldn't respond to allegations that she was involved in the dismantling of the motorbike.

Wheeler put all the allegations to her – that she had an active part in Paul's murder, and that she had disposed of the body. 'I have no comment,' she replied.

Wheeler charged her with murder.

While three of the key players were being charged with murder and remanded into custody, two forensic experts went to the Morwell CIB. Crime scene examiner Sergeant Brian Gamble and forensic scientist Nigel Hall from the Applied Biology Department examined the couch, which had been relocated to the Morwell CIB office. Gamble photographed the couch while Hall examined it. While they were there, the two forensic investigators examined the Maslins' Subaru, which police had taken to search.

After looking at the couch and the Subaru at the police station, Gamble and Hall went out to Rhona Heaney's house in Nicholls Road. If Ian had been telling the truth, Paul had been sitting on one of the remaining armchairs and had bled onto the carpet. Rhona had cleaned the carpet, but getting rid of blood completely was very difficult.

Hall quickly found bloodstains on one of the armchairs and stains on a section of carpet near the armchair. The two forensic experts carefully cut out the section of carpet and on the underside, both men could see a large stain almost a square metre in size. It was later examined and determined to be blood. Blood was also detected on one of the green armchairs in the lounge room.

After the interviews at the Homicide Squad offices earlier in the day, detectives McLoughlin, Wheeler and Robertson drove Ian Gillin to the Maslins' house in Mirboo North. It had been a long day for the detectives and by the time they arrived, it was a little after 6 pm.

Ian again took the detectives through his statement. He had little new information to add, but he did say that when Irene Maslin had dropped him and Jano off at the house on the night of the murder, she had said, 'We're just going to get rid of the body.'

At the end of the re-enactment, Ian was asked if he had anything to add.

'Um, a few weeks later, I asked Irene where the body was and she said, "It's out near Shady Creek area. I'm not going to tell you whereabouts."'

On 11 January 1990, an application was made in the Melbourne Magistrates' Court under Section 646B for the detectives to talk further with Rhona Heaney after she was arrested and remanded into custody. Rhona was taken before a magistrate and asked if she understood the nature of what she had agreed to do. She said she did, and agreed to help the detectives try to locate Paul Snabel's body. They drove to the area as she remembered it, but the search was unsuccessful. While in the company of the police she also agreed to do a re-enactment of the murder at her house in Nicholls Road.

Considering that Ian and the Randall sisters had accused Rhona of being one of the instigators of the crime, her story seemed to minimise her own involvement. She didn't mention the afternoon attempt to poison Paul with speed and battery acid, and implied that the day had been completely normal until Jano and Ian had arrived in the early evening. They had all been sitting around having a chat. She said Ian was standing at the doorway with a baseball bat and she left the room and went into her son's room. She said she thought it would have been a better idea to simply take Paul outside and have Ian punch him and send him home.

Rhona said that she had heard a 'clunk' sound from where she was in the bedroom. She came back into the lounge room because it had been her job to inject Paul with battery acid, but she said that she was too nervous and couldn't do it. She joined Ian outside and said, 'This is really fucked. I want to get out of here.'

Rhona said that she then went back inside. When she saw Paul bleeding, she left and went into the laundry for most of the time.

'And then all I remember is getting in the Subaru after that.' She didn't mention Jano hitting Paul or the plastic bag being put over his head, nor did she admit to cleaning the blood from the carpet. She said that it had been her job to inject Paul 'because I was into speed years ago so I knew how to put it into your veins but I hadn't used it in so long, but they thought I should be able to still do it.'

Rhona claimed to have spent the rest of the time either in her son's room or in the laundry and the next thing she knew, she was in the Subaru heading out to Shady Creek in the middle of the night. She knew that Paul's body was in the back of the Subaru but didn't know how it got there. When Irene found a good spot to dump the body in the bushes, Rhona said she had felt too ill to help. She admitted dragging some bushes over to the Subaru but didn't remember what happened after that.

Later at the Maslins' house, she said that she tried to help strip the bike but because she didn't know what she was doing, they all sent her away. She went inside and went to bed.

Rhona couldn't think of anything else to add to her statement and the video recording ceased.

A little after 11 am on 19 January, Donna Randall sat opposite Detective Wheeler in one of the Homicide Squad interview rooms. He read Donna her rights. Not surprisingly, she had yet more to add to her story.

A couple of days before her house-warming party on 4 November, Donna had met with Jano and Irene Maslin, Rhona and Karen. The five friends had discussed the problem of Paul Snabel. Apparently, Paul had followed Karen's son home from school that day and Irene was worried that he might hurt the young boy. According to Donna, Irene had told the group that something needed to be done. At first, they had joked that they could break both his legs.

'Rhona and Irene started discussing what they could do about him in a more serious way ... they'd come up with the idea that they'd get some speed and put something into it and then make him take it or inject it into him.'

At the meeting, they had all discussed Paul's past strange behaviour and the violence he'd perpetrated on Karen. Karen had also told them about how he had once tried to shove sleeping tablets down her throat. Even though they had split up three months earlier, Donna said that Paul still came around to see Karen and hassled her. One time Karen had suffered a black eye and she told Donna that Paul was responsible. Another time, he had been down at the pub drinking and had come banging on Karen's door in the middle of the night. They'd told him to leave, but he'd walked around the house banging on all the windows and yelling at the top of his voice. Donna said that she remembered Karen having two black eyes and a badly twisted arm during her time with Paul.

Donna told the detectives that they had all agreed Paul was a danger to both Karen and her son. It was decided that Donna would lure Paul to Rhona's house on the night of her party. Donna presumed that when Karen rang Paul while he was at her party, she had made promises of getting back together again if he came out to Nicholls Road.

'And you've all decided on a certain course of action that you were going to take, a plan or something had been formulated?' asked Wheeler.

Donna said that she was supposed to talk Paul into going to Mirboo North. Karen was supposed to entice him out there, and Irene and Rhona would inject him with speed mixed with battery acid. Jano hadn't said much in the planning.

After her house-warming party, when she finally got Paul to Rhona's house, Donna said that she felt scared for him, but at the same time, it was 'just like a dream' and 'a bit too unreal'. When Rhona and Irene indeed injected him with the mixture of speed and battery acid, Irene had whispered, 'We got him to take it,' before telling Donna that if she didn't want to see him fall down, she'd better leave.

Irene and Rhona had taken Paul on the long walk after injecting him, figuring that if he was moving, the dangerous cocktail of drugs would go through his system faster. But they figured wrong. Paul had returned to the house looking none the worse for wear, and had then hopped on one of the motorbikes and gone joy-riding around the paddocks. Things certainly were not going to plan for the would-be killers. Seeing Paul out of the window racing around the paddock, the women all concluded that their plan had failed. Donna had got the impression that Rhona and Irene were going to go out and bash Paul. Karen was shaking and nervous, and it was then that she had decided to leave.

Wheeler asked Donna if she had since been told what had happened to Paul after they had left.

'I didn't know what they'd done. I didn't ask. I didn't really wanna know. First thing that come to mind was they've bashed him and put him somewhere. Just ... maybe he had to find his way to a hospital or something like that 'cause I didn't think they could do something like kill someone. As time went on I presumed that he was dead and that they had killed him.'

Donna said that when Karen had her house-warming party a couple of weeks after the event, she had got drunk and 'made a fool of herself', resulting in a falling-out between Karen and Irene. Donna recalled that after that, when she was talking to Karen on the phone, Irene said to tell Karen that she was 'polishing both barrels'. Donna took this as a threat towards Karen.

During the stay in Corio, Donna had overheard Rhona and Irene talking about possibly moving the body but discussing that it would by now be rotting and smelly and quite possibly had been dragged away by animals.

As the interview drew to a close, Wheeler asked Donna whether she was aware in advance of what was going to take place at Nicholls Road.

'Yeah,' replied Donna.

'You've also indicated that each person had a specific role. You've already indicated your role. Now, at any stage, have you said to any of the people at the discussion, "No, this is wrong. I don't want to do it."?'

'Um, I don't think so ... no.'

'And I'll put it to you that as a result of what was discussed by all of you on that day, that you knew Paul was going to be killed when he was taken out to Nicholls Road?'

'I really don't know if I knew that he was gunna be killed ... I don't know.'

'Well,' said Wheeler, 'I further put it to you that at no stage have you gone to the police or alerted anyone of what was going to take place as a result of that discussion?'

'No, I didn't really.'

'Well, can you explain why you haven't done that?'

'Because I was scared. I don't know whether you'd believe me or not, but I was scared. I've never come across anything like it before. I didn't know what to do. I thought if I'd said something to anyone that they would have probably killed me and if I'd gone to the police that they'd probably arrest me anyway.'

Wheeler asked if she had at least tried to warn Paul. She admitted that the reason she had kept putting him off when he'd wanted to leave her party and go to Nicholls Road was because she was trying to delay what was going to happen. But Wheeler persisted, saying that even if she had been reluctant, she still ended up delivering Paul to Irene and Rhona and their plan of the speed syringe laced with battery acid. He then told Donna that she would be charged with causing the death of Paul Snabel.

After they had finished with Donna, Robertson and Wheeler next interviewed Karen Randall. She was read her rights before the interview started. Referring to a few pages of handwritten notes, she recapped her previous statement, this time speaking about her relationship with Paul.

She said that he had given her a black eye after an argument when she had accused him of seeing other women. He had hit her, and Rhona and Irene had seen her with the black eye. They were angry at his behaviour. According to Karen, Irene had been interested in star charts and she had done Paul's chart and then announced that Paul was crazy and dangerous and that she felt he would kill Karen.

One day, not long before the murder, Paul had come around to Rhona's house and he and Karen were arguing on the porch. Next thing Karen knew, Irene, Jano and another man pulled into the driveway. Apparently, Rhona had called them for support. Paul had left as soon as they arrived.

A few days before the murder, Karen said she had received a postcard from Paul with the words *You make me see red* printed on the front of it. The postcard had been pushed under the door of her new house. She said she had been shocked because she didn't think that Paul knew her new address. Irene had been with her at the time. Karen had been upset, but Irene had been angry. Afterwards, the two women had joined Rhona and Donna and discussed the situation. During the discussion, Karen said that Irene had discussed 'disposing of Paul'. The general discussion had quickly turned to specifics when Irene started talking about luring him out to Rhona's house and injecting him with battery acid. The plan was to be enacted that coming weekend.

Karen played her part and rang Paul at Donna's party, asking him to come to Rhona's house. Rhona had got some syringes from the chemist. Karen said that before she rang Paul, Rhona had injected her with speed and then injected Irene. The rest of Karen's story was similar to her other statements. Paul had arrived, he had gone on a bike ride to Leongatha, come home, been talked into an injection of speed, which Rhona and Irene had administered, and then Karen and Donna had left when Paul got Irene's motorbike bogged in the paddock.

Back at the Maslins' house, Jano and Ian had left shortly after Donna and Karen had arrived. They were gone for several hours. When Jano and Ian returned, Jano had said to Karen, 'Well, he's not going to bother you again.' Karen had asked him to explain and according to Karen, Jano had told her there had been a fight and Paul had taken off. She hadn't believed him and figured that Paul was dead.

Towards the end of the interview, John Robertson cut to the chase. He asked again about each person having a role to play in the plan. Karen agreed. Robertson asked Karen if she realised what might happen if the plan to inject Paul with battery acid took place.

'Um ... that ... that it'd kill someone – I knew that.'

He asked if Karen had contacted Paul any time between the meeting and the night of Donna's party.

'Um ... I don't think so.'

'Didn't ring him up or warn him?'

'No.'

'Didn't tell anyone else that he shouldn't go to the party or anything?'

'No, I didn't um ... contact him at all.'

'Right,' said Robertson. 'And in that interim period as well, did you phone the police and tell them what was going to happen?'

'No.'

Karen tried to back-pedal. She said that maybe Irene was big-noting herself and that while she believed that something would happen, she didn't necessarily think that the plan would be carried out.

But Robertson insisted that she knew that even the plan to inject battery acid could prove fatal.

'I knew that the battery acid would kill someone.'

Robertson replied by saying, 'You're going to be charged with causing the death of Paul Snabel. You're not obliged to say anything unless you wish to do so but whatever you say or do may be recorded and given in evidence ...'

Karen and Donna Randall were both remanded into custody.

❖ ❖ ❖

On 25 January 1990, in the early hours of the morning, Detective Sergeant Shane Downie coordinated a search for Paul's body using a large number of police and State Emergency Service (SES) members. While the Homicide Squad held little hope that the body would be found in the dense bushland, Downie knew the area well and was a little more optimistic. Not only was it important for him to find the body to solidify the case against the people responsible for the murder, but it was also vital for closure for the victim's family. Until a body is located, family members always cling to the possibility that a missing person is still alive.

According to Rhona's re-enactment interview, she and Irene had driven the Subaru into the area and dumped the body from the car. She had said that the body had been dumped off a dirt track in dense bush on the left-hand side of the road. The police bus took all the SES volunteers on a journey through the bush in the Noojee State Park, east of Springsure Hill, searching any track where you could drive a car.

Russell was a local dairy farmer and SES volunteer from the Leongatha Branch. He walked up the main track for nearly a kilometre from where the police bus had dropped off some of the searchers. He saw a track on the northern side, which he judged was wide enough for vehicle access. Up the track, he could see that ferns and grass had been flattened, which indicated that a vehicle had been up there relatively recently. Further up the track, he could smell a foul odour that he later described as smelling like a decaying animal. He could see that a car had done a three-point turn up the track a little and there were some tyre marks right next to a sawn-off log. Russell saw a pair of blue jeans lying on the ground in the long grass. About a metre away from the jeans was what looked like a rib bone. Russell made his way back down the track and whistled loudly to attract attention to his find. One of the police officers appeared and the two inspected the site together. The police officer radioed for assistance.

As soon as the remains were located, Homicide detective John Robertson contacted Dr David Ranson from the Victorian Institute of Forensic Pathology and asked him to come to Shady Creek. It was critical that the forensic pathologist attend the scene to get an impression of the conditions in which the remains had been located. Dr Ranson drove with Wheeler and Robertson, as well as fellow pathologist Dr Alison Cluroe, to the bush location. The four arrived at 5.20 in the afternoon. At the scene, they met up with crime scene examiner Tony Kealy, and the party made their way to the Sweetwater Creek track. Around 6 pm, the group arrived at the inconspicuous piece of bushland surrounded by flattened grass, a pile of logs, and a small tree. Near the pile of logs, Ranson saw a collection of bones. They were photographed and put into a plastic evidence bag.

Underneath the pile of logs, Ranson could see more human bones. These too were examined and bagged. In a grassy area nearby, the experienced pathologist found a portion of human skull; he found the greater part of the skull a bit further down the flattened grass track. Ranson found bones located in eight different areas around the search site, as well as pieces of material scattered among the vegetation. Some of the material looked like a pair of blue jeans.

While Dr Ranson collected human bone fragments, crime scene examiner Tony Kealy looked for any other evidence. Kealy collected and bagged some more pieces of clothing around where the bones had been scattered. About sixteen metres from a tree that the crime scene examiners had used as their central reference point in the search, Tony Kealy found a log lying on the ground, which had a small area of damage. He could see that the damage was relatively fresh and there was a pink-coloured substance on the log. He collected it for evidence.

Once the pile of logs was moved, David Ranson found more bones and noted that the soil under the logs was very dark in colour, in contrast to some of the surrounding soil. The search finished when darkness fell around 9 pm. As soon as the search was over, Shane Downie drove to the home of Paul's parents. Downie didn't want the family to hear the news through the media. He informed them that human remains had been found and that there was a possibility that they could belong to their son. He told them that police would need their son's dental records.

At the morgue the following morning at 11 am, Dr Ranson began his examination of the remains found at Shady Creek. Working through the evidence bags one by one, Ranson laid out the bones that had been found in different locations around the bush and made note of each fragment, what it was, and where on the body it came from. Many of the bone fragments, while not showing signs of any ante-mortem injury, had been subjected to post-mortem chewing – most probably from bush animals.

The skull fragments told more of a story. Ranson examined the skull and noted that 'examination of the edges of these bone fragments showed crush artefacts together with entrapped hair on some surfaces, features indicating that the injuries that had resulted in these fractures occurred prior to the complete decomposition of the soft tissues of the body. Similarly, the lower jaw contained fourteen teeth. Although the jaw showed no evidence of injury, Ranson noted that 'one of the teeth towards the front of the jaw was missing and a sharp-edged tooth socket indicated that the loss of the tooth had occurred recently and it is possible the tooth was lost at some stage shortly before or after death'.

After Ranson had examined all the bones and documented his results, the skull bones were stuck together using wax so that the pathologist could get a more complete picture of the injuries to which the victim had been subjected. He concluded that the skull had radiating fracture lines in the vicinity of the left ear, fractures in a circumference from front to back of the skull, and that 'force had been applied from a sideways direction to the head'. The presence of hair in some of these fractures meant that they occurred while the victim still had hair, and not after the body had decomposed. Ranson felt that the skull fractures were caused by 'a number of occasions of significant force to the left side of the head which were inflicted when there was hair on the head. The nature of the damage to the skull is of a type that is usually associated with very severe underlying brain trauma and would be expected to lead to unconsciousness and death, although death may not occur immediately'.

Because teeth had been found in the upper and lower jaws, a forensic dentist was consulted to compare the teeth in the skull to some X-rays that Paul had taken in 1988. He concluded that the skull belonged to Paul Snabel.

On Wednesday 7 February 1990, crime scene examiner Tony Kealy examined Irene and Jano Maslin's Subaru station wagon. On the lip underneath the passenger-side door, there was some damage and a portion of the lip was bent flat. Kealy postulated that the damage to the passenger-side lip could have been caused by the passenger side wheel running over an object larger in height than the clearance between the ground and the sharp lip, causing it to land on this object. He collected a sample of paint from the lip. Considering a damaged log had been found directly adjacent to the tyre tracks where Paul's body had been found, it was worth comparing the paint of the Subaru with paint found on the logs. They were a match. This link definitely tied in the Maslins' Subaru to the exact area where Paul's body had been found. With the lack of any admissions by the Maslins, any forensic link was important.

Predictably, the trials of the six accused contained as many twists and turns as the investigation.

At the committal hearing, Rhona Heaney, Ian Gillin, Donna Randall and Karen Randall were committed to trial but Irene and Jano Maslin were discharged on the grounds that there was insufficient evidence to warrant their trial. Rhona, Ian and the Randall sisters had all admitted their involvement, whereas the Maslins had refused to cooperate with the police at all. Their lack of cooperation had stood them in good stead. For the time being.

After the committal hearing, Ian offered to plead guilty to manslaughter and give evidence against Jano and Irene Maslin. The Maslins were served notice of a trial but the Director of

Public Prosecutions did not accept Ian's plea of manslaughter. All four were sent to trial for murder. After the ten-week trial, Rhona and the Randall sisters were found guilty of murder and Ian was found guilty of manslaughter. All four defendants made pleas for leniency in their sentences. In December 1991, the judge sentenced 38-year-old Rhona to fifteen years in prison with a ten-year minimum. Karen and Donna were both sentenced to fourteen years in prison with a minimum of nine years. Ian got six years with a four-year minimum.

All four appealed. Karen and Donna Randall were granted a retrial and were found guilty of attempted murder and each sentenced to four years in prison with a minimum of two years. Ian Gillin's sentence was reduced to four years with a three-year minimum. Rhona Heaney appealed all the way to the High Court of Australia to no avail, with her sentence remaining as originally imposed.

In June 1993, Irene Maslin finally went to trial and pleaded guilty to the murder of Paul Snabel. She was given fifteen years in prison with a ten-year minimum. Jano Maslin was found not guilty.

Neither Peter Wheeler nor John Robertson had ever had so many defendants for one victim. The whole case had echoes of Agatha Christie's *Murder on the Orient Express*, when the whodunit turns into they-all-did-it.

The most extraordinary thing about the Snabel case was that so many people could take part in a murder and not one of them thought that it was wrong. Perhaps with the exception of Ian Gillin, who detectives believed was roped in at the last minute, they had to wonder how the others could think that the killing of Paul Snabel was the only solution to Karen's problems with him.

After the trial and her imprisonment, Rhona Heaney contacted Detective Robertson every now and then. She hinted to him that there was more to the story than met the eye and that perhaps one day she would give him the missing pieces to the puzzle. But Peter Wheeler says today that you can never drill down deep enough to get to the underlying things that go on with a case like the murder of Paul Snabel. He says that even if any of the key players now gave a different version, he would find it difficult to believe. 'These people lied to us all along and changed their stories so often. At what point do you turn around and believe everything they say?'

For country detective Shane Downie, the Snabel case was one of the most bizarre cases of his career. Years after it happened, and after all the convicted players had served their time and been released back into the community, Downie says that Paul's family are the forgotten victims in the story. They lost a son and because the circumstances were so sensational, the fact that a young man lost his life became almost a minor detail.

Chapter Four

❖

THE VIOLET TOWN COLLISION

*Secrets push their way up through the sands of
deception so that men may know them.*

– From a poster on the wall above Carsten Schultz's
desk at the Major Collision Investigation Unit

It was impossible not to notice the huge truck driving dangerously
late at night, weaving snakelike across double lanes of the Hume
Highway. Luke and Angela were heading to Albury for Easter,
driving right behind the truck. On the approach to the Violet Town
exit, Luke tried to overtake the truck. He figured it was best to put
some distance between their car and the huge red truck with the
white trailer. Luke moved into the right lane to overtake, but just
as he drew near, the truck veered over into his lane.

Luke hit the brakes and pulled back.

'This guy must be asleep or something,' said Angela after the
tense moment had passed.

Once the truck was back in the left lane, Luke tried again to
overtake. The truck swerved again. It took three attempts before
Luke was finally able to plant his foot and get the hell away from
the dangerous truck.

Once the moment was over, Luke and Angela settled back into
their journey, hoping that if the truck driver was drowsy, he would
have the sense to stop for a rest-break.

After six months in the Major Collision Investigation Unit, Senior Constable Carsten Schultz hadn't become used to the phone ringing in the middle of the night. At 12.15 am on Good Friday, 1998, the phone rang and it took Schultz a moment or two to register what the noise was. Schultz had worked a 3 pm – 11 pm shift and had only just fallen into a deep sleep when he got the call. On the other end of the line was his sergeant, Brian Sweetman, who told him that there had been a fatal collision near Violet Town on the Hume Highway between Euroa and Benalla.

Schultz, Sweetman and Senior Constable Chris Harris were the on-call crew during the night and calls like this were common. Schultz struggled out of bed and Sweetman picked him up 20 minutes later. The two officers met up with Harris at the Glen Waverley Major Collision Investigation Unit office on Springvale Road. Information already received told them that a truck had collided with a Mazda Bravo four-wheel drive towing a caravan and a child had died in the collision.

Since the truck didn't stop after the collision and was headed north, there was a good chance the driver would be apprehended at the border. Inside the office, Brian Sweetman called the Wangaratta Communications Centre and requested they contact the local police to set up a roadblock on the New South Wales border between Albury and Wodonga on the Hume Highway. Sweetman also instructed the State Emergency Service (SES) to set up lights at the crash scene. Coordinating the scene from Glen Waverley, Sweetman radioed instructions to the local police officers to divert all traffic off the Hume at the closest turn-off before the collision site. The area on the Hume Highway where the collision had occurred had to be treated as a crime scene and it was crucial that evidence not be disturbed.

Brian Sweetman also called his senior sergeant, Jeff Smith, and informed him that his crew was heading to Violet Town and wouldn't be available for any other jobs. Jeff Smith told Sweetman to keep him informed.

Schultz, Sweetman and Harris loaded their equipment into their specially fitted four-wheel drive, known as the 'crash truck'. The drive to the Violet Town collision site took two hours, lights and sirens. En route, the three police officers discussed what they might find. Attending a fatal that involves a child is never easy. Each of the officers had children of his own and comparisons were inevitable – *That could be my child* ...

Through local cops at the scene, Sweetman heard that there had been no sign of the truck at the border, so while Schultz drove, Harris checked the road map and the officers discussed possible directions the absconding truck might take.

A couple of kilometres from the collision, the crash truck took to the gravel, bypassing the huge traffic jam caused by cars slowing down to take the turn-off. It looked more like peak hour than the small hours of the morning. Once they'd spotted the scene in the distance, Schultz slowed down to a crawl and stopped well clear of the debris. It was 3 am and cold enough for the officers to zip up their thick police-issue leather jackets over their white crime scene overalls. They approached on foot. In the pitch-black country night, visibility was almost zero, and though the SES had set up a light to illuminate the scene, it didn't really help much and the officers had only a partial impression of the entire scene.

Traffic Operations Group (TOG) Sergeant Ron Kennedy met them as they got closer to the debris that had been strewn along the highway. Kennedy filled them in on the story so far. Witnesses reported a truck with a big white trailer disappearing in a cloud of dust immediately after the collision. The victim, twelve-year-old Nicky Fleming, had died on impact. His father, brother and sister had all been taken injured to hospital.

Thawing out over a cup of coffee courtesy of the SES van, the officers walked the scene slowly. Kennedy offered any assistance that he and the TOG officers could give, but was relieved to hand over the responsibility of the investigation to the experts.

The car and the caravan had separated on impact and both rolled in different directions – the caravan to the right, the Mazda to the left side of the road. The officers walked to the caravan, which had come to rest upright on the median strip in the middle of the highway. A rectangular section was torn cleanly from the back right-hand panel of the caravan and lay on the same side of the highway as the Mazda. The caravan had in all probability been clipped from behind. Schultz's torch beam illuminated a tartan mattress visible through the gaping hole in the rear of the caravan.

Across the other side of the highway, the Mazda Bravo had come to rest on its roof with debris scattered all around. In his torch beam, Schultz saw a Peter Pan colouring book, children's sneakers, empty McDonald's drink cups, thongs, a hubcap, and a scattering of personal belongings that had tumbled from the car as it rolled. The body of Nicky Fleming, clothed in a colourful hooded windcheater and tracksuit pants, lay face down on the roof inside the upturned vehicle, his sandy-coloured hair streaked with blood. One of his little hands lay curled near his head, making it look like he might be sleeping. In his left hand was an Easter egg wrapped in gold foil. Around the other side of the car, Nicky's blood-streaked feet protruded from the shattered window. A child dead at Easter. The police officers took a moment to acknowledge the loss of a young life, but they didn't have time to dwell on it; they had a job to do.

Brian Sweetman called Jeff Smith around 4 am to give him an update.

'It's a big scene,' he told his senior sergeant. 'Can you send Bellion up?' Sergeant Peter Bellion was the squad's engineer and an expert in collision scene analysis. Jeff Smith agreed and told Sweetman to keep him posted.

Peter Bellion arrived just as the sun rose. The police officers realised for the first time how far the scene extended. Double-tracked tyre marks arched blackly across both northbound lanes of the road and continued onto the median strip, indicating that the truck had travelled for some metres on the grass. Schultz wondered if the truck would have had enough time to slow down, veer to the left and take the Violet Town exit. Or perhaps the driver had continued straight up the Hume. None of the witnesses could say for sure. Brian Sweetman called Jeff Smith, who had gone in early Good Friday morning to the Glen Waverley office to monitor the situation.

'We've got a problem,' he said. 'There are tyre marks that make the scene twice the size we originally thought it was.'

With this information, Jeff Smith knew that his men needed help with the scene coordination and the media so that they could get on with the job. Going up the chain of command, Senior Sergeant Smith contacted the Collision Squad inspector, Chris Ferguson, who worked out of the squad's Brunswick office. He explained the situation: a fatal collision involving a child, the Easter weekend, and the Hume Highway was blocked – possibly for the best part of the day. Ferguson agreed that Jeff Smith should travel to the scene in the police helicopter.

Ferguson got a call from his superintendent who had heard a media report that the Hume Highway was blocked at Craigieburn. He'd put two and two together and thought that the Hume was blocked from Craigieburn to Violet Town – a distance of 150 kilometres. Ferguson radioed the police helicopter officers who assured him that the highway wasn't blocked off all the way. The block at Craigieburn was caused by a traffic-light malfunction, and the Violet Town traffic, while it was backed up about a kilometre, was slowly diverting onto the old Hume Highway. Ferguson was able to phone his superintendent and assure him that the two traffic jams were not connected.

Chris Ferguson knew it was always problematic to block off sections of major roads, especially at holiday times when thousands of cars travelled them. But the area was now a crime scene and it must be preserved. His officers needed time to process it properly.

Brian Sweetman drove to the Benalla hospital to speak with Nicky's dad, Ian Fleming. Ian's forehead was lacerated and his nose had a deep gouge. His other son, fourteen-year-old Glen, had sustained a fractured skull, while his eight-year-old daughter Kimberley had minor cuts and grazes. Ian Fleming explained to Sweetman that he had slowed down to take the Violet Town turn-off. He had needed petrol. He'd been hit from behind just before the exit.

Bellion, Schultz and Harris began the daylight crime scene examination. On the right front panel of the Mazda Bravo, the three officers noted one horizontal and two vertical indentations, which looked like they could have been made by a bull bar. The position of the vehicle on the left-hand side of the highway, and the caravan on the median strip, led them to speculate that the truck had hit the caravan on the back right-hand side, causing the car and the caravan to jack-knife. As the caravan veered left, the car was flung to the right towards the median strip. When the truck swerved to the right after impact with the caravan, it collided with the front right-hand panel of the car, sending it into a roll. The caravan was wrenched free and flung to the right, coming to rest on the median strip. The Mazda rolled with such velocity that it left perfect impressions of its side in the bitumen. The caravan had bitumen scrapings on one side, making it look like it had slid across the road on its side and then somehow righted itself. Apart from a few minor dents and scratches, it was in remarkably good condition. The same couldn't be said for the vehicle.

As Carsten Schultz walked the highway slowly, he hit the accident investigator's version of a jackpot: some pieces of amber glass – one with a serial number on it. It looked clean and fresh enough that it probably came from the collision. Schultz bagged it as evidence. Crime scene officers from Wangaratta swept the surrounding area and bagged debris to be examined later at the Forensic Science Centre in the hope of finding further evidence.

Looking closely at the back right-hand panel that had been torn from the caravan, the officers noticed a rectangular indentation with an inverted *V*, or perhaps the top of an *A*, imprinted on the aluminium. Could it be the impression of a number plate? Above the impression was a clean tear, a hole punched straight through.

On both the caravan and the car, the police investigators noted smears of red paint – probably transferred from the truck on impact. On the ground near the back of the Mazda Bravo, among the debris, lay a piece of mudflap from an International truck. As Schultz turned the piece of evidence over in his hands, he noticed that the broken edges were worn and dirty, indicating that it was not a fresh break. It was possible the missing truck was an International, but then again, the mudflap could be old and just here by coincidence.

As Jeff Smith approached by helicopter, he could see what Sweetman had meant by it being a 'big scene'. Scattered debris was clearly visible strewn hundreds of metres up the highway, as were the black skid marks of the missing truck. He landed to confer with his investigators while Chris Harris boarded the helicopter to take aerial photographs of the scene.

At this point, the investigators knew a truck had rammed the caravan, and the officers showed Smith the International mudflap. The position of the mudflap was consistent with it being flung off the truck on impact. If it was an International truck, it was one of tens of thousands traversing Australia's roads.

One of Jeff Smith's jobs at the scene was to handle media inquiries. Radio host Neil Mitchell went live-to-air talking to Smith about the situation. Smith knew that the media could help in two ways; the first was that someone listening could hold vital information about the collision, and secondly, people caught in the traffic jam on the Hume would understand the reason for it – and their anger at the delay might turn to sympathy. Any law-abiding citizen would put up with a bit of a delay so that the police could gather their evidence to catch the callous truck driver whose actions had killed a child.

Once the photographs of the car and the caravan had been taken in daylight, undertakers gently removed Nicky Fleming's body from the wreck and transported it to the morgue for post-mortem examination.

All up, collecting evidence and documenting the scene took over twelve hours – double the time a scene usually takes. When the officers were finished, the car and caravan were towed to Benalla for storage until they could be picked up after Easter and taken back to the Forensic Science Centre in Melbourne for testing. Peter Bellion took the caravan panel with him for immediate examination. If the indentation was a number plate, they needed to get onto it right away. The Hume Highway was opened for business at 2.55 pm.

Back at the office at 5 pm on Good Friday, their Easter cancelled, Smith, Sweetman, Schulz, Harris and Bellion went to work. Not being trucking experts, the officers began a steep learning curve. Initial inquiries at state motor registration boards told the investigators that there were 160,000 trucks registered on Australian roads. The crash investigators knew that they had to narrow the field, or they would be looking for a needle in a haystack. The red paint scrapings on the car and caravan suggested that the truck could be red but then again, the officers knew that it could also be another colour with red stripes.

The first thing Schultz did was to fill out a job-card – a summary of the job to submit to his superiors. Schultz contacted D24 and asked for tapes of all calls logged regarding Violet Town – just in case the truck driver had called triple 0 himself. The officers also began contacting any witness who had left their names with the police first on the scene.

In discussion, the investigators wondered if the hit-run driver, heading north along the Hume Highway just before Easter, was heading home because all the truck depots would be closed over Easter and therefore, he would hardly be heading north to sit outside a closed depot and wait four days for them to open again. But it was only a guess. At this stage, there wasn't much else to go on.

After working nearly 36 hours straight, Sweetman, Schultz and Harris finally went to their respective homes to sleep only to be back on deck Easter Saturday to continue the investigation. Some information had come in through Crime Stoppers, and each call was checked out.

Over at the Brunswick branch of the Collision Squad, Sergeant Peter Bellion calculated the exact measurements of the collision, and found that the truck had been travelling at 106 kilometres per hour at the beginning of the skid, and it had hit the Mazda that had been travelling at 88 kilometres per hour. This was consistent with Ian Fleming's statement that he had slowed down to take the turn-off.

The International mudflap had to be investigated. Officers contacted mudflap distributors and told them to be on the lookout for a truck seeking a replacement mudflap.

Late Saturday afternoon, Schultz rang Hella Australia – the maker of the amber light fragments from the collision. He knew no-one would be working on the Easter weekend, but he luckily got onto a helpful security guard who put him in touch with an engineer called Heinz Schulte, who had worked at Hella for 40 years and was a veritable expert in glass. Carsten Schultz rang Schulte and told him about the fragment of glass with the serial number K12642A2254. Schulte noted the number and promised to check Hella's catalogues.

As Carsten Schultz's young son woke to check if the Easter Bunny had been, his dad had gone into the office to check if the hit-run driver had given himself up. Experience told him that these types of offenders often gave themselves up in the days following hit-runs. They either took the time to come to grips with what they'd done – or sobered up or came down from pills. Schultz also knew that hit-run offenders almost always told someone what they'd done. Word would get around, and eventually, he'd get dobbed in. Worst-case scenario was that the truckie wouldn't tell a soul, and they all could be in for the long haul.

As promised, Heinz Schulte rang the squad office after his Easter lunch and said, 'Yes, it's one of ours.' But the glass expert explained that Hella fitted that kind of light to boats, cars and some trucks. They did, however, have a contract with Western Star trucks to fit their lights since 1994.

'Are you telling me it's a Western Star truck?' asked the police officer.

'No, the light could be fitted to anything. Don't hang your hat on a Western Star truck,' said Schulte.

On Tuesday 14 April, the results from Nicky Fleming's post-mortem results came through. Nicky had suffered from fractured ribs, a broken leg and broken collarbone, and had died from severe head injuries.

On Wednesday 15 April, Jeff Smith scheduled a debriefing in Seymour with the volunteer SES and CFA members and uni-formed police who had attended the collision scene. He drove up the Hume and made his way to the TOG office at the Seymour police station. The group of about fifteen gathered in the TOG mess room. After coffee and introductions, Smith took charge of the meeting. He wanted to find out what the volunteers had seen before the Collision Squad members had arrived. Often, they held vital clues to an investigation because they were first on the scene. And often, they didn't realise that what they knew was important.

Smith opened the debriefing by explaining how the investigation was going and then looked around the room. 'So, what did you blokes see?'

Over the next hour, the men discussed the collision. When the meeting was drawing to a close, one of the SES volunteers, almost as an afterthought asked, 'Did you get that mudflap that the motorist moved?'

'*Moved?*' Smith spluttered. 'Did you say, "moved"?'

'Yeah,' said the volunteer without realising the significance. 'One of the passing motorists who'd stopped after the accident found it near the caravan. He moved it over near the Mazda so you blokes wouldn't miss it.'

Smith went quickly over to the whiteboard in the mess room and drew a rough outline of the Hume Highway and marked the spots where the caravan and the Mazda had ended up.

'Where exactly did he pick it up from?' he asked the volunteer, who drew a mark behind the caravan on the median strip. Smith saw from the diagram that it was unlikely to have come from the truck. And the mudflap was only significant as evidence because of where it had been found near the upturned Mazda. Now it was almost certainly a red herring. These things can happen in an investigation, but the investigators had spent the last four days chasing up information on International trucks. Valuable time had been wasted.

After the meeting, Smith drove to the stretch of road where the collision had occurred and inspected the site where the SES volunteer had said the man picked up the mudflap. He suspected immediately that a southbound truck had dropped the mudflap and that it indeed had nothing to do with their collision. He also saw other mudflaps littering the highway – 'a mudflap graveyard', he would call it later. Smith concluded that mudflaps must come off trucks fairly easily. Back to the drawing board.

Early in an investigation, information floods in. With the deluge of information from Crime Stoppers, Jeff Smith quickly concluded that if there was a world champion profession for gossip, trucking had to be it. Truckies were dobbing in each other. Disgruntled neighbours were dobbing in truckies who parked their rigs in the street. Ex-wives got in on the action and dobbed in truckie ex-husbands.

Each report had to be followed up and all the officers at the Collision Squad were used to interview truckies. It all led nowhere.

Carsten Schultz bought as many trucking magazines as he could find and scanned the pages for makes and models that could fit the scant details they had of the offending vehicle.

Schultz contacted the New South Wales Roads and Traffic Authority to get the Safe-T-Cam photos. Unbeknownst to most car drivers, a gantry on the New South Wales border photographs all trucks that cross the border. Thirty kilometres further up the road, the truck is rephotographed and its speed is calculated from the time elapsed between photos. Infringement notices are sent to truckies who speed. Within a week he received 50 black-and-white Safe-T-Cam photos of trucks taken in the period between 10.30 pm and 6 am on the 9th and 10th of April. Schultz was looking for a truck with a bull bar and damage consistent with the Violet Town collision. He found nothing.

When the Mazda and the caravan had arrived at the Forensic Science Centre for extensive examination, forensic officer Senior Constable Lorelle Denham photographed them and sent the photos to Schultz. Schultz arranged to get a blown-up photograph of the caravan panel with the impression on its surface. The strange rectangular shape pressed into the metal of the aluminium panel was puzzling. It had to have been made by something on the face of the bull bar. Initially, it had looked like the impression of a number plate, but it was the wrong size. A hundred times a day, Schultz examined the photo. He felt that it had to hold the answer. The impression was rectangular with an inverted *V* in the middle of it. There were some circles and then a rectangular tear. Over and over, Schultz pondered what the shapes could be. He knew trucks had all sorts of signage on their fronts, *road train* and *hazchem* just to name a few. Schultz had a gut feeling that if he could identify what caused the strange impression, he could identify the type of truck that killed Nicky Fleming.

On 24 April, forensic officer Ted Kennedy-Ripon examined the wreckage of the Mazda and the caravan. He was surprised. For the truck to have hit first the back of the caravan and then the Mazda Bravo, it was sheer luck that so little evidence had been left behind. Kennedy-Ripon examined the paint smears that the investigators had noticed at the collision site. He carefully took samples and looked at them under the microscope. He found an automotive paint sequence – an iron-based undercoat with an epoxy primer and a topcoat. The topcoat was made from an organic red pigment. Kennedy-Ripon studied the red pigment and got a good professional handle on exactly what type of red it would be. He knew that most people see a red car or truck and can't differentiate between different shades and colour bases. This was purplish-red. With the help of investigators, Kennedy-Ripon requested and received paint samples from Australia Post, Mack trucks, paint manufacturers – and even from the truck that Wayne Gardner used to transport his racing cars. It had been travelling north on the day of the collision. None of the paint samples was the same as the one from Violet Town.

Reporting back to Schultz and Brian Sweetman, Kennedy-Ripon could give them little that could help.

'You guys are useless unless we find the truck,' Sweetman said, realising that unless Kennedy-Ripon had something to compare it to, his colour analysis was merely academic.

And Kennedy-Ripon had to agree.

By the end of May, Carsten Schultz had hit a frustrating series of dead ends. Until now, every piece of information had led somewhere else and now it seemed that the case had stalled. On 29 May, he and Brian Sweetman organised a round-table meeting with the forensic examiners at the forensic science lab.

Sweetman requested that the bull bar measurements be further examined. The bull bar had left clear dents in the caravan panel and the Mazda so perhaps that could be something to go on with. Nonetheless, Schulz left the meeting feeling frustrated. Maybe he'd watched too many cop shows on TV; he felt like Forensics should have more answers, like they should have looked at the paint scrapings and been able to tell instantly whodunnit. But he was slowly realising that they worked in response to very specific requests from the police. If he didn't ask the right questions, they couldn't give him the right answers. Eight weeks had passed since the collision and Schultz felt his stress levels building. Working full time on Violet Town gave him the lion's share of the responsibility – self-imposed, nonetheless. He was also finding that he couldn't leave the case at work. At home at night, his head would buzz with details and truck data, always thinking about what he needed to do next.

Schultz drove back from the meeting, finished his shift, and then picked up his wife and child. Wanting to show them exactly what he'd been working on, he drove to an industrial estate in Rowville containing a number of trucking yards. After he and his family had a look around, Schultz noticed a big red truck parked up the road. What caught his eye were two small canvas covers on the right- and left-hand side of the bull bar under the headlights. The insignia on the covers was a big white *W* with a red star in the middle – the logo for Western Star trucks. Schultz had looked at pictures of the caravan panel thousands of times and all of a sudden, it clicked. This was the pattern indented onto the panel.

Above the canvas cover was an eyebolt. Schultz knew he had found the right type of truck – but not the right truck. The eyebolt was in the wrong place to have made the tear in the caravan panel, and it showed no sign of damage or repair. He took the truck's details and registration number, and took his family home.

The following Monday at work, Schultz tracked down the owner of the truck and went to interview him. The truck driver showed Schultz that the covers were placed over the words *road* on the left and *train* on the right. In other states, big trucks are required to display the words *road train*, signifying that they are longer and heavier than normal trucks. In Victoria, however, these signs had to be covered. The truck driver was really helpful, and he even removed one of the Western Star covers and gave it to Schultz.

Back at the office, Schultz strode silently into the mess room and picked up a whiteboard marker. Without a word, he drew the Western Star insignia on the whiteboard and announced, 'I found the type of truck!' Schultz explained how he'd come across the truck, and recognised the impression from the caravan panel. Schultz got a round of applause.

Then Schultz rang Ted Kennedy-Ripon.

'Ted,' he said, 'I can tell you what type of truck it is.'

Kennedy-Ripon could tell from Schultz's voice how excited he was. It took a further day for the forensic science lab to test the cover against the marks on the caravan panel. It was a perfect match. Schultz's enthusiasm for the case just got a turbo-injected boost.

Once the make of the truck was established, the Collision Squad officers could further narrow down their search by finding out which Western Star trucks were fitted with the model of Hella light that would match the fragments found at the scene. After an exhaustive search, the records indicated that 1732 trucks built since 1993 were fitted with the Hella amber light. The cops were getting closer.

It was now that the bull bar became significant.

As Schultz established his Western Star lead, Lorelle Denham faxed through the measurements of the indentations left by the bull bar. The vertical sections were 75 millimetres wide. Investigators contacted a bull bar manufacturer, who examined the measurements. They were unusual. Most vertical uprights on bull bars were between 90 and 100 millimetres wide. There were only a few manufacturers who made 75-millimetre uprights. One of them was King Bars in Queensland. Western Star trucks were manufactured in Queensland so it stood to reason that King Bars might be the supplier of choice for Western Star trucks.

Carsten Schultz immediately contacted King Bars and spoke to Lester Strasburg, the manager. Strasburg explained that yes, he did manufacture 75-millimetre uprights on bull bars and yes, his company had the contract to fit bull bars to Western Star trucks. Chances were that the elusive truck had been through the premises at King Bars.

This new information was a bonus, but it came with a price. King Bars made 75-millimetre uprights, but did anyone else? Together, Sweetman and Schultz realised that someone would have to contact every bull bar manufacturer in Australia with their measurements to see if any other bull bar fitted the bill. Senior Constable Jamie Lynch was seconded to the Collision Squad to spend a month on the phone. As he hung up the phone for the last time, he was able to say with considerable authority that there were only three manufacturers in Australia who made bull bars with 75-millimetre uprights. There was one company in South Australia and another in northern Queensland, but their eyebolts were in the wrong place and didn't coincide with the tear in the caravan panel. King Bars was the one.

According to King Bar's Lester Strasburg, the only bull bar that fitted the forensic measurements with the eyebolt in the right place was a 4964F heavy duty road train bar. Schultz got a mock-up wooden bull bar made to the King Bar specifications and on 9 July, he took it to the lab to put it up against the caravan panel. As he pressed the model into the caravan indentations, it fitted like a glove. Same with the Mazda panel. Bingo.

As soon as Schultz was able to confirm that the 4964F heavy duty road train bar was the one they were looking for, Lester Strasburg agreed to send his receipt books to Melbourne. They arrived a fortnight later with a thump on Schultz's desk. There were over a thousand scrawled entries in the receipt books and most of them had scant details about the trucks onto which the bull bars had been fixed, but Schultz was excited to think that his truck could be somewhere in these books. After three weeks of painstaking work, the records revealed that 679 Western Star trucks had been fitted with the 4964F heavy duty road train bull bar. Out of these 679 trucks, 206 of them were fitted with the bull bar and the Western Star canvas covers.

Each of the Western Star trucks on the list had to be located and checked and the investigators appreciated how difficult this would be. These trucks travelled the country, they didn't just sit around waiting for the cops to eliminate them. However, trucks on the list were put in order from most likely to least likely according to all the criteria that investigators had amassed over the months. Schultz would enlist the help of interstate collision squads, who were always willing to lend a hand.

Another idea Schultz had was to get all traffic cops around the state to target Western Star trucks. He and Jeff Smith gathered a representative officer from every Traffic Operations Group (TOG) in the state at the Police Academy and explained the case to them. Schultz had developed a four-page questionnaire that he wanted filled out each time a Western Star truck was pulled over, listing make, model, colour, and most importantly, any damage it might have to its side and bull bar. Now the hit-run driver would have every TOG officer in the state looking for him. And the beauty of this plan was that every harassed truck driver would also be looking for the culprit. Some Western Star drivers would get pulled over four or five times in the course of the blitz.

Five months into the investigation, it was cause for celebration that the investigators had narrowed the field from 160,000 to 206. Carsten Schultz had worked full time on the Violet Town case, and at work, he barely took a break; now, finally, he could see the light at the end of the tunnel.

At the end of August, Schultz took leave to be with his wife, who was due to give birth to their second child. As much as he wanted the case solved, his biggest fear was that it would be solved while he was on leave. Senior Constable Rod Oldfield, the officer who took over Schultz's position, joked that he would solve it. Schultz was not amused.

Also on leave from the forensics lab was Ted Kennedy-Ripon. Ted and his family were holidaying with his in-laws in Echuca. Around lunchtime on Saturday 12 September, Kennedy-Ripon and his father-in-law took a drive and pulled into the Marulan Service Station to fill up. When Kennedy-Ripon got out of the car, he noticed a large red truck parked on the other side of the station. As his father-in-law filled the tank, Ted went over to get a better look at the truck. His father-in-law, who had heard all about the frustrating search for the red truck, laughed at Ted as he wandered off.

Kennedy-Ripon walked over, trying to look casual. There was no sign of the truck driver and he approached cautiously from the side. The big silver logo caught his eye – it read 'Western Star'. Right sort of truck, thought Kennedy-Ripon, and, after looking at the paint sample over the previous months, he also knew it was exactly the right colour. Kennedy-Ripon had a look at the bull bar to see if there were any signs of damage. It was then he spotted a crack in the bottom rung of the bull bar on the right-hand side – certainly consistent with the Violet Town collision. Kennedy-Ripon also noticed that the truck had a Western Star canvas cover on its *road train* sign, and that the eyebolt was in the correct position to have made the tear in the caravan panel. This was looking good. He walked around to the other side of the truck to see if there was any damage to the paintwork and found a scrape the size of a ten-cent piece close to the Hella light. Everything was consistent with Violet Town. As he examined the scraped paintwork, the truck driver stepped down from the side of the truck. Kennedy-Ripon hadn't noticed him there and nearly jumped out of his skin. This could be the bloke they'd been hunting for six months. Ted said the first thing that came to mind: 'How big's your engine?'

The truck driver was tall and average-looking; looked like a bit of a battler. Kennedy-Ripon told him that he was a trucking enthusiast. To the truck driver, it was two blokes making small talk. To Kennedy-Ripon, it was a forensic officer pumping a possible suspect for information.

'Do you own it?' Ted asked, knowing that the detectives were looking for an owner-driver rather than company driver, figuring that the collision damage would be easier to hide if the driver wasn't answerable to anyone.

'Nah, the bank owns it,' the driver laughed, but it meant the same thing – he was an owner-driver.

Back in the car with his father-in-law, Ted Kennedy-Ripon wrote down the truck's details. As soon as he'd got it all down, he used his mobile phone to call the Collision Squad. Speaking to Chris Harris, he told him that he might have found the truck. Later, when Kennedy-Ripon reached his final holiday destination, he faxed through a detailed account of the truck to the Collision Squad and waited anxiously to hear something.

What Ted Kennedy-Ripon didn't know was that Sergeant Richard Solty from the TOG in Victoria pulled over the same Western Star truck three days later and filled out the questionnaire that Carsten Schultz had provided.

The driver's name was Brett Killmore – and two hits on Killmore's truck in five days pushed it from twenty-fifth on the list of possible suspects to number one.

Impatient for news, Ted Kennedy-Ripon rang Carsten Schultz at home. Schultz thought it sounded like a strong possibility – but there had been so many 'strong possibilities' and 'definite maybes' over the months that he'd learnt not to get too excited. Even so, he couldn't resist a quick trip to the squad office to check out the details of Ted's fax. The other investigators were there checking insurance companies to see if any repair claims had been made on the truck after the Violet Town collision. It was a slow process, and Schultz took his son off to the Royal Melbourne Show.

Senior Constable Rod Oldfield, who'd joked he'd catch the Violet Town offender while Schultz was on leave, happily rang Schultz at the Show and said, 'I've got him!'

In the end, it came down to a check on Brett Killmore's mobile phone records. During the day of Thursday 9 April, in the lead-up to the collision at 10.40 pm, Brett Killmore's phone records placed him at Clayton in the morning. Just after 3 pm, he made a phone call from Dandenong, then one from Keysborough, then one from Braeside. By 9.15 pm, he was in Kilmore and half an hour later, he was in Seymour – heading towards the collision site at just the right time. His last phone call was made from Nagambie at 10.09 pm. Then nothing until 1.49 am on Good Friday morning. The call went through the Shepparton transponder. Not only did the phone calls put him at the collision site at precisely the right time, but they showed that he had left the Hume Highway and travelled up the

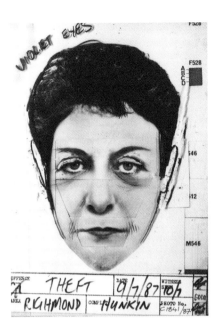

UNOLIET EYES

OFFENCE THEFT DATE 9/7/87 WITNESS 10h
AREA RICHMOND COMPLT HUNKIN PHOTO No. C184/87

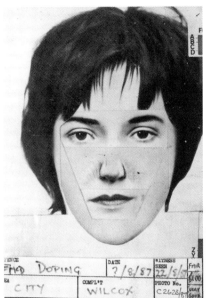

FENCE DOPING DATE 2/8/87 WITNESS SEEN 22/8
EA CITY COMPLT WILCOX PHOTO No. C2628/87

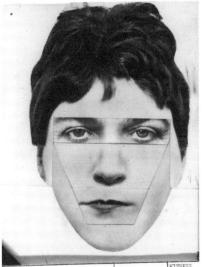

FENCE POISONING DATE 3/9/87 WITNESS SEEN 7/9/8
EA FITZROY COMPLT GUEST PHOTO No. C 2804/8

Poison Ivy

The mysterious woman who successfully drugged and robbed a series of Melbourne people, mainly lonely men, was dubbed 'Poison Ivy'. These identikits were assembled by three of her victims. By the time police saw the third one, provided by victim number five, they felt sure the crimes were all committed by one woman.

The crime scene examiner
Sergeant Trevor Evans has worked on a wide variety of cases during his years as a crime scene examiner. Pictured in Bali, where he was part of the Disaster Victim Identification team in the aftermath of the 2002 terrorist attack, he stands in front of a poignant piece of graffiti: *There's no place like home.*

One of Evans's cases included a murder at St Albans, in Melbourne's western suburbs. A body was found in this empty house.

A brick had been recently removed from the pile stacked up against the house.

The backpack and the missing brick found by a creek would provide crucial evidence in the murder investigation.

Where is Paul Snabel?
When Paul Snabel was reported missing from the small Victorian town of Mirboo North, near Moe, Inspector Peter Wheeler had a gut feeling that something sinister had happened to him. But he couldn't have guessed just how bizarre the circumstances of his disappearance would prove to be.

The area around Shady Creek, where Paul Snabel's remains were found, was littered with forensic evidence, including a log marked with paint from the Maslins' Subaru, tattered remnants of the victim's clothes and an SEC plastic bag, which played a key role in Snabel's nightmarish murder.

Death at Violet Town

A 12-year-old boy died in a hit and run accident when a truck hit his family car, which was towing a caravan. After months of painstaking investigation, detectives narrowed down the field to a Western Star truck like the one above, with covers to conceal the words *road* and *train*.

The panel that covered the words *road* and *train*.

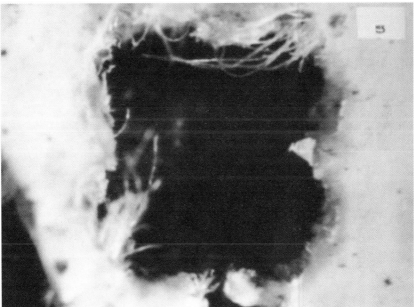

The piece of canvas found in a bolt on the caravan panel (top) was a perfect match for the tiny hole in the Western Star cover on the hit-run driver's truck (above).

The truck ripped this panel from the caravan. Note the strange indentations.

Only from the air could the accident investigators get a full picture of the extent of the scene they were faced with.

A mock-up of the truck's bull bar is matched
to the dents in the caravan panel.

The blooding

Miss Rita Knight's home in Wee Waa, NSW. The rapist who brutally attacked the 91-year-old woman first turned off the electricity from the power box, seen on the left of the veranda. On the right is the plastic chair in which the old woman sat waiting for help.

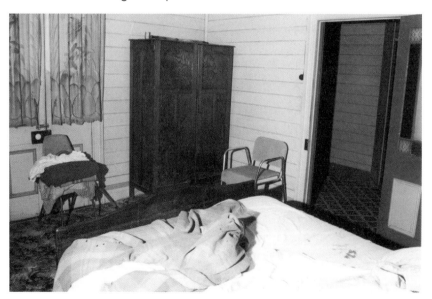

Police found the victim's blood on the bed where the attack took place, but the rest of the house was undisturbed.

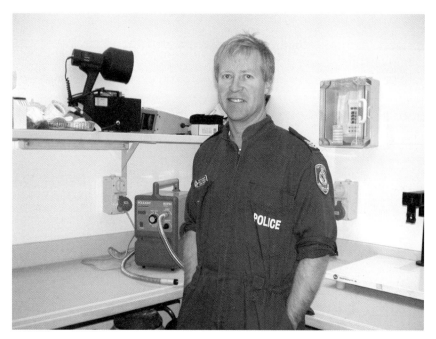

Police took the unusual step of DNA-testing all the males within the profiler's demographic in the small town of Wee Waa. Crime scene examiner Detective Sergeant Greg Carnell stands in front of the Polilight machine used to detect and enhance evidence, using wavelengths of light.

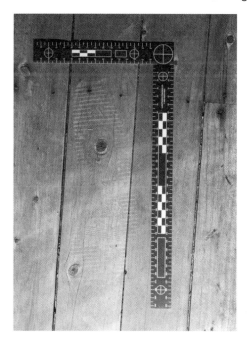

A shoe impression left by the offender on Miss Knight's porch.

Jenny De Gruchy and two of her children, 13-year-old Sarah and 15-year-old Adrian, were found bludgeoned to death on the morning of 13 March 1996. Jenny De Gruchy's Toyota Seca, parked outside their Wollongong home, contained some important clues.

Although the jack was in place, the wheel brace was missing from the car.

Fingerprints were later found on this jerry can in the garage.

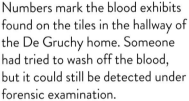

Numbers mark the blood exhibits found on the tiles in the hallway of the De Gruchy home. Someone had tried to wash off the blood, but it could still be detected under forensic examination.

Torn pieces of a note were found in a backpack recovered from a nearby water catchment. When pieced together, they formed a chilling murder to-do list, which played a vital part in the conviction of 18-year-old Matthew De Gruchy.

On the floor of the back seat of Jenny De Gruchy's car, Steve Hodder found a thread of carpet wool similar in colour to that of her bedroom carpet. It was stained with blood.

The contents of the backpack. Among them, investigators found almost every item that Matthew De Gruchy had listed as stolen from the house.

The carpet in Jenny De Gruchy's bedroom, showing the patch that was removed. The missing piece of carpet was among the items found inside the backpack.

Matthew De Gruchy's mugshot, taken after his arrest. The 18-year-old was charged with the murder of his mother, sister and brother.

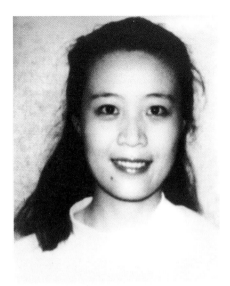

The murder of Gong Qi

Chinese student Gong Qi, 26, was murdered in the quiet bayside Melbourne suburb of Mentone just six weeks after her arrival in Australia.

The police artist's sketch of the victim, in the clothes she was wearing at the time of the fatal attack, was published in the press in the hope of obtaining more information from the public.

Neighbours reported seeing Mark Hastie Brown, 22, sitting on the brick wall outside his Mentone unit around the time of the murder, although he claimed to have gone inside at 5 pm.

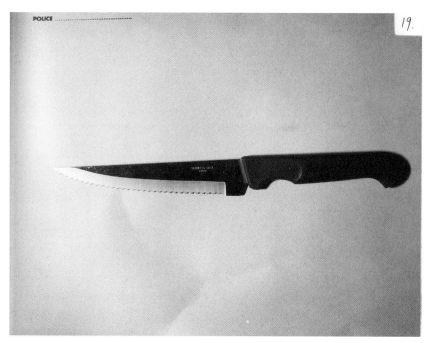

The kitchen steak knife that was used to stab Gong Qi.

(left to right): Detectives Bob Ryan, John Robertson, Peter Phelan and Peter Wheeler flank Gong Qi's parents, who presented them with plaques inscribed in Chinese. The translation is: *Maintain justice and drive away evil.*

Newell Highway – not the route that truck drivers take to head north. It also showed that for some reason, the truck had stopped for quite some time in the middle of the night. Perhaps in the aftermath of the collision. Certainly looked good.

That was enough to convince Carsten Schultz to come off leave and see this through to the end. He had devoted six months of his life to finding this guy and now he was probably within arm's reach.

Back at his desk the next morning, Schultz contacted the National Transport Insurance Company. According to their records, Brett Killmore had had two collisions in Adelaide and one in New South Wales since Violet Town. A couple of phone calls later, and Schultz found out that Killmore's red Western Star truck was currently in for repairs. This information mobilised the troops. If damage on the truck was being repaired, then possible evidence from Violet Town could be lost. It was imperative that the truck be impounded and forensically examined without delay.

Jeff Smith rang Inspector Chris Ferguson to find out if the budget would support sending officers to Queensland to question Killmore. Keen for a result, Ferguson said, 'How many for how long?' Jeff Smith told him he wanted to send Schultz and Sweetman. Ferguson okayed it and Smith immediately made the arrangements. Forensics paid to send Lorelle Denham and Ted Kennedy-Ripon to go too for the forensic examination of the truck.

Schultz was nervous on the flight. Would this finally be the end to the most gruelling case of his career? Was Killmore the one? Brian Sweetman was nervous on the flight because he didn't like flying. Discussing the suspect, the investigators didn't miss the irony of Killmore's name, and his address was equally odd – Cemetery Road.

The four officers arrived at Brisbane Airport on Sunday 4 October and met with their colleagues from the Brisbane Accident Investigation Squad to plan their course of action. Officers from the Brisbane squad had organised warrants to seize the truck, and all of the paperwork was done in advance.

Early Monday morning, accompanied by local police, the four Melbourne investigators arrived at the truck repair centre where the truck was being fixed. Queensland police served the warrant of seizure to the repairer and Schultz got his first look at the big red truck.

Brian Sweetman found a strange device wired to the engine and hidden in a compartment in the sleeper cabin. None of the officers knew what the device was until a mechanic from a neighbouring repair yard explained that it was a 'whizzer' used to override speed limiters on trucks. Because the officers knew that the truck was travelling at 106 kilometres per hour prior to the collision at Violet Town, and that Western Star trucks were speed limited to 100 kilometres per hour, there had to be a device overriding the speed limiter, and here it was.

Now that they had the truck, they had to find as many ways as they could to link it to the caravan and the Mazda. The scientific officers began their examination. The cracked bull bar, which Kennedy-Ripon had noticed at the service station, was certainly consistent with Violet Town. Kennedy-Ripon examined the three huge round fuel tanks located on the right-hand side of the truck under the driver's door. One of the fuel tanks had a huge dent in it but had been turned around so that the dent faced inwards and couldn't be seen. Kennedy-Ripon remembered standing right next to the fuel tanks when he had spoken to Killmore at the service station. This was definite evidence of Violet Town.

When he had first seen the truck, Kennedy-Ripon had noticed among the flyspecks a tiny hole in the canvas Western Star road train cover. He now inspected it closely. Since they knew that the Western Star cover had hit the caravan panel, leaving the impression, it was possible that fibres from the cover could still be found on the caravan panel.

While Kennedy-Ripon and Denham examined the truck, Schultz and Sweetman headed for Cemetery Road. Schultz knocked on the door of the average Queensland suburban home, a weatherboard on stumps, and it was anticlimactic when no-one answered. The place looked deserted. They conferred again with their Queensland counterparts. Since Killmore was being investigated for three other collisions since Violet Town, they decided to ask the officer who was investigating his New South Wales collision to phone Killmore and tell him to report to the Inala police station, close to where he lived. They didn't want to spook him.

A few minutes after 1 pm on Tuesday 7 October, a tall lanky man walked into the Inala police station and gave his name at the front desk. Schultz and Sweetman were out the back and were notified immediately that their man had arrived. It was just shy of six months since the Easter collision and the death of little Nicky Fleming.

'Are you Brett Killmore?' said Sweetman.

'Yep,' replied the man looking from one police officer to the other.

The Victorian officers were in plain clothes. They introduced themselves and ushered him through to an interview room. Schultz couldn't fail to notice that Brett Killmore was rubbing his hands together and not making eye contact. This is not a bloke with nothing to hide, he thought.

'We're from the Victoria Police and we would like to ask you some questions about a collision at Violet Town on 9 April this year.'

'What Victorian collision?' said Killmore, looking increasingly nervous. 'I thought I was here about a New South Wales collision.' It was then that Killmore began to shake. 'Should I ring a solicitor?' he asked in a cracking voice.

'It's up to you,' said Sweetman and then cautioned the suspect that anything he said would be used as evidence. Killmore stared at the floor.

'I've been waiting for you blokes to come around for six months,' he said finally. It was like opening a floodgate. Killmore told them how he had collided with the caravan and veered off the Violet Town exit and then stopped his truck up the road, where he could see the cars screeching to a halt in the aftermath of the collision. Some cars, however, didn't stop and continued on around the collision site, so Killmore explained that he thought it mustn't have been that serious. He also said that he hadn't seen the caravan till it was too late.

Schultz thought, *It's pretty hard to miss a bloody big white caravan looming up in front of you.*

Killmore denied driving erratically and he also denied being on any kind of drugs to keep him awake. There was nothing that the officers could do to prove or disprove whether Killmore had indeed taken any illegal substances in the lead-up to Violet Town. Considering that he had had four collisions in the past six months, he may have just been a really bad driver. Or, had he deliberately collided with the other vehicles so that he could have a legitimate reason for claiming repairs to the truck for damage that would have occurred in the Violet Town collision? Killmore had in fact had the truck's bull bar repaired the week after Violet Town. He told the officers that he'd called, made an appointment, and paid a repairer on the Gold Coast a hundred dollars to have it repaired.

During an interview that lasted over four hours, Killmore made a full confession.

Rather than charging Brett Killmore and facing the process of extraditing him to Victoria, Schultz and Sweetman decided to issue him a summons for him to appear in a Victorian court to face charges at a later date. There was still a lot of work to be done to put the case together.

Back in Melbourne, Jeff Smith was having a barbeque at his house for some of the blokes from work. Smith stood at the barbie, having a quiet drink and wondering how Schultz and Sweetman were going. As Smith turned the sausages and browned the onions, he heard the phone ring. It was Sweetman.

'You're not gonna believe this. He's confessed.'

'*What?*' Smith couldn't believe it. He was sure that Killmore would have kept his mouth shut.

Smith congratulated Sweetman on a job well done. He grinned as he hung up the phone. In the backyard, he repeated the news to the boys.

'That was Brian. Killmore's confessed.'

The officers all had the same response, *You're kidding*. No-one could believe it. After years at the squad, they were all a bit cynical.

Schultz's first duty when he returned to his hotel was to contact Nicky Fleming's dad, Ian. Schultz had kept the grieving father up to date on the investigation all the way through. Ian Fleming thanked Schultz for the work the police had done, and he was glad that the truck driver had been caught.

After the phone call, the officers went to a local Chinese restaurant to celebrate. Back at the motel around 10 pm, Schultz knew he wouldn't sleep and told Brian Sweetman that he was going to take a walk. For the next three hours, Schultz wandered the streets of Brisbane with a feeling of absolute relief.

Back in Melbourne, Schultz had to locate the bull bar repairer who'd fixed Killmore's bull bar after the Violet Town collision. Checking through Killmore's mobile phone records for the week after Violet Town, Schultz rang every number with the Queensland 07 prefix. Eventually he located a bull bar repairer. Carsten Schultz introduced himself over the phone and said, 'I'm making inquiries about a hit-run in Victoria where a young child was killed. I believe you may have repaired a truck that was involved in the collision.'

There was a pause at the other end of the phone. 'You're not going to tell me that the bloke who came in here killed that kid at Violet Town? I had a feeling about that bloke. I even told my mate in the factory next door that it might be him.' The repairer's voice shook and Schultz could tell that he was really upset. Schultz felt sorry for the repairer, but at the same time knew that if he'd picked up the phone six months ago to report his suspicions, he would have saved a lot of people a lot of work.

Examining his evidence in the lab back in Melbourne, Ted Kennedy-Ripon hit the jackpot. Embedded deeply into one of the Phillips head screws from the panel in the caravan, he found a tiny patch of canvas. He photographed it in place and then gently removed it with tweezers. Laid out flat, the piece of canvas was a perfect match for the hole in the Western Star road train cover. Even though Killmore had confessed, the police still needed to build a case against him. Every connecting piece of evidence was vital. Even with everything else – the mobile phone records, the truck damage and the Hella light – this piece of canvas left in the caravan screw said without doubt that the Western Star canvas from Killmore's truck had hit the back of the caravan.

Nearly two years after his truck killed Nicky Fleming, Brett Killmore went to trial. He was charged with culpable driving and a string of other offences relating to the injuries to Ian Fleming and his other two children. Killmore received a five-year sentence with a three-year minimum.

Carsten Schultz and Ted Kennedy-Ripon both received commendations from then–Chief Commissioner Neil Comrie. And Ted Kennedy-Ripon was ever after known as 'Truck Stop Ted'.

Several years after the Violet Town collision, Carsten Schultz tried to articulate why he and his fellow officers were so dogged in their pursuit of Killmore and his Western Star truck. He thought for a moment and said: 'It's an affront that somebody could just not come forward. It goes against honour and standing up for yourself and taking responsibility for what you did. You have to be held accountable. It will never be all right for the family because it won't bring their child back; but you can do the next best thing for them by catching the bloke.'

Chapter Five

✦

THE BLOODING

On 22 November 1983, a schoolgirl was found raped and murdered in the small town of Narborough, Leicestershire, in England. The body of fifteen-year-old Lynda Mann was discovered in the grounds of Carlton Hayes psychiatric hospital. She had been attacked while walking down a path alongside the hospital.

Police investigations led nowhere, but a forensic pathologist was able to get a semen sample from her body left by her attacker. The sample was analysed and found to belong to a person with A-type blood. About ten per cent of the population has A-type blood, so the evidence had the potential to narrow down any suspect lists. This was the only lead police had.

Three and a half years later, on 31 July 1987, the body of Dawn Ashforth was discovered in the same area. She too was fifteen years old and had been raped and strangled. Police suspected the same man was responsible for both murders. During the investigation, a seventeen-year-old youth called Richard Buckland was taken into custody. In his often-garbled account when interviewed by police, he finally admitted to killing Dawn but not Lynda.

Because police thought that the same person had killed both girls, they got the idea to use a new forensic technique known as 'DNA fingerprinting'. The technique had nothing to do with fingerprints, but rather used advanced technology to record a person's unique genetic code, which then could be compared and matched to other samples from the same person.

Leicestershire police contacted Dr Alec Jeffreys at Leicester

University, who had developed the technique. Jeffreys compared semen samples from both murders against a blood sample from Richard Buckland. The test proved conclusively that semen from both girls' bodies had come from the same man – but that man wasn't Richard Buckland. His confession had been false. As a result of the negative test, Richard Buckland became the first person in the world to be exonerated by DNA.

When the DNA test established Buckland's innocence, Leicestershire police decided on a bold move – they would take DNA from all adult males in three surrounding villages. Five thousand men were asked to volunteer a blood sample. All the samples didn't have to be DNA tested because police knew that the killer had A-type blood and so only A-type blood samples needed to be tested. Even so, the testing took six months and failed to produce a match.

Drinking in a pub with some co-workers, a woman overheard a man named Ian Kelly admit that he had given a blood sample for another man. The woman passed the information on to police and Kelly was interviewed. He told the investigators that a man called Colin Pitchfork had asked him to take the test in his place. Pitchfork had told Kelly that he in turn had already taken the test for a friend who had a police record for flashing. According to Kelly, Pitchfork was worried that if he took the test twice, he could be caught out in his deception.

When police visited Colin Pitchfork, he admitted that he had killed both girls. His DNA was later compared to the semen samples taken from the victims and matched. He was sentenced to life in prison for the two murders and had the dubious honour of being the first person in the world to be convicted with the help of DNA evidence.

In those days, DNA was extracted mostly from blood samples, and because around 5000 men gave a blood sample to Leicestershire police during the mass screening, the Pitchfork case became known as 'the blooding'.

❖❖❖

Crime scene examiner Detective Senior Constable Greg Carnell of the New South Wales Police Force has a Diploma of Applied Science in Forensic Investigation and has been investigating crime scenes since 1993. His cases have numbered over a thousand.

Carnell got called to a job in the early hours of New Year's Day 1999. He was based at Tamworth Forensics, and the crime scene he had to examine was in a small town called Wee Waa, which is about 40 kilometres from Narrabri, or about 650 kilometres north-west of Sydney. He was told that an elderly woman had been bashed and raped in her home. She had barely survived the brutal attack.

Calling by his office first, Carnell collected a crime scene kit and also packed a small square machine called a Polilight, which produces infrared, ultraviolet and white light, and can detect blood, semen, hairs and fibres not visible to the naked eye. Carnell and fingerprint expert Detective Senior Constable John Stanford drove to the Wee Waa police station for a briefing.

The victim, Miss Rita Knight had been asleep in bed in her Cowper Street home when a man attacked her and raped her. When he left, Miss Knight had staggered out to her front porch, bleeding from her many injuries, and sat in a garden chair calling for help. Luckily, some New Year's Eve revellers walking past heard her and came to her aid.

Leading the investigation into the attack on Rita Knight was Detective Senior Constable Greig Stier. He had been working on New Year's Eve and got the call from the police station. He went to the local Wee Waa hospital to see Rita Knight and met her niece, Nola Cherry, there. Miss Knight was still being treated for her injuries and was in no condition to speak to the detective.

When Nola spoke about her aunt, it was obvious that she was the most innocent and vulnerable of victims. Rita Knight was 91 years old, had never married, and lived alone in the Cowper Street house that had been her childhood home. She was a pillar of the community.

Early reports from doctors suggested that because of her age and injuries, Rita Knight might not survive the attack.

After their briefing, crime scene examiner Carnell and fingerprint expert Stanford drove from the Wee Waa police station to the Cowper Street house. On the way, they drove past a down-and-out-looking man walking down the street, minutes from Rita Knight's house. They gave him nothing but a cursory glance.

Miss Knight's house was a well-kept old weatherboard surrounded on all sides by a veranda. The house was on a double block of land with no front fence and tall trees on either side that gave it privacy – unfortunately, it had also given her attacker privacy. Across the road was a large park, and there were only a few houses spaced out along the street. The rapist had turned off the power at the power box on the front veranda to ensure that his victim hadn't been able to turn on a light and see him.

At the house, the crime scene examination started from the outside. When Carnell and Stanford arrived, they spoke to a uniformed officer guarding the property out front, who was keeping a log of all who had entered the scene since the attack. Walking around the veranda, the two investigators could see the power box where the offender had flicked the main switch to turn off the power to the house. The box was at the front of the building on the left-hand side and didn't have a cover. Anyone could have gained access to it.

The investigators followed a trail of dusty shoe impressions leading along the wooden decking of the veranda. The shoe impressions looked like they had been made by someone wearing thongs and led to a pair of French doors near the back of the house. A jagged pane of glass had been broken from the right-hand door and it looked like the offender had removed the glass, reached through and slid back a bolt to gain entry.

John Stanford dusted the French doors for prints but could only find a fabric impression, which, if it was made by the offender, could have meant that he was wearing gloves or that he had pulled his sleeves down over his hands before he broke the glass. On the kitchen floor inside, there was not enough broken glass to account for the size of the piece missing from the door. There was no sign of the missing glass in the immediate area. Stanford then visually examined items that the offender might have touched on his way from the back door to the front bedroom where the attack on Rita Knight took place.

Leaving Stanford to search for fingerprints, Greg Carnell examined the rest of the house and took photographs of each room from different angles. He then videoed each room. When he was finished, it was time to process the scene. Both Carnell and Stanford could see that the rest of the house looked undisturbed. Furniture from another era, wicker chairs, a piano, overstuffed low armchairs and antique wooden dressers decorated the house. In a spare room, pastel-coloured frocks hung from hangers on hooks on the wall, and several were neatly draped over the end of a spare bed. Religious icons were prominently displayed throughout the house. Neighbours would later say that Miss Knight attended church every day. There was nothing out of place and it seemed that the attacker had come into the house with only one thing on his mind – raping the defenceless elderly woman; he hadn't searched around or opened drawers looking for money or valuables.

While the house remained neat and tidy overall, Rita Knight's bedroom told a violent story. Her bed was splashed with blood and Carnell photographed the disturbed blankets and bloodstained pillows. Pulling back the blankets and sheets, he saw a pair of bloodstained dentures in the bed. It was yet another reminder of the age of the victim. A pair of bloodstained underpants had been stuffed under the pillows. He photographed each item and made notes as to what he found and where he found it.

Aside from the blood and the messed bed, nothing else in the room seemed to have been disturbed. China ornaments on an old dressing table were still standing, and there was nothing to suggest that the offender had done anything else but walk into the house, go straight into the victim's room, and rape her. Rita Knight's handbag was sitting undisturbed on a table. No money had been taken. In a second bedroom, an old wrought-iron bed was laid out with clothes and bags and items of jewellery. None of it had been disturbed. Robbery definitely wasn't the motive here.

Carnell pulled the curtains shut in the bedroom to make the room as dark as he could, then donned a pair of protective goggles. He plugged in the Polilight machine and swept the metal arm of the torch around the dark burgundy Axminster carpet. Any semen would fluoresce under the light, but although he swept the entire area of carpet in the room, he could find no traces of it.

After the attack, Miss Knight had left the house through the front door, which was right near her bedroom at the front right-hand side of the house. She had sat down in her nightgown on a white plastic garden chair to call for help. Examining and photographing the chair, the investigators could see that it was smeared with the victim's blood. It told a sorry tale; the seat was bloodied, and so were both arms.

Halfway through his examination of the house, Carnell was called to the local hospital. Rita Knight had now been treated and was judged well enough for him to see her. It was his job to photograph her injuries after the doctor had finished his forensic examination using a sexual assault investigation kit (SAIK).

As soon as he entered the hospital room and saw the battered elderly woman lying in the hospital bed, he was reminded of just how important his job was; if he and his colleagues could find the evidence to catch her offender, they could prevent him doing this to anyone else.

The first thing Rita Knight said to the crime scene examiner was: 'I want you to get him, and I want you to whip him.'

No-one in the presence of the elderly victim could disagree with her sentiments.

Miss Knight had a huge bruise to the right side of her face from when the rapist punched her during the attack. She remembered screaming when she had awoken to find the man in her bedroom. He had punched her and then pushed a pillow over her face to stop her from screaming. Miss Knight had lost consciousness around that time. She also had a hearing impairment and either the man hadn't said anything or if he had, she hadn't heard him. She hadn't seen his face and had little to offer the police to help identify her attacker. She said that the rapist had smelt like he had been drinking alcohol.

Rita Knight's body was a mess. Because of her age, her skin was paper-thin and it had torn where the rapist had touched her roughly. Her arms and legs were red raw and bleeding. A laceration in her hand had proved difficult to suture because her skin was so frail.

The doctor explained Greg Carnell's role to her – the policeman needed to photograph her injuries in order to have a record of what had been done to her. She readily agreed. In the presence of a doctor and a nurse, he took photos of her bruised face, and injured arms and legs.

To Carnell, it seemed Rita Knight was as angry as she was upset. Her home had been violated and she had been attacked. Newspapers would later report that she never returned to her house after the attack, moving straight into a nursing home. She had lived in that house all her life.

When Carnell finished taking his photographs, the doctor handed over the SAIK evidence in a sealed bag. He had taken swabs from the victim that police hoped would yield evidence that would help catch whoever had done this to her. Carnell would pass the evidence on to Michele Franco, who worked at the Division of Analytical Laboratories. If Franco was able to get DNA evidence from the swabs, this could be matched to the rapist – if his DNA was on file or when they eventually caught him.

Back at the house, Carnell and Stanford finished their examination of the crime scene. Carnell bagged the bed sheets and pillowcases to examine later back at the office, where conditions were more conducive to finding minute traces of evidence. Outside the house, in the garden near the back door, Carnell found the missing pieces of broken glass from the kitchen door. It looked like the offender had thrown it there after breaking the pane.

❖❖❖

Minutes after Carnell and Stanford had seen the down-and-out man when they'd first driven to Cowper Street that morning, a Toyota HiLux ute was reported stolen from that very area. The theft was to provide the first red herring of the investigation. Cotton farming is the biggest industry in Wee Waa, and there are a lot of wealthy farmers. One farmer offered to use his private aeroplane in the search for the missing ute the suspicious man had stolen. He spotted the ute in a remote area, and the man, who had been seen so close to Rita Knight's home the morning after her rape, was caught and brought in for questioning.

When asked if he had been near Cowper Street the night before, the man told police that he had spent some time in the park across the road from Miss Knight's house. When asked if he'd had sexual intercourse the night before, he replied that he had. The investigators asked him who he'd had sex with and he told an odd story. He said that he had been making a phone call from a phone box in the park when a woman had approached him and asked him for sex. He said that they had sex in the phone box. Even considering it was New Year's Eve, and people had too much to drink, police thought his story unlikely – until they located a woman who admitted that she had indeed asked the man for sex in the phone box. So in the end, the suspect had done nothing more than steal a car.

On New Year's Day, it was all hands on deck. Senior Constable Ken Anderson, a well-respected local cop who knew his area well, was called in to help investigate the crime. He spent the day making inquiries to see if any of the locals had returned home the night before with blood on them, or if any of the locals hadn't returned home at all. Anderson met with Detective Greg Stier and the two discussed the case.

Ken Anderson had worked in Wee Waa for around fifteen years when Rita Knight was attacked. He knew the locals well, and there was something strange about the immediate aftermath of the rape – no-one in town had any knowledge of it. He joked that the townsfolk know everything that happens in Wee Waa – sometimes before it even happens – and the fact that no-one had any knowledge of it meant that whoever had done it hadn't told anybody.

The immediate reaction from the public was that it must have been an outsider or perhaps one of the itinerant labourers, but after having a look at the elderly woman's home, Senior Constable Anderson knew that it must be someone who knew she lived alone and knew that the power box was on the front veranda.

There were seven police stationed at the Wee Waa police station before the influx of detectives and crime scene examiners. Wee Waa was the kind of small community where most people knew each other and there was a good community feel. The population was about 70 per cent people of Caucasian background and 30 per cent Aboriginal people. Relations between the police and the citizens were positive. Wee Waa cops practised the type of country policing where if they were out patrolling in the van with no pressing duties, and they saw a bunch of kids playing a game of handball, they would pull up and join the game and have a chat. Over the years, Wee Waa police had been involved in charity fundraising and had raised over $300,000 for local organisations. And when they came calling, the cops would take their boots off at your front door. That was the way things were done in Wee Waa.

In the early days of the investigation, Ken Anderson talked to many people. An Aboriginal woman told him that a man she knew, Stephen Boney, had a conviction for rape and had served time in prison. Anderson knew Boney, a man in his early forties who was part of the Aboriginal community. He was a loner who people didn't really notice. He didn't really drink and didn't say much, and never drew attention to himself. Boney had separated from his partner recently and had been living by himself a couple of streets down from Rita Knight. He hadn't been seen around the town since New Year's Eve. Anderson made a note to talk to Stephen Boney. But when he checked Boney's police record, he was surprised to find that there had been no sexual assault convictions. There was a rape conviction recorded against a relative of his with the same name; perhaps the woman who had spoken to Anderson had her facts confused. Boney slipped down the list.

In the days immediately after the attack on Rita Knight, it became obvious that her wounds wouldn't prove fatal and there were signs she might even eventually recover from her injuries. Detective Greig Stier met with her a number of times and took her statement. Miss Knight could remember little except that she had gone to bed around 10 pm – she knew that because she had looked at a little clock that she kept beside her bed. She remembered that she hadn't fallen asleep straightaway, and when she was awoken, there was a man in her room. He had hit her and then put the pillow over her face. She didn't remember much after that. Nonetheless, Stier hoped that as she regained her strength and recovered, she might remember something else that could help police.

What impressed the detective about Rita Knight was that she was so alert, but she also had a calmness about her. She told him that she had been praying to God that her attacker would be brought to justice and was confident that the police would catch him. Indeed, every conversation between the elderly victim and the detective ended with her saying, 'I know you'll get him.' Perhaps it was her age, or her wisdom, but she never indicated anything but complete faith in the investigators. And that boosted the faith they had in themselves.

Another thing that impressed Stier was that Rita Knight was held in such high esteem that it seemed that the whole town turned out in support. Everyone wanted the rapist caught as much as the police did. Another dynamic at play was that many of the farms in Wee Waa were now being run by second-generation farmers; that meant that many of the first-generation farmers were now elderly and had moved into town. With the callous attack on one elderly citizen, the community was nervous that the offender would strike again.

But despite Rita Knight's confidence and prayers, the rapist proved elusive. Police had set up Operation Ramat, which was a strike force to catch the offender. The crime was considered so heinous that Greig Stier had any resources that he needed placed at his disposal. Local politician Ian Slacksmith provided every assistance he could right from the start. He would often come in for a chat with the police and promised to do everything that he could to help. One day, he even suggested DNA testing every man in town. But the detectives knew that such a thing was unheard of in Australia. And in the beginning, although swabs had been taken from Rita Knight after the rape, there was no certainty that the long process of DNA extraction would yield any results. They would just have to wait.

Stier relied heavily on local cop Ken Anderson for his knowledge of the men of Wee Waa. Suspects were brought in and their alibis were checked. The locals tended to blame the itinerant workers, but Stier had a feeling that the perpetrator was a local. Who else would know that Rita Knight lived alone, and that breaking into that particular house on Cowper Street would yield a defenceless old lady? Ken Anderson agreed.

Many of the early suspects could be eliminated by providing an alibi, but some couldn't. Stier and his fellow detectives spent over five weeks in Wee Waa checking alibis, tracking down leads and talking to locals. But it all led nowhere. When the leads petered out, the detectives returned to their own hometowns but still visited Wee Waa at every opportunity.

Then on 12 May, over five months after the rape on New Year's Eve, the detectives received the best possible news. The rape swab had tested positive to semen, and DNA had been extracted.

The population of Wee Waa was around 1900 people at the time of the attack on Rita Knight. The male population would be about half that, and discounting children, the possible suspects could number around 600. Despite the passage of time, Rita Knight could shed no further light on the identity of her attacker, and the one piece of evidence the police had was his DNA, which was only important once the offender was caught.

Some of the suspects who couldn't be eliminated with alibis were located and volunteered swabs of their DNA. On no occasion did Detective Greig Stier encounter any man unwilling to give a DNA sample. About a dozen samples were taken, but none proved a match and all the suspects were eliminated. Locals still clung to their theory that the rapist must be one of the many itinerant workers who flooded into Wee Waa to work in the labour-intensive cotton-picking industry. They couldn't fathom that the callous attack could have been committed by one of their own. Almost everybody in town knew old Miss Knight. Nobody could believe that someone they knew could have attacked her so viciously.

But time passed and when the DNA tests cleared any suspects, police realised that they were no closer to catching the callous rapist. And then several things happened that injected a new energy into the investigation. Firstly, the case was featured on *Australia's Most Wanted* in May. The widely watched TV show featured unsolved cases from around the country and called for members of the public to come forward with any information they might have.

Secondly, crime scene examiner Greg Carnell had attended a seminar and heard a police officer by the name of Detective Senior Constable Kris Illingsworth speak. Illingsworth had trained as a criminal investigative analyst profiler a couple of years earlier as part of the FBI training program and it was her area of expertise to prepare psychological profiles of unknown offenders based on the known facts of the case. She was one of only a few such experts in Australia. Carnell was so impressed with her that he suggested to Stier that she might be able to help the Wee Waa investigation.

Carnell told him that if they wanted to utilise Illingsworth's expertise, she would need extensive amounts of information to complete a profile. She needed Rita Knight's statement, all investigation notes, all crime scene photographs, forensic analysis, a Wee Waa town map, and local demographics. Stier was just about to take annual leave and he felt that the report needed his full and undivided attention. Using the couple of weeks' leave, which he was spending staying with his parents, he worked on the report for a couple of hours every day. Since the New Year's Eve rape, he had become friendly with both Rita Knight and her extended family. He'd even taken his wife and kids to visit Miss Knight in the aged care facility where she now lived. The more he got to know her, the more he was driven to catch the man who had hurt her.

When he returned from leave, Stier handed his lengthy report and a copy of the story on *Australia's Most Wanted* to Kris Illingsworth and left her to develop the profile. She took the case material with her to Adelaide, where she and her profiling understudy colleagues were to undertake a month of field training with their profiling sponsor, South Australian police officer Bronwyn Killmier. As part of their training in criminal investigative analysis, they all looked at a number of unsolved cases, including the Wee Waa rape. In group consultation, they developed the crime scene analysis and offender profile, and Illingsworth wrote up the analysis of the Wee Waa case report when she returned to Sydney.

The scope of possible suspects Illingsworth included in the report was small. The behavioural analysis indicated the offender knew the victim and had been to her house before. This meant that there were a small number of people who could possibly be responsible for the offence. In the investigation strategies, she recommended that four particular men who met the criteria be interviewed, including two gardeners who mowed Rita Knight's lawns.

Not every cop believes in methods that don't burn shoe leather, but if Stier faced any criticism over the use of the profiler, he always had the same response: 'There are many tools to do our job and this is one of them. We've got to try everything we can.'

Kris Illingsworth finished preparing the profile and gave it to Stier. Her findings were common sense, but they served a vital purpose of drawing attention to a range of people who were more likely to be the offender.

The offender had committed a crime that was in the low-risk category for him. There was little chance of him being caught inside the elderly woman's home, and because it was New Year's Eve, the sound of breaking glass and an old woman's screams, if they were heard by anybody, could have easily been mistaken for revelry. The victim was elderly and hearing impaired, and to make doubly sure, the offender had turned off the mains power to the house, preventing her from turning on a light and identifying him. The fact that he was worried that she could identify him also pointed to him being local. It was likely the offender was a local man, familiar with the house and perhaps known to Rita Knight.

Because no weapons were used, and there was no evidence of the offender wearing a disguise, Illingsworth believed that the crime was spontaneous rather than planned. Despite the injuries to the victim, the only time that the offender had struck Miss Knight was once to the face. She concluded that the injuries suffered by the victim were control injuries – meaning that the offender had only done to her what was necessary to control her. He had ample opportunity to beat her further, but he didn't. He also had the opportunity to strangle her, but he didn't. From this, she reasoned that he needed to control the victim without causing unnecessary harm.

Illingsworth concluded that the offender probably had a history of break and enter offences that were unlikely to have involved violence. Because he hadn't used a condom to prevent leaving his DNA behind, he probably had no priors for sexual assault.

Looking at the assault from a lateral perspective, Kris Illingsworth theorised that the offender was someone who lacked power in his life both at work and socially. When someone or something had triggered a negative response in him, making him feel powerless, he had sought to gain power and control over someone less powerful than himself. The fact that he chose a 91-year-old woman meant that he was pretty low on the power scale.

Finally, Illingsworth listed traits that she thought the offender would possess. According to statistical data and all the information that she had, she believed that the offender would be Caucasian, 20 to 35 years old, would live within the township or surrounding area but most likely close to the victim, may be unemployed or have intermittent work, and was probably in a relationship or married. However, the relationship would be unsatisfying and the offender would be the subservient partner.

Sex with a consenting partner would have been unavailable that night; this may have been due to an argument with the partner, or the partner might have been unavailable for other reasons. The offender would not be popular, and would be a loner with introverted or selfish tendencies, would be weak in character, perhaps had a minor criminal history involving breaking and entering, and was probably left-handed, since the injuries were to the right side of the victim's face.

Illingsworth concluded that the pre-offence behaviour leading to the crime was likely to be a triggering event, probably involving his partner, which stressed the offender and led him to act out while intoxicated. She believed that the triggering events probably occurred shortly prior to the events and in close proximity to the victim's residence.

While the investigation in Wee Waa was taking place, an interesting development was unfolding in Federal Parliament. Politicians were attempting to introduce the Crimes Amendment (Forensic Procedures) Bill. The purpose of the Amendment was to give authorities the power to conduct forensic procedures on certain convicted offenders and on volunteers, and to create a national DNA database. Both the politicians involved and senior police officers were looking for a test case to sway public sympathy towards the new legislation.

Superintendent Robin Napper was a British police officer who had worked in the National Crime Faculty at Bramshill, near London. He and another British police officer had been invited to join the New South Wales police force by the police chief, Commissioner Peter Ryan, who had also come from Britain.

Napper had been involved in DNA screening operations in Britain, and one of his portfolios as a high-ranking cop was to help develop support for the introduction of DNA legislation in New South

Wales. He did a lot of work to achieve this and was instrumental in the eventual introduction of DNA legislation in Australia.

It was Napper's idea to use Wee Waa as a test case. He consulted profiler Kris Illingsworth and asked her if she thought that the offender was local to Wee Waa. The two police officers discussed the case and agreed that the geographic isolation and the size of the town would provide a good opportunity to demonstrate the value of DNA in how a mass screen could solve an otherwise unsolved case.

Napper then spoke to Greig Stier about the possibility of using the Wee Waa rape as a test case. Stier thought it was a great idea for a number of reasons. Firstly, a mass DNA screening could catch or flush out Rita Knight's rapist, and secondly, he was hard-pressed to think of a community more pro-police than Wee Waa. He had spent enough time there to know that locals badly wanted the rapist caught and had willingly given police assistance every step of the way. And finally, Stier knew that with the eyes of the nation directly on the town, every resource available would be put towards catching the offender.

Stier had been impressed right from the start with how generous the police hierarchy had been with police resources. This case, after all, was a rape rather than a murder or a multiple murder. Thousands of other women were raped without the media attention and police work hours behind their investigations.

He felt that there were a number of reasons why this case got so big. Rita Knight's standing in the community had a lot to do with it. People had admired her before the rape, and they certainly admired her stoicism afterwards. Many people her age simply wouldn't have survived it, but she did. And of course her age was a factor, as was the fact that she had never married. Stier felt that you couldn't think of a more innocent and vulnerable victim. Perhaps what happened to Rita Knight was everyone's worst nightmare – if it had happened to her, it could happen to anybody's parents or grandparents.

Behind the scenes, Robin Napper was instrumental in gathering support for the DNA screening operation. He and Kris Illingsworth gathered maps and housing information to help estimate the scope of the operation, while the Forensic Services Group estimated the screening needs and scope. Crime agencies supported the operation and provided valuable resources for it.

The wheels of bureaucracy turned slowly and by the time a mass DNA screening was agreed upon for the township of Wee Waa, over a year had passed since the rape. When the news became public, the little town became the centre of international attention. Representatives from the worldwide media began phoning the Wee Waa police station for comment. For the local country cops, the attention was a bit daunting. For several weeks, they didn't know when they answered the station phone whether it would be a local in need of assistance or a journalist from London's BBC. They left all comments to the media to the senior officers.

When the actual logistics of the mass screening were considered, the authorities realised that it was all very well to order a screening with potentially five or six hundred men giving DNA samples, but analysing the samples was a different matter altogether. The lab analysis capacity was for around five hundred samples every six months. If the lab concentrated just on the Wee Waa case to the exclusion of all others, it could still take up to six months to identify the perpetrator.

To address this problem, Illingsworth came up with a possible solution. In addition to volunteering a DNA sample, she suggested that the men of Wee Waa should be asked to fill out a questionnaire. She would then analyse their answers to the questions, and earmark more likely suspects to have their DNA tested first. The questions would be designed to elicit a certain emotional response in the offender. Officers in charge of the testing agreed and Illingsworth prepared the questions.

Many people involved in the mass screening helped put together hundreds of screening kits in brown paper bags. The bags contained swabs and sealed containers, barcodes so that evidence could be labelled, forms to check for identification, and the questionnaire. On a sheet accompanying the questionnaire was the consent form. Volunteers were asked to provide two types of identification. They gave a thumb print and had a Polaroid photo taken. The use of photos, fingerprints and barcodes in the Wee Waa case was the result of Superintendent Robin Napper's previous experience with screenings in Britain. He wanted to ensure that the situation in the UK where Colin Pitchfork had avoided taking the DNA test by getting a friend to take it in his place didn't happen in Wee Waa.

On Friday 7 April 2000, a little over fifteen months since the attack on Rita Knight, police met at Wee Waa for a comprehensive briefing and training session. Around 30 extra police, including seven detectives from the Sydney-based Homicide and Violent Serial Offenders Agency, had been brought in to help with the screening. Also returning to Wee Waa was crime scene examiner Greg Carnell, who had been a part of the investigation at the beginning.

Among the speakers was Kris Illingsworth. She showed the police the questionnaire and gave them instructions on how to use it. She would remain in Wee Waa over the week of testing and would go over each response immediately.

When she had first arrived in Wee Waa, local police had shown Kris Illingsworth around town. She could see first-hand what the demographics were. The proportion of Aboriginal residents to white was more significant than the demographics had suggested, particularly in the built-up areas of town. Although she had profiled the offender as Caucasian, she began to wonder if, in fact, she should also consider whether he was an Aboriginal person.

Superintendent Napper was also part of the police contingent converging on Wee Waa for the mass screening. Greig Stier took Napper and Illingsworth to meet Rita Knight at the nursing home. They were both impressed with her strong and spirited character and her determination that the offender would be caught. They all hoped that the mass screening would be the answer to her daily prayers.

Local police officers who were present in Wee Waa on the evening of 31 December 1998 offered to be the first to volunteer a DNA sample. The media was there to photograph them doing so and their smiling faces appeared in the next day's newspapers. Also appearing in response to media interest was Rita Knight herself. Police had suggested one interview by one journalist, which could be shared among the media. They didn't want to tax the elderly woman who by then had celebrated her ninety-third birthday.

At 7 am on Saturday 8 April, the mass screening began of every man aged between eighteen and 45 present in town on the night of the rape. There were a number of ways that local men could participate. A police caravan with a large awning was set up outside the Wee Waa police station, and teams of police were systematically making their way around town knocking on doors. Parliamentarian Ian Slacksmith organised for the local footy team, the Wee Waa Panthers, to attend the screening in their football jerseys and pose for the media. They did so willingly.

In the first three days, 330 men had volunteered their DNA at the police station caravan, and the rest were being tested in their homes. Illingsworth sat in an office set aside for the purpose, surrounded by questionnaires, and read through each one thoroughly. Some of the questions were related to name, age and address to see if the person fitted into the demographic she was seeking. Another question asked if the respondent was right- or left-handed. This was important because Rita Knight had been punched in the right side of her face by the man standing by her bed. This meant that he could be a left-handed man. Other questions asked the respondent things like what kind of person they thought the offender might be, and whether he deserved a second chance.

Given that the offender might leave town over the screening weekend, Illingsworth knew it was vital to check that all men in the demographic had been approached by police for their DNA samples. If anyone was out of town, they needed to be tracked down. In all, only eight men objected and refused to give a sample. During this time, the media made much of the event. Civil libertarians raged against the screening, but by and large, the men of Wee Waa were just glad to help try to catch the man who had assaulted an innocent elderly woman.

After going through the first 330 questionnaires, Kris Illingsworth could say with confidence that the offender wasn't among them.

This wasn't surprising because it was unlikely that the offender would be among the first volunteers. While her profile might fit a number of men, she knew that post-offending behaviour would affect only one of them. It was likely that the offender would be extremely anxious over the mass screening. He alone would have something to fear.

Ken Anderson worked with Greig Stier and other officers and compiled a list of men that he knew around town who hadn't been DNA tested. Anderson prepared a list of 30 men who he felt most needed to be tested. Police began working through Anderson's list one by one. On top of the list was Stephen Boney, whom he'd considered early on in the investigation.

Anderson had bumped into Boney a couple of months earlier in a town a few hours away from Wee Waa. He had greeted him and asked him if he'd been into Wee Waa lately. Boney said he hadn't. Anderson had told him that detectives would like to speak to him about the rape, just like they were speaking to many men around town. The week before the screening, he had seen Boney at the local post office, so he knew he was back in town. On a second examination, it transpired that the conviction for rape under the name of Stephen Boney had been incorrectly entered into the system attributed to a relative bearing the same name. This explained why there was no record of prior convictions for sexual assault against him.

Profiler Kris Illingsworth was also shown the list of suspects generated by local police that included Boney's name. She was told of Boney's history of break and enter convictions, and also of his history of committing sexual offences. She thought it suspicious that he had left Wee Waa immediately after the offence and again when the screening operation began. She agreed with local officers and that Boney's DNA be sought as a matter of priority. Ken Anderson was directed by the officers in charge of the screening to find Boney and request he provide his DNA sample.

On Tuesday 11 April, Anderson began the task of tracking down Boney. He made some inquiries with local police in a town called

Brewarrina, where Boney's sister lived. The local police drove around and checked the sister's house and confirmed he was there. Anderson drove the two and a half hours specifically to get Boney's DNA. It wasn't so much that he had left town that worried Anderson; Boney's absence at the screening was significant because Anderson had recently been told by another local Aboriginal woman that Boney had indeed been imprisoned for rape. Not only that, she said that when he raped two young women, he had cut the power to their house and removed light bulbs. Anderson had also had a chat to the local gardening contractor who was mowing a lawn across the street from his house. The contractor admitted employing Stephen Boney on occasions and remembered that they had last mowed Miss Knight's lawns on Christmas Eve – a week before the rape.

'Did you collect the money, or did he?' Anderson had asked. 'Boney did,' the contractor replied, explaining how he would have gone around to the side doors – the same doors through which the rapist had entered.

By the time Anderson met up with Boney in Brewarrina, he was more than interested in him as a suspect. Boney was a mild man, quietly spoken and neatly dressed, but Anderson could see that he was very nervous. Anderson could also see that Boney was reluctant to give a DNA sample, but with his family members around, it would have been awkward for him to refuse. He filled out the questionnaire and swabbed the inside of his cheek with the swab stick and handed over his sample to Anderson, who put it straight into a cooler. Anderson made the 240-kilometre trip straight back to Wee Waa.

When Illingsworth read Stephen Boney's questionnaire, she could see that his answers were quite unlike the hundreds that she had already read. The questions were designed to elicit an emotional response in the offender, and Boney had responded emotionally. He went to the top of the list of suspects.

❖ ❖ ❖

On Monday 17 April 2000, six days after he had given his DNA sample and filled out his questionnaire, 44-year-old Stephen Boney walked into the Wee Waa police station and asked to speak to Ken Anderson. He was holding a Bible.

'I'd like to give myself up,' he told Anderson. 'I've put my trust in the Lord and I was baptised before I came here today. The reason why I done it is because a lot of people have evil in them and I wanted to get the evil out of me. That's why I turned Christian ... when I was baptised, that washed away all my sins.'

Anderson advised Boney of his rights and then the elusive Wee Waa rapist told his story. He explained that on New Year's Eve, he had gone looking for his partner and mother of his children. They had been arguing and she had moved out of the house they had shared. He couldn't find her because she'd gone to another town to spend New Year's Eve. Boney had then gone to a friend's place to watch a video.

'As I was walking back downtown, it was raining ... and at the time, I was going home but I don't know why I went to the old lady's house. I went to her place and she was awake. I could see her through the window. She was having a cup of tea,' Boney explained. 'Then I could see her walking into another room and she sat down and watched TV.

'All the doors on the side of the kitchen were locked but one of the doors had a cracked glass on it, and I pulled it out because it was loose. I then put my hand through it and unlocked the door. I got inside the house and I waited for a couple of minutes, but this had happened after the old lady had finished watching TV. I then walked to the door where she slept ... the door was open and she was lying on the bed. I walked up to the bed and just put my hand on her leg ... sort of grabbed her leg and sort of ... she sort of sat up.'

It was here that Anderson stopped the interview. If this was to be done, it needed to be done properly. Stephen Boney had a chance to call and organise a lawyer to represent him.

Three hours later, a formal taped interview began. Anderson sat in on the proceedings with Detective Senior Constable Paul

Jones, who ran the interview with Stephen Boney and his legal representative.

For the purpose of the taped interview, Boney repeated his name and address and went over the confession he had made to Anderson earlier. Paul Jones began with Boney's responses to the questionnaire that he filled out when he had given his DNA swab the previous week. Boney admitted that his responses to questions like 'Do you know who sexually assaulted Rita Knight?' were incorrect and that he was in fact the culprit.

Jones asked if Boney had been to Miss Knight's house before. He said that he had mowed her lawns a couple of times.

'Did you ever speak to Miss Knight while you were mowing the lawn?'

'No,' replied Boney quietly.

'Did she ever come out to the yard while you were mowing the lawn?'

'No, she just was sittin' down on the veranda.'

The detective established that Boney had never entered the house before the night of the rape.

'Did you know how old Miss Knight was?'

'No,' replied Boney. 'I didn't know.'

'Do you agree that she's an elderly woman?'

'Elderly woman, yeah.'

Jones established that Boney had gone to a friend's place on New Year's Eve and watched a video. And then he had left to go home but made a detour.

'What happened?' asked Jones.

'I don't know ... I just started ... I don't know what sort of ... what made me change my mind, and I started walkin' across the park ... I dunno what sort of made me go to that old woman's place.'

'You don't know what made you go there?'

'No.'

'Okay, but you did go there?'

'Yeah.'

'And what did you do when you got there?'

'I didn't do anything. I was just standing outside ... on the veranda.'

'What did you do when you were standing on the veranda?'

'I wasn't doing anything. I just was looking in.'

'And what did you see when you looked inside the house?'

'The old lady.'

'And what was the old lady, Miss Knight, doing?'

'She was havin' a cup of tea.'

Boney described how he had stood on the veranda and watched Rita Knight have a cup of tea in the kitchen and then she went into another room to watch television. He said he had watched her for over half an hour. After that, she had gone to bed. He said that she had turned all the lights off in the house. He had then cracked the glass in the door, pulled some of the pieces out and threw them out into the garden. He knew that Rita Knight wouldn't be able to turn on a light and see him because he had turned off the power at the main switch.

Boney described walking into the kitchen and then down the hallway towards her bedroom. Once again, he described grabbing her leg and her waking up screaming. He said that he put his hand over her mouth to stop her screams.

'Did you do anything else to stop her from screaming?' Jones asked.

'Yeah, I grabbed a pillow.'

'And what did you do with the pillow?'

'I put it over her face.'

'Did you at any stage strike Miss Knight to the head?'

'No, no, I did not.'

'Okay. When you put your hand over her mouth, how much force were you applying to her?

'Oh, just enough to stop her screaming.'

'Okay. When you put the pillow on top of her head, how much force were you applying on top of the pillow?'

'I just pressed with one hand.'

'Once you placed the pillow over the top of Miss Knight's head, did she stop screaming?'

'Yeah. I didn't have the pillow on her face too long.'

'Did you remove the pillow from her face?'

'Yeah.'

'Did Miss Knight scream then?'

'Yeah, she was still screaming, yeah.'

Boney described how he raped her while she screamed. He denied hitting her or causing her any injuries, even though she clearly suffered severe physical trauma during the attack.

'When did you decide that you were going to have sex with Miss Knight?'

'Probably when I got inside the house,' replied Boney.

'Can you recall if you made the decision to sexually assault Miss Knight before you went into the house?' asked the detective. This was the logical assumption. He had stood on the veranda for at least half an hour and waited for Rita Knight to go to bed. But Boney denied this was his motive for entering the house.

'What was your motive for going inside the house then?'

'To see if she had any money.'

'Did you look in any of the rooms for money?' asked the detective, knowing that there was no evidence that the intruder had done anything else but rape Rita Knight.

'No,' admitted Boney.

'So it was obviously shortly after entering the house you changed your mind about the money. Is that right?'

'Yeah.'

'Do you agree it would have been difficult to look for money when you turned the power off ... considering you didn't have a torch?'

'It was, yeah.'

'After you had sex with Miss Knight, what did you do then?'

'I left the place.'

'How did you leave the place?'

'The same door what I got in.'

'Once you left the place and out that door, where did you go?'

'Well, I walked out the front and I walked down Cowper Street.'

'Did you hear or see Miss Knight after you left the house?'

'Oh, I could still hear her screaming.'

Again in the interview Boney denied hitting Rita Knight. He suggested that she might have got the injuries to her cheek by

falling over. He said that he'd seen her interviewed on television
soon after the attack.

'Do you agree,' asked Paul Jones, 'that those injuries ... you've
seen on TV were quite serious?'

'Looked serious.'

'Did you feel anything in relation to seeing those injuries?'

'Oh, I feel ... feel ashamed.'

Boney then told the police officers how he had left town
the following day ostensibly because of a death in his family.
He explained how he had thrown out the clothes he had been
wearing on the night of the attack because he had bought new
ones. He said that he hadn't noticed any blood on his clothes
before he threw them out.

Jones then asked if Boney would complete a video reconstruction
the following day at Miss Knight's house. His solicitor explained to
him what that would entail. He would walk through the house and
show the police what had happened. The solicitor explained that
Miss Knight no longer lived at the house and assured Boney that
he wouldn't be seeing her at the house.

At the end of the interview, Jones asked Boney if he had
anything to say.

'Yeah, all I can ... I'd like to say that, yeah, I'm sorry, ... I'm sorry
for what happened ... it shouldn't happen, and I'd just like to say
that I am not a violent person, and I did not hit Miss Knight that
night ... and that's all I'd like to say. I'm sorry.'

After the interview, which lasted six hours, Boney was charged with
aggravated sexual assault, aggravated break and enter to commit a
felony involving violence, and break and enter to commit a felony.

Crime scene examiner Greg Carnell was again called back to
Wee Waa – this time to video Stephen Boney's re-enactment
of his crime. What struck him most about the rapist who had
proved so elusive for the past sixteen months was that he was so
softly spoken and so meek and mild. Boney was small in stature,

portly around the middle, and neatly dressed. Perhaps with the brutality of the attack, investigators were expecting someone more forceful.

Because the media had started to gather at the house in Cowper Street, police accompanying the video re-enactment team held up a large white screen to protect Boney's privacy. He also had a pink towel, which had been given to him at the Wee Waa police station to cover his face from the media. He was then escorted out of the police car in handcuffs. He was asked if he had any connection to the house and he said that he had twice been employed there to mow the lawns.

The old house, which in the intervening time had been sold, looked essentially the same. Boney walked up the front steps with his police entourage and spoke so quietly when questioned that he had to be asked several times to speak louder so that the video's microphone could pick up what he was saying. He walked to the power box while the two officers holding the white screen shuffled along between him and the front of the street. Standing in front of the power box, he was asked to indicate the switch he had turned off on the night he attacked Rita Knight. Raising both handcuffed hands, Boney pointed to a switch on the left-hand side of the box.

The group then made their way down the left-hand side of the veranda and stopped at the door where Boney had entered. In a quiet murmur, he described watching Rita Knight make herself a cup of tea in the kitchen and then he had waited while she drank her tea and watched television for a while. He said that he stood on the veranda for around half an hour before he entered the house. He could hear a loud party going on in the house behind Miss Knight's. Boney again claimed that his original thought was to rob the old lady and he'd only decided to rape her when he stood outside her bedroom door. He was no different from the many rapists who minimise their crimes. It wasn't the last time in the re-enactment that he would do this.

For the camera, Boney explained how he had broken the pane of glass in the French door and then slid back the bolt to gain entry. When he stepped inside the house, he looked at the floor and told the investigators that he had seen the broken glass on the floor and had picked it up and thrown it out the door. He made a movement with his cuffed hands to indicate an area in the side garden.

He described making his way through the kitchen and down the hallway to Rita Knight's bedroom. It was standing at this door, he said, that he had decided to rape the old lady. He had entered her room in the dark and saw that she was lying in her bed asleep. The police officers and Boney all crowded into the front bedroom. He described how he had grabbed Rita Knight on the leg and how she had woken up.

'She sat straight up and started screaming,' Boney explained.

'What did you do when she screamed?' asked one of the investigators.

'Put my hand over her mouth.'

Again, Boney didn't mention hitting the elderly woman, but did describe how he had put the pillow over her head to stop her from screaming. When the questioning began to cover details of the sexual assault, Boney hung his head, whether out of shame or embarrassment it was hard to tell.

There were long pauses between the investigator's questions and his responses. He struggled to answer questions about what he had done to expose his penis before the attack. He mumbled that he had pulled down his trousers and when questioned further, he said that his trousers remained around his ankles during the attack.

'I removed her pants and started to ... have sex with her.'

For the record, Boney was asked whether he was aware during the attack and Miss Knight's struggles and screams that she was not consenting.

'In all the circumstances that were going on here with Miss Knight screaming, did you know that she didn't consent to having sexual intercourse with you?' asked a detective.

'Yes.'

'And that was before you started having sex with her?'

'Yes.'

'And it was whilst you were having sex with her?'

'Yes.'

'And it was after you'd finished having sex with her?'

'Yes.'

'Okay.'

And then Boney volunteered the only bit of information that he had volunteered during the entire re-enactment. He sounded annoyed when he said, 'I mean it only happened for ... it wouldn't even have been ten minutes.' As if that made it okay.

After Stephen Boney's confession, profiler Kris Illingsworth had time to look over the investigation and evaluate its effectiveness. Boney was nine years older than her upper profile age limit; she feels that age is the most difficult aspect to profile – often offenders can be less emotionally mature than their chronological age. Boney was Aboriginal, not Caucasian, and Illingsworth feels that if she had gone to Wee Waa when she was compiling the profile, she would have made different conclusions considering the demographics. But aside from that, Boney was everything she thought he would be. He was in a relationship, but lacked power in his life. He lived within a couple of streets of Rita Knight, and he knew her because he had mowed her lawns while working for a local gardening contractor. Illingsworth was also correct in anticipating that something triggered the offence on the night of the rape. Boney had been trying to contact his partner, ready to confront her about their domestic difficulties, and had been unable to find her.

Illingsworth also feels that the value of her work was evident in the fact that she knew that the man police were seeking was not among the first 330 respondents. Stephen Boney was not caught with DNA evidence – his confession came *before* his DNA could even be tested. But he, like Colin Pitchfork before him, knew that the DNA would prove he did it, and confessed. This perhaps illustrates the power of DNA and other forensic evidence – sometimes it catches offenders, and other times, it simply flushes them out.

Boney was sent to trial and received a twelve-year sentence. He would have to serve eight years before he would be eligible for parole. It was ironic that he'd found God and was baptised before he came in to confess. Perhaps he had found the same God that Rita Knight had been praying to every day since she was attacked, praying that her rapist would be caught.

When Stier visited Rita Knight after the long investigation was over and Boney had been arrested, her response was typical. She looked keenly at Stier and said, 'I knew you'd find him.'

Even though Boney said that he had mowed her lawn a couple of times while working for the man who did her garden, Rita Knight couldn't place him except for a vague recollection of a man fitting his description mowing her lawn.

Greig Stier knows Rita Knight's case gave the community a reason to support and embrace the new use of DNA in the fight against crime. The result was good for her, but it was also good for the entire community to know for sure who had committed the terrible crime against her.

In the early months of 2005, Rita Knight passed away in her nursing home. She was a couple of years shy of a century. Greig Stier attended her funeral and paid his final respects to the elderly woman of whom he'd grown so fond. He thought of her spirit, and her plucky nature. She had never been defeated by what had happened, even though it had taken a terrible physical toll on her. He remembered what she'd told him over and over again, 'I'll get over this.' And in many ways, she had.

Chapter Six

✦

THE DE GRUCHY CASE

Steve Bailey was talking to a neighbour in Shearwater Boulevard in Albion Park Rail, an outer suburb of Wollongong in New South Wales. It was early in the morning of Wednesday 13 March 1996. Suddenly his eighteen-year-old neighbour, Matthew De Gruchy, came running out of his house.

'Something's happened to Mum and Sarah!' Matthew yelled.

Steve Bailey followed the young man back inside his house and entered the front bedroom, which was to the left as he walked in the front door. In the seconds he remained in the bedroom, he could see that Jenny De Gruchy – Matthew's mum – was battered and bloody and obviously dead. He ran back outside again.

Detective Sergeant Danny Sharkey was on duty that day. He was in charge of a crew of eight detectives covering the Albion Park Rail area. He and a colleague, Ron Smith, and two other detectives drove to the house in Shearwater Boulevard.

When Sharkey pulled up near the De Gruchy house, he could see an ambulance parked on the road outside, and a young man doubled up on the lawn with an older man attending him. Sharkey spoke to neighbour Steve Bailey, who told him what had happened.

At a crime scene, the fewer people who enter the scene, the better, but Sharkey had to first ensure that there was in fact a body inside the Shearwater Boulevard home, so after getting directions from Bailey, he made his way into the front bedroom. A woman lay on a double bed under the covers. Her head was such a bloodied mess that Sharkey thought she might have been killed with a shotgun blast.

The neighbour had also said that Matthew De Gruchy had told him that there was something wrong with Sarah, his thirteen-year-old sister. Detective Sharkey thought it prudent to check the sister's bedroom. He found Sarah lying dead on her bed. She too had received severe head injuries. Oddly, considering their injuries, there wasn't much blood around their respective beds. Over the sister's head lay a cushion from a chair in another room. It looked as if the killer had placed the cushion over Sarah before the attack, keeping blood splash to a minimum. The cushion might have been used to cover the mother as well.

Sharkey and his detectives did a quick walk through the house to ensure that there weren't any further victims inside, and that the offender was no longer there. They didn't touch anything and left the house immediately to call in the crime scene examiners.

Matthew De Gruchy was so distressed at the killing of his mother and sister that the ambulance took him off to hospital. Apparently, he had come home from spending the night at his girlfriend's house and discovered the bodies. Detective Sharkey calculated that De Gruchy, the neighbour, Steve Bailey, and the detectives were the only ones who had entered the crime scene – apart from whoever had killed the two victims. That meant that the integrity of the crime scene hadn't been tainted any more than was absolutely necessary.

Detective Senior Constable Barry Doherty was the first crime scene examiner on the scene. His job was to record the scene and collect any evidence that might indicate who killed Jenny and Sarah De Gruchy. When Doherty entered the house, he could see that the scene was huge. Both the mother's bedroom and the daughter's bedroom needed to be examined, but so did the rest of the house. A cursory inspection of the tiled floor in the hallway showed that someone had tried to clean up what looked to be blood. In various other rooms, cupboards were open, and disconnected cords in a cabinet under the television indicated that a video recorder might have been recently removed. There was no sign of forced entry, but not every window in the house was locked, and the back sliding door was closed but not locked.

Doherty called his boss, Detective Sergeant Steve Hodder, at the Wollongong Forensic division and explained the situation. In cases like this, it was all hands on deck and Hodder made his way straight to the scene. Assisting Hodder and Doherty was a fingerprint expert and a video operator.

With Matthew De Gruchy in hospital, and his mother and sister dead, there were two members of the family unaccounted for. There was no sign of his father Wayne De Gruchy or his fifteen-year-old brother Adrian.

Being a Wednesday, Detective Danny Sharkey figured that Adrian might be at school. Sharkey sent police to the school Adrian attended but they were told that he hadn't turned up for classes that day. When Sharkey heard this, he and the other officers began to wonder if perhaps Adrian had killed his mother and sister and vanished. It was very important that they locate the missing fifteen year old.

Because the scene was so large and evidence was spread all over the house, it was some time before anyone got around to looking in the garage. Detectives Sharkey and Smith and crime scene examiner Doherty walked through a neighbouring property and out their back gate so that they could access the De Gruchy house from the rear. All the backyards on that side of Shearwater Boulevard backed on to a large nature reserve, and that meant it was important to organise a large line-search as soon as possible to look for any evidence that might have been left by the killer in the parkland. The three investigators saw a spa underneath a pergola in the De Gruchy backyard and then saw the access point for the double garage – a door from the back pergola led into it. Sharkey opened the door and the three investigators made a shocking discovery.

The garage was awash with blood, and lying on the floor was the body of a teenaged boy. Since Matthew De Gruchy had gone to hospital, chances were that his missing brother, Adrian, had just been found. His body was visible but his head had been covered by a doona in a red and white motorcross cover with trail-bike riders patterned across it. There was a glue gun oozing glue on Adrian's right side, and a small wooden chair underneath his right hand. It looked like he had been fixing the chair.

After the body had been photographed in situ, investigators pulled back the doona. Adrian's injuries were as brutal as those of his mother and sister. He had been severely beaten around the head; lying next to his head was a number of teeth. Blood evidence in the garage told the story of a brutal, prolonged attack.

Cast-off blood is a term used to describe blood spattering that occurs when a victim is hit a number of times and bleeds. When the weapon connects on subsequent blows, the blood adheres to the weapon and then flicks off as the weapon is thrown back before it strikes again. This cast-off blood was evident on the garage ceiling. Many blows had struck the dead teenager. Unlike his mother and sister, nothing had been used to cover his head during the attack and there was blood everywhere.

At some point in the chaotic morning at the Shearwater Boulevard house, the telephone rang. Danny Sharkey answered it. On the other end of the line was Wayne De Gruchy. Over the course of the morning, detectives had tried to locate the missing husband but the company where he worked told the detectives he was on the road. Now, he was obviously back at the office and ringing in to check on his family.

Given the tragic nature of the news he had to break to the father, Danny Sharkey asked Wayne if he could put his secretary on the phone. He obliged and a woman came on the line. Sharkey introduced himself and said, 'Stay with him because I've got some very, very bad news for him.' The secretary agreed and put Wayne back on the line. Sharkey gently broke the news to the shocked husband that his wife, daughter and younger son were all dead.

Immediately after the phone call, Sharkey rang the police at Parramatta, which was close to where Wayne De Gruchy worked, and organised for some officers to go to his office, collect him and take him to the Warilla police station.

Emotions were running high all around. Neighbours were distressed and gathering outside the house. The sight of Jenny, Sarah and Adrian lying dead in their home with horrific head wounds was difficult for all the investigators and crime scene examiners. Sharkey organised for a mobile command post to be set up in a police van outside the house, and for grief counsellors to talk to anyone who needed it.

Sharkey enlisted a large contingent of State Emergency Services volunteers to search the nature reserve behind the house. Nothing of any evidentiary value was found. He also sent one of his detectives to visit Matthew De Gruchy in the hospital to try to elicit further information from the young man who had found the bodies of his mother and sister. Unfortunately, the detective was diverted to another urgent case and Sharkey couldn't spare any other members to visit Matthew; by the time he could, an aunt had collected the teenager from hospital and taken him away.

Crime scene examiners Doherty and Hodder began to process the house. The front bedroom was furnished with a double bed and a dressing table. There was an exercise treadmill against one of the walls. The room was fitted with holland blinds and the window behind them was closed and locked. Two other doorways leading from the room went into a walk-in wardrobe and an ensuite.

Lying against the northern wall was the double bed. It was fitted with a wooden bed-head and had wooden bedside tables on either side of it. Above was a ceiling fan fitted with a light, which was turned off. Jennifer De Gruchy lay dead in the bed. A blanket was pulled to her chin but her head, neck, right shoulder and arm were still visible. The head and facial injuries that she had suffered were so severe that she was unrecognisable. Her head was lying on the pillow leaning against the bedside table and there was a lot of blood soaked into it and down into the mattress. Lying on the floor next to the body was a broken denture plate.

On the floor was grey-coloured carpet. Strangely, a large piece of carpet near the side of the bed had been cut out and removed. Doherty noted that two other sections of carpet in the room were also missing, though they were much smaller than the one near the bed.

Given the severe nature of Jenny's injuries, and the lack of blood anywhere but at the immediate scene, Doherty formed the opinion that something had been held over her head during the attack. His boss, Steve Hodder, agreed. There was only a spray of fine blood spatter on the wall above the body, and Doherty swabbed the blood for further analysis.

Later, when the bodies were removed, Doherty would collect all the sheets and pillows in the room for further analysis. But for the time being, the bodies would have to stay where they were until the crime scene had been thoroughly processed. In the adjoining ensuite, he found a small reddish stain at the bottom of the wash basin near the plug hole. He took a swab of it.

Next to be examined was Sarah's bedroom. A big white teddy bear sat on the floor by the door. Sarah's body lay on pink sheets on a single bed. Posters of her favourite bands were stuck to the wall above where she lay. A Walkman was on the floor by the bed. Resting on Sarah's head was a blue and white seat cushion from a chair in the dining room. The cushion was heavily bloodstained. Since something must have been placed over Jenny when she was attacked to account for the lack of blood anywhere but around the immediate area of the body, it seemed that the cushion from the dining room chair had been used for the same purpose with Sarah.

The girl had sustained the same severe head and facial injuries as her mother. In addition to the head injuries, Barry Doherty noticed what he described as a 'tram track' bruise on Sarah's right forearm. The bruise was about fifteen centimetres in length and five millimetres in width, consisting of two parallel lines that seemed to close off at the end. This kind of bruise, which was obviously the shape of whatever weapon had been used to make it, could help investigators narrow their search for the weapon.

In the hallway connecting the bedrooms, Doherty examined the faint reddish-coloured stains on the white tiles. He placed numbered markers along the hall and photographed the locations of the marks. Presumptive tests proved positive for blood. He then swabbed the areas and put the evidence in sealed containers.

While Doherty continued the detailed examination of the interior of the house, Hodder instructed members of the Police Rescue Squad to search the backyard of the house, which included a fish pond and fountains. He also had members of the squad get up into the roof space of the house to see if anything had been hidden up there. Nothing of any evidentiary value was found.

Well-respected forensic pathologist Dr Allan Cala from the Institute of Forensic Medicine was called to the scene. It was Dr Cala's job to examine the bodies where they'd been found, and he set about trying to determine an approximate time of death.

Estimating the time of death can be done in a number of ways. After a body has been dead for several hours, rigor mortis sets in, which means that the body and limbs go stiff. Rigor mortis lasts for several hours, then dissipates. Another way to determine time of death is by looking at post-mortem lividity. This is when the blood starts to settle at the lowest points of the body, turning those sections a deep shade of purple. The third method involves taking the body's temperature and calculating it against the ambient or room temperature at the time of the discovery of the body. The doctor used all three methods, checking each of the bodies for signs of rigor mortis and lividity, and taking body temperature readings. He estimated the time of death to be somewhere between 8 pm and 1 am.

Dr Cala also noted the tram track mark on Sarah's arm, which looked as if it had been caused by a long thin weapon with a squared-off end. When he examined Adrian and lifted the dead boy's T-shirt, he saw the same parallel marks on the boy's chest, but in addition to the tram track bruises, there was also a circular mark on Adrian's chest. It was Dr Cala who concluded that the three victims hadn't been shot – instead, he said, they had been beaten to death with the weapon that had left marks on both Adrian and Sarah. It suddenly dawned on the doctor and the investigators that the circular wound and the long parallel bruises could have been caused by a wheel brace – the device used to loosen and remove the nuts on a car wheel before changing the tyre.

Hodder and Doherty went straight outside and inspected the boot of the white Toyota Seca, which had been sitting in the driveway all morning since the police had arrived. It was Jenny De Gruchy's car, and apparently Matthew had driven it to and from his girlfriend's house. Police guarding the outside of the house were able to say that the car hadn't been touched since they arrived. Hodder opened the boot and saw that the small opening to the hatch that contained the jack was in the closed position but not clicked shut. Opening the hatch, he could see the jack was where it should be, but there was no sign of the wheel brace. From an investigative point of view, this was looking promising.

Steve Hodder lifted the boot carpet and located the spare tyre in the tyre storage cavity. The spare tyre of the late-model Toyota was brand new and had never been used. The crime scene examiner could see that the tyre still had the flashing – or the tiny rubber pieces – around the edge. These would break off once the tyre was used. The deduction here was elementary. Why would anyone open the jack hatch of Mrs De Gruchy's car? To get the jack to change a tyre ... but if the tyre had never been changed, then why would someone open the hatch ...?

If the wheel brace from the Toyota had been the murder weapon, then the next question was: who had access to the car? According to early reports, Matthew De Gruchy had used the car to drive to his girlfriend's house the night before and had returned home that morning to find the bodies. If this was so, then how could the murder weapon have been taken from the car?

Examining the car more closely, Hodder noticed a small piece of what looked like a tuft of carpet fibres on the floor near the back seat. Given that a section had been cut out of the bedroom carpet in Jenny De Gruchy's room, he collected the tuft for further examination. To the naked eye, it looked to be a similar colour to the carpet in the bedroom. Doherty also looked at the tuft and pointed to a tiny reddish-stain on the fibres. Both crime scene examiners thought the stain might be blood. Hodder organised for the car to be towed to the Wollongong Crime Scene Unit for further examination.

When he heard that Wayne De Gruchy had arrived at the Warilla police station, Detective Sharkey took one of the grief counsellors from the police command post outside the house and drove to the station. By this time, Sharkey had also located Matthew De Gruchy and had him brought to the police station. After Wayne had spent some time with the grief counsellor, he was reunited with his only surviving offspring.

Matthew was questioned by detectives and confirmed that he was at his girlfriend's house on the night his mother and Sarah and Adrian were killed. When his girlfriend was questioned, however, she told police that Matthew had telephoned her around 8 pm and said he would be at her house shortly, but he hadn't shown up. She told the detectives that she had tried ringing the De Gruchy house at 10 pm but there was no answer. Matthew finally arrived at her house at 11 pm. He told her that his family had received some crank calls to the effect that three members of his family would die that night. This information was highly suspicious – Matthew hadn't mentioned anything about crank calls to the police.

Back at the house, Doherty continued his work. In the laundry, there was a washing machine and above it, a clothes dryer. When he examined the laundry, he found a number of blood smears on the floor. He labelled them, had them photographed and took swabs. Inside the washing machine were two towels and a pair of green and yellow rubber gloves, which had all been washed. There was some faint staining on the towels that could have been blood. All in all, it looked like someone had tried to clean up the scene – not the likely actions of a random attacker.

Examining the family bathroom, Doherty found some reddish-coloured stains in the bottom of the wash basin and on the mirror behind the vanity unit. He had these photographed and took swabs. On one of the doors of the vanity unit, Doherty found some faint reddish smears that appeared to be blood. In one of the smears was what appeared to be a partial fingerprint. This was examined and photographed, and then, in consultation with the fingerprint expert, the cupboard door was removed as evidence.

There was not much in terms of evidence in Adrian's bedroom apart from a couple of smears of what appeared to be blood just inside the doorway near the light switch. In Matthew De Gruchy's bedroom, some drawers in a wall unit were open, as were the doors to the wardrobe. A number of items lay on the floor, including a metal money box. In the lounge room, Doherty examined the area around the television for clues. While the video recorder had apparently been taken, its cord was still attached to the back of the television. In front of the television cabinet, a number of video cassettes and an empty box from a Sega video game system lay on the floor.

Aside from where the apparent ransacking had taken place, the house in Shearwater Boulevard was neat, tidy and clean. This was good for crime scene examiners because most of the things that were out of place in the house looked like they were connected with the crime.

After many hours of crime scene examination, it was finally time for the bodies to be moved. Barry Doherty organised with Dr Cala for the three family members to be transported to the Institute of Forensic Medicine in Glebe, where they would be examined the following morning.

When it was time to move Adrian's body, both Doherty and Dr Cala noticed large areas of skin peeling off his left arm in sections that had been in contact with the concrete floor of the garage. As soon as the body was moved, a strong smell of petrol became obvious. It came from underneath Adrian. A closer examination of his clothing revealed that both his shorts and shirt appeared to be soaked with petrol. Nearby in the garage was a red jerry can. Did the killer pour petrol on the boy intending to set him alight, then change his or her mind? The jerry can was examined for prints and a number were found on its handle.

Right from the start, there was something about the De Gruchy murder scene that wasn't quite right. Jenny De Gruchy had been killed in her bed. She was wearing a nightie and lying under the covers, indicating to the investigators that she was in bed, possibly asleep, when she was murdered. Sarah De Gruchy was also attacked in her bed. The Walkman and headphones next to her indicated she was in her room listening to music when she was attacked. In the garage, Adrian had probably been fixing the little chair. The fact that you could only get into the garage by a door from the back patio or by opening either of the double garage's tilt-doors meant that the killer had sought him out.

Some drawers around the house had been opened, and a number of CDs were scattered around the floor of the otherwise neat suburban home. If robbery was the motive, then why hadn't the robber simply packed up his booty and left the house? It seemed unlikely that a robber had been disturbed because both Jenny and Sarah had been attacked in bed and Adrian was in the garage. In the collective experience of the investigators, a disturbed house-breaker might assault a home-owner in order to leave the house quickly, but a triple murder seemed an extreme way to cover up the theft of a video recorder. Indeed, the robbery looked staged. The most likely scenario was that someone wanted members of the De Gruchy family dead and left the evidence of the robbery in an attempt to throw police off the track.

Also curious and telling were two things: firstly, the pieces of carpet that had been removed from the bedroom, and secondly, that someone had tried to clean up after the murders. The blood on the tiled hallway floor was diluted with water, which meant that someone had tried to wash it. The investigators wondered if the killer bled at the scene and was worried about leaving his blood behind. Why else would they go to the trouble of cutting out a section of carpet and washing the tiled floor? What the killer didn't realise was that the crime scene examiners had tools that could detect blood even in minute amounts. The floor had been examined with a Polilight machine, which found traces of blood on the floor. Stains on the towels washed in the washing machine were also suspicious, as was the fact that someone had put rubber gloves through the wash. A random killer without any connection to the family would hardly have bothered to put on a load of washing before leaving the house.

The following morning, crime scene examiner Barry Doherty started work at 7 am. The previous day, he had worked from 8 am till 1.30 am in the house, and after snatching a couple of hours' sleep, he was back on duty – this time to attend the post-mortem examinations of the three dead members of the De Gruchy family. It was his job to collect forensic samples from Dr Cala, who would examine the bodies. The intense working hours immediately following a murder were crucial for all investigators.

Seeing the three bodies lined up on adjoining steel tables in the mortuary brought home the enormity of the loss to the De Gruchy family. Mother, daughter and son were all examined and found to have massive head injuries from repeated blows, probably with the wheel brace, which hadn't been located. A similar wheel brace had been procured from a local Toyota dealer. It was the same as would have been supplied with the Toyota Seca model belonging to Jenny De Gruchy. The handle matched the tram-track bruises on Sarah and Adrian, and the round head matched the round bruise on Adrian's chest.

Dr Cala found multiple fractures all over Jenny De Gruchy's skull and facial bones. He found the cause of death to have been the 'result of severe blunt force head trauma and resultant haemo-aspiration [aspiration of blood]. Severe facial and skull fractures were present, which were associated with extensive, severe underlying brain trauma'. Dr Cala wrote in his report that he believed that Jennifer was possibly asleep at the time of the attack, given the position of the body, as well as the blood spatter patterns and blood pooling around the body. He found defence injuries on Jenny's hands, indicating that early in the attack she may have tried to defend herself.

Chillingly, he wrote towards the end of his report: 'The injuries sustained would have been caused by a large amount of force. The facial bones, in particular, were grossly fragmented. I believe that numerous blows were delivered to the face and head of the deceased. Death was not instantaneous given the amount of blood aspirated into the lungs. This could only have occurred whilst the deceased was alive.' This meant that Jenny De Gruchy had survived long enough during the attack to breathe in a large amount of blood.

Examining Adrian, Dr Cala found that his skull was grossly fractured. Blood had haemorrhaged into his brain. Many of Adrian's teeth were either broken or missing. Adrian's head injuries were similar to his mother's, and Dr Cala concluded that they could have been caused by the same weapon. The doctor mentioned a wheel brace as being most consistent with the type of injuries and bruising sustained by the victims.

Dr Cala wondered if the petrol that had been poured on Adrian might have been an attempt to set the deceased alight, given the strong smell of petrol and the open jerry can in the garage. The skin peeling that was present on Adrian's left arm and left hip region was consistent with petrol being poured on him after he had died. Aside from the peeling skin, there was no other physical reaction to the petrol. He described Adrian's injuries as coming from a 'blitz-type' attack and wrote in his report: 'It would appear that Adrian De Gruchy was working in the garage at the time of the attack, and may have been struck from behind initially. There were no defence-type injuries to his arms or elsewhere.'

Dr Cala listed Adrian's cause of death as: 'complications of severe blunt force head and facial trauma'.

Next, the pathologist examined Sarah's body. He concluded that 'this 13-year-old girl died as a result of severe blunt force head trauma, however there were some aspects of the scene in conjunction with the post-mortem findings which were suggestive of smothering ... frothy clear fluid was present around the nose and mouth, and in conjunction with the finding of the flat pillow adjacent to the deceased's head at the crime scene, was suggestive of smothering'. The pillow also could have been used to muffle her cries. Dr Cala noted the defence-type injuries on her right arm, reporting that her right arm was probably raised to fend off the attack. In his report, the pathologist wrote: '... the injuries on the deceased's head were similar to those on her mother's and brother's heads and were probably caused by a heavy, possibly metal object such as a crowbar or wheel brace'.

In many murder cases, members of the immediate family fall under suspicion and since three members of the De Gruchy family were now dead, that left husband Wayne and son Matthew as possible suspects. It is more usual for a husband to be the perpetrator in this type of killing, and so it was vital that Wayne De Gruchy's whereabouts for the time of the murders be ascertained. It turned out that he'd stayed with his parents in Sydney the previous night.

One early red herring was that a neighbour reported seeing a car similar to Wayne De Gruchy's in Shearwater Boulevard in the early hours of the morning before the murders were discovered. It was driven by someone fitting Wayne De Gruchy's description. Could it be that Wayne had driven back to his house in the middle of the night and killed his family? But then investigators found out that the car Wayne De Gruchy usually drove was in for repairs during the time in question and the car he was driving at the time was different in make and colour than the one seen in the street on the night of the murders.

While Wayne De Gruchy had a cast-iron alibi, Matthew De Gruchy's whereabouts at the time of the murders was less certain. He didn't get to his girlfriend's house till 11 pm, but no-one had answered the De Gruchy phone at 10 pm when she had tried to call him.

On Friday 15 March, Danny Sharkey arranged for a number of the De Gruchy extended family to attend the police station. It was obvious to the detective that the family thought he and the other investigators were suspicious of Matthew and they were not happy about it. Wayne De Gruchy's brother Paul had even advised Matthew not to cooperate with the police. Nonetheless, Sharkey took Matthew into an interview room.

'Matthew, I want you to understand very clearly what I am now about to say to you,' he said to the young man. 'I want to ask you questions about the death of your mother, sister and brother. Do you understand me?'

'Yes,' Matthew said in a quiet voice.

'Matthew, you have been given some advice by your uncle Paul. I understand that his advice to you was that you do not have to speak to me or any of the other police or answer my questions. What you have been told by your uncle is true; you do not have to answer any of my questions. I want you to clearly understand what I have just said to you.'

Again Matthew said, 'Yes.'

Sharkey pushed a little harder. 'Matthew, I believe that you know a lot more about what happened to your mother, brother and sister the other night. More than what you said in the statement you made. Is there anything you want to say to me about what happened the other night?'

Matthew sat with his arms across his stomach, rocking back and forward with his head bowed. He said nothing. One of the other detectives asked if Matthew had anything to say about the night of the murders. Again he said nothing.

'Matthew, this is not going to go away,' said Sharkey. 'We will be investigating this for as long as it takes. Do you understand what I'm saying?'

After a long silence, finally Matthew spoke. 'I told the policeman the other night what I know.'

'Matthew, I believe that you had something to do with the deaths of your mother, brother and sister. Do you understand what I have just said to you?'

Matthew repeated himself. 'I told the policeman the other night what happened.'

Another detective said, 'We think you know a lot more about

this than what you told the policeman. Firstly, can you tell us why you didn't come home until after 8 o'clock in the morning?'

Matthew said nothing.

'We have been told that you have to be home earlier than this so that your mum can use the car to take your brother and sister to school. What can you tell us about that?'

Matthew didn't answer.

'The wheel brace and jack handle are missing from the car that you had possession of on that night. Do you know where they are?'

Matthew remained silent and sat with his arms hugging his stomach, rocking back and forth in his chair.

'Are you feeling all right?' asked the detective.

'No, I feel sick,' replied Matthew.

'We will speak to you later on this,' said Sharkey. 'We found a lot of blood through the house and also some hair. We will need to get some blood and hair samples from you for elimination purposes. You better speak to your uncle about this.'

When Sharkey opened the door to the interview room, Matthew's uncle, Paul, was right outside the door. Matthew was taken back to the rest of his family while Paul De Gruchy expressed his displeasure at the questioning of his nephew to the detectives. As far as the family was concerned, the loss of Jenny, Sarah and Adrian was being compounded by the suspicion of the boy. Sharkey could understand how they felt. The family had been through so much in the past few days, but he had a job to do, and everything so far suggested Matthew knew more than he was letting on.

Arrangements were made for both Matthew and his father to attend the local hospital where both men would give samples of blood and hair.

Detective Sharkey wanted a record of Matthew's exact movements in the house when he discovered the bodies because then his account could be matched against the evidence that was turning up under analysis. Under questioning, which was video-recorded,

Matthew leant his chin on his hand and showed little emotion. His answers were often monosyllabic. His father and uncle were present during the interview.

Matthew said that he had arrived home at 8.30 in the morning of Wednesday 13 March and walked inside to get his wallet. He then left straightaway to go to the shop to buy cigarettes. He hadn't seen any members of his family at the time. When he returned, he said that the house seemed quiet so he had gone past Sarah's door and then into his mother's room. It was then, he said, that he had discovered his mum's body and had immediately run outside.

Sharkey asked Matthew whether he had gone into Sarah's bedroom. Matthew said that he hadn't. This was one of the first anomalies in Matthew's account. Neighbour Steve Bailey was certain that when Matthew had come running out of the house on the morning of the murders, he had said, 'There's something wrong with Mum and Sarah.' But according to Matthew, he hadn't gone into Sarah's room at all. How could he have known there was anything 'wrong' with her?

The detectives also asked Matthew to make a list of stolen property. By then, Matthew and his father had been allowed back into the house. Matthew listed CDs, the video recorder and a number of other items including two calculators as belonging to him and his brother. Detective Sharkey secretly wondered how a young man who had just lost three members of his family would notice that his brother's pocket calculator was missing. Most people who are robbed can list obvious things that are missing, but a precise list of things was rare.

The detectives had heard that Matthew had fought with his mother about using her car. Often, he would drive his father's car, but that was in for repairs. There were also stories that he had been violent towards his mother. When asked if he had argued with his mother about using the car, Matthew replied: 'I wouldn't call them arguments.' Since he drove her car on the night of the killings, the detectives wondered whether the whole terrible incident could have been over something as trivial as an argument about the use of the car.

The case was starting to build up against Matthew De Gruchy. Blood on the floor in the hallway had by now been analysed and was found to be his. He was the last to use the car, and a carpet fibre with blood on it had been found in the car. The partial fingerprint in blood on the door handle in the family bathroom also belonged to Matthew. His fingerprints were found on the jerry can of petrol – he did use the jerry can to put petrol in both the family cars, but the last person to use the jerry can would have been the person who had poured petrol on Adrian's body.

According to Matthew's girlfriend, and a police examination, he didn't have any wounds on his body that could account for his bleeding, but experts agreed that when under intense pressure, people could suffer from spontaneous nose bleeds. Perhaps that could account for Matthew's blood being found in various places around the house.

Detectives working on the case checked incoming and outgoing calls from the De Gruchy house around the time of the murder. Matthew's calls to his girlfriend appeared on the phone company's records, but there was no record of a call coming in when Matthew had said he received the crank call threatening the deaths of three members of his family. More holes in Matthew De Gruchy's story.

While some detectives are lucky enough to never have to investigate a murder, Danny Sharkey had had more than his fair share. Beating the De Gruchy case in terms of body count was a case that he'd investigated in 1990, when a farmer had shot his wife and two young daughters and then killed himself. That case had been fairly cut and dried and in many ways the De Gruchy case was too. But even with the evidence pointing to Matthew, the detectives still had to build a strong case before any arrest was made. This careful process couldn't be rushed. Detectives had to wait for evidence analysis results and fingerprint results. But the community and the media were crying out for a quick arrest.

When the solid evidence began to mount up against Matthew De Gruchy, Sharkey had him brought in for further questioning. He wanted to put certain allegations to the young man to see how he responded. Unfortunately for the detectives, Matthew again arrived at the police station with his father and a number of other relatives in tow.

Because he was over eighteen years of age, Matthew could be interviewed without another adult present. While he was taken into an interview room and questioned, his relatives were shown into an office down the corridor. They were angry with the police because they felt that while the detectives were focusing on Matthew as a suspect, they weren't out there 'catching the real killer'. Cases like this are fraught with difficulty for both police and families. Trying to explain to a family dealing with the murder of three of its members that another member could be responsible – especially a teenager – is almost impossible.

In the interview room, Matthew was starting to feel the pressure and Detective Sharkey thought the young man was weakening and on the verge of making admissions. Just then, one of his uncles burst into the room and said that was enough. Even though the detectives escorted the uncle out again, explaining that Matthew was an adult and the police had every right to question him alone, the moment was lost forever.

Because there was no confession, it would be up to forensic evidence to prove that Matthew was a killer. There were over a hundred exhibits and specimens and they all had to be examined. The carpet tuft found in the car Matthew had driven was analysed and an expert concluded that it was 'highly probable that the carpet tuft had its origin in the bedroom carpet.' In even more damning evidence, Matthew's DNA was found on the carpet tuft, on the hallway tiles, and also in a blood droplet from the wall above his mother's bed.

With Matthew De Gruchy fairly and squarely in the crosshairs, Sharkey looked at his known movements on the night of the murders. Matthew had spoken to his girlfriend from the house in Shearwater Boulevard around 8 pm and then arrived at her house around 11 pm, so the only route that detectives knew that he had definitely driven was the one between his house and hers. After some checking, Sharkey found that there were fifteen creeks and waterholes between the two houses – including one directly behind the De Gruchy house. He organised for Police Rescue Squad officers to search each watercourse to a distance of 500 metres from the banks. If Matthew De Gruchy had ditched evidence on the way to his girlfriend's house, Sharkey hoped that the police divers would find it.

A couple of days after the triple murder, a group of young boys were riding their BMX bikes alongside a dam at the old Boral Brickworks on the western side of the Princes Highway in Woonona. They spotted a bag in the shallow water on the edge of the dam. They fished the bag out and went through its contents; the bag contained a hammer and a big piece of carpet, among other things. The boys took a couple of items from the bag and then tossed it back in the water. They thought nothing of it.

Nine days after losing his mother, sister and brother, Matthew De Gruchy attended their triple funeral. He wore a white shirt, dark trousers and dark sunglasses. His long hair was tied back in a ponytail.

It would take police exactly two months from the date of the murder to find the evidence that would lead to Matthew's arrest.

Eventually, the father of one of the boys who had found the bag near the old Boral Brickworks alerted the police. The thought had occurred to him that the bag might have some significance to the investigation. On Monday 13 May, police went to the area indicated by the BMX riders.

Police divers were called in and Detective Sharkey supervised the search. In the dam water, police divers located two bags. One of them was a red and white sports bag, and the other was a black backpack. Crime scene examiners Hodder and Doherty were called to the dam and supervised the removal of items from the bag. These were laid out on sheets of plastic, photographed and documented. Other items were found loose in the mud. Among the items in the bags was a video recorder, a calculator labelled 'A De Gruchy', various CDs and videos, and Jenny De Gruchy's purse – all of the things Matthew De Gruchy had said were stolen from his house when the murders were committed.

One bag also contained a piece of carpet that looked identical in size to the piece cut out of the carpet in Jenny De Gruchy's bedroom. Among the other items recovered was a small zip-lock bag containing a number of bandaids in their wrappers and what looked like pieces of a torn-up note. One of the police officers involved in the retrieval of the items joked, 'Wouldn't it be funny if that note was a how-to list!'

And that's exactly what it was.

Later, when the items were taken back to Forensics to be examined, Barry Doherty carefully dried out the torn note and put the pieces together like a jigsaw puzzle. The letterhead on the flipside of the paper read: 'Noah's on the Beach'. Pieced together, the note revealed a chilling list. It read:

*Open gate
* throw bottle down the track
* throw things down wall in roof
track suit pants 1
Knife 1
T Shirts 2
Shoe's 2
hanky
pole
towel
* open blinds to see through
Sarah mum Adrian

head but ~~mirror~~ bench
Have shower
* throw hifi down back
* hit arm with pole
* hit leg with pole
* cut somewhere with knife

The note specifically tied Matthew De Gruchy to the murders. Who else would refer to Jenny as 'mum' except for one of her children?

Because of the evidence found at the dam, police made arrangements to drain it to search for anything else that might have been thrown into it. On 27 May, the draining process began. Again, Steve Hodder was on hand to examine any items they might find, and also to photograph the search.

A Sega case was located in mud on the western side of the dam; a video tape and a handkerchief were found on the western bank.

Danny Sharkey drove the distance between the Shearwater Boulevard house, the old Boral Brickworks dam and Matthew De Gruchy's girlfriend's house. The 31-kilometre drive could be comfortably completed in 26 minutes, travelling five kilometres below the speed limit. Matthew certainly had time between his phone call to his girlfriend at 8 pm and his arriving at her house at 11 pm to drive via the dam and ditch the evidence.

A handwriting expert would later find twelve points of comparison between the writing on the how-to list and Matthew De Gruchy's handwriting. He stated in his report that 'there were many significant similarities between the note and samples of Matthew's writing and no significant differences'.

'It is my opinion,' his report continued, 'that the person who wrote the specimen writings also wrote the questioned writings on item 1 ...'

Matthew was taken into custody at 7.30 am on Saturday 22 June. Detective Sharkey found him at his girlfriend's house and told him that he wanted to speak to him again about the murders.

'When?' asked Matthew.

'I want you to come back to the Warilla police station with me now,' replied Sharkey.

'I need to speak to my dad.'

'That's fine. Get dressed and you can ring him before we leave.'

Matthew got dressed and then rang his dad. He turned to the detectives and told them that his dad wasn't home but the answering machine was on. Sharkey left a message for Wayne De Gruchy and then Matthew was taken to the Warilla police station. Wayne arrived soon after his son, and called his brother Paul to come to the station as well. Wayne De Gruchy used the phone at the police station to arrange legal representation for his son.

After recording another police interview during which Matthew made no admissions of guilt, Sharkey charged the eighteen year old with the murder of his mother, brother and sister.

Later that day, Hodder and Doherty went back to the house in Shearwater Boulevard accompanied by detectives investigating the case. They were there to search Matthew's bedroom. They found a single sheet from a notepad bearing the words 'Noah's on the Beach' – the same letterhead that was on the back of the how-to list. They took some more samples of Matthew's handwriting to compare against the list, and just to make sure, they checked the roof space again, through an access hole in the garage. The note had indicated that evidence was to have been discarded down the walls through the roof. A search of the area revealed that the internal wall cavities could not be accessed because of timber capping nailed over the top of the wall frames.

In the immediate aftermath of the arrest, headlines in the *Illawarra Mercury* screamed: 'Father vows to stand by his son'. In the court appearance after his arrest, Wayne De Gruchy was quoted in the media as 'offering to put up $100,000 surety for his bail, to open his home to him and to drive him to and from work each day in an effort to acquire his freedom'.

Matthew De Gruchy's Legal Aid solicitor Justin Hutchinson applied for bail for Matthew, and told the court the accused youth had the full support of his father and the remaining members of the family. He said that the family had found the allegations against Matthew 'unbelievable'. The solicitor said that Matthew had continued to live with his father in the Shearwater Boulevard home where the murders had happened.

Despite his father's unswerving loyalty, Matthew De Gruchy was denied bail and remanded into custody.

By the following day, the family had appointed a QC, Malcolm Ramage, to represent Matthew in court. Ramage came in guns blazing and was reported in the media as having 'angry outbursts' about the 'disgraceful' long delays in the DNA testing relevant to the De Gruchy murders. Ramage was also critical that the entire police case was based on forensic evidence. He was quoted as saying that it was 'dangerous stuff' when people were convicted on forensic evidence alone. Ramage claimed that there were 'numerous convictions' in England based on forensic evidence that had to be 'sorted out' by the appeals courts. He didn't elaborate on what these cases were.

Despite Ramage's appeal for bail to be granted to Matthew, at the end of the hearing, the magistrate summed up: 'I am also not satisfied he's not a danger to the community or that he would not commit further offences.' Matthew was again denied bail.

Matthew went to trial for the murder of his mother, brother and sister. He never admitted to committing the murders, and the wheel brace was never located. Matthew was found guilty and received a maximum sentence of 28 years. The judge set a minimum sentence of 21 years before he could be eligible for parole.

Seven years after the murders, Wayne De Gruchy contacted Danny Sharkey. There had been a lot of bad feeling between the De Gruchy family and the police; many members of the extended family felt that Matthew had been unfairly 'stitched up' by the investigators. It is sometimes impossible for families to come to terms with the fact that one of their own has killed other family members. Wayne De Gruchy was no exception.

At the trial, Wayne was a witness, and because of court rules barring witnesses from being in court until after they've given evidence themselves, Wayne had never heard the full case against his son. Enough time had elapsed for the bereaved husband and father to want to know the truth. When he contacted Detective Sharkey, the experienced investigator knew that Wayne had reached the point where he just wanted to know. The two men arranged a time to meet, and Sharkey promised to give him as much time as it took; it ended up taking nearly a whole day.

Sharkey showed Wayne statements, photographs and evidence lists, and patiently explained why the detectives had targeted his son in the investigation. Right from the start, everything had pointed to Matthew. Sharkey detailed the holes in Matthew's story until it became obvious to the father that his son was a killer. Danny Sharkey knew that it was a lot for Wayne De Gruchy to take in all in one go. He told Wayne to get in touch if he needed any further information. Sharkey didn't hear from him again.

Matthew De Gruchy was released from prison in August 2019. He had served 23 of the 28 years of his prison sentence, having spent the first two decades of his adult life in prison. He was 41 years old when he stepped out of the gates, a free man.

Chapter Seven

✦

THE MURDER OF GONG QI

Ben was talking to a friend on the telephone at his flat in the south-eastern Melbourne suburb of Mentone on Wednesday 26 April 1989. His fiancée was out, and his 26-year-old Chinese boarder, Gong Qi, hadn't yet returned from classes at Melbourne's International College of English in the city. It was around 8.20 in the evening and he had been on the phone for half an hour when he heard a noise and looked out through the kitchen window. He saw Gong Qi waving her arms and he could hear her crying. He hung up the phone and ran to get his keys to unlock the flyscreen door to let her in. Gong Qi was sobbing and speaking in Chinese, which he couldn't understand. She was grabbing at her back with her right hand. The young woman stumbled into the flat and tried to pull her jumper off. Ben asked her what had happened but she couldn't speak. Her breathing was heavy. She got as far as the lounge room before falling forward onto the floor.

Ben raced for the phone book and looked up the number for the police and rang them, telling them to ring an ambulance. He returned to Gong Qi and saw that she was bleeding from the mouth and nose. He grabbed some rags from the laundry and placed them under her head.

'What happened?' he asked her urgently.

'Boy, boy!' she gasped.

Ben tried his best to comfort the stricken woman but she was getting worse. Her eyes began to roll back and she tried to grab his hand. Gong Qi had pulled her jumper up and Ben saw blood on her back. He ran to the phone and called the police again and told them that he thought that Gong Qi had been stabbed. By the time Ben got back to the lounge room, he could see flashing lights through the window. The ambulance and the police had arrived at the same time. He ran outside and called them over.

Constable John Barbour and his partner saw Ben in the driveway of the flat in Levanto Street and followed him inside. The ambulance officers entered with them. The police took Ben into the kitchen while the paramedics worked on the by now unconscious woman on the lounge-room floor. When they lifted her jumper, they found a visible wound in her upper back. She was pale, unconscious and cold. Her breathing was shallow.

Leaving Ben in the kitchen, Constable Barbour returned to the lounge room. He could see the woman lying on the floor and the blood-soaked blue rags lying near her head. The ambulance officers asked Barbour to help them lift the woman onto the stretcher to take her to the ambulance.

By this time, a second patrol car pulled up outside. Constable David Banks from the Mordialloc police arrived in time to help manoeuvre the stretcher out of the flat and down to the driveway to the waiting ambulance. Barbour returned to the flat while Banks went with the ambulance officers as they loaded the unconscious woman into the back of the ambulance. Suddenly, she stopped breathing.

For 30 minutes, Banks and the ambulance officers tried CPR to revive her. A MICA ambulance arrived to assist, but by the time they got there, 26-year-old Gong Qi's pupils were fixed and dilated, she had no vital signs, and her heart had stopped beating. She was given adrenaline, and the ambulance officers inserted a suction tube to clear large amounts of blood from her airway. They also tried to establish intravenous lines but were unable to.

Despite their resuscitation efforts, Gong Qi did not respond and died in the back of the ambulance outside the Mentone flat where she had lived for six weeks since coming to Australia from Shanghai. Resuscitation attempts ceased at 9.10 pm.

After Gong Qi died, there was no hurry to get her to a hospital and her body remained where it was in the back of the ambulance outside the Mentone flat for several hours while the police called in the troops – CIB detectives, a crime scene examiner, photographics, a video operator, and then the Homicide Squad.

Around 10.15 pm, Detective Sergeant John Robertson and Detective Senior Constable Peter Wheeler from the Homicide Squad arrived at the Levanto Street flat. They spoke to the police officers already in attendance and viewed the body of Gong Qi in the back of the ambulance. They also spoke to Ben, who was distraught with the death of his housemate.

At 10.50 pm, crime scene examiner Senior Constable Tony Kealy arrived at the scene. Inside the flat, he collected Gong Qi's handbag and its contents. Using a torch, he walked around the surrounding streets close to where she lived and found a number of tissues, some stained with what appeared to be blood. He found no sign of a knife or any other weapon that could have been used to stab the young woman.

When the scene was cleared, the ambulance drove Gong Qi's body to the Alfred Hospital, where an attending physician pronounced her dead at 1.18 am. Constable Banks then followed the ambulance to the city morgue, where the body was taken into storage to await a post-mortem examination.

At 6 am the next morning, forensic pathologist Dr Shelley Robertson prepared Gong Qi's body for the autopsy. Before any internal examination begins, the pathologist performs a visual examination. Dr Robertson described Gong Qi's body while a police photographer recorded the procedure on film.

Gong Qi was 166 centimetres tall and weighed 57.8 kilograms. Dr Robertson noted that she was of Asian appearance with black hair and brown eyes. Contact lenses were present in both eyes. She noted a small amount of dried blood present around the nose and in the mouth. The body was still dressed in the clothes she had been wearing – blue jeans and a mustard-coloured jumper with a brown floral pattern on it. The back of the jumper was stained red with blood.

Observing the post-mortem examination was Detective Senior Constable Peter Phelan from the Homicide Squad. He asked Dr Robertson to align the stab wound with the natural fall of the shirt and jumper Gong Qi had been wearing when she was attacked. Dr Robertson did this and both the doctor and the detective saw straightaway that there were rolls of material up near her shoulders. Since the stab wound was up near her right shoulder blade, and the corresponding hole cut in the jumper was in its waist band, it was obvious that the jumper was not in its natural worn position when the stab wound was inflicted. It was likely that the offender had grabbed her by the jumper and she had tried to get away, and the jumper had been pulled right up when the stab wound was inflicted.

Once the initial visual examination was completed, Dr Robertson had an assistant remove the clothes and clean the wounds and she was able to see Gong Qi's injuries. On both sides of her neck were tiny puncture wounds with some bruising around them – these were caused by the medical intervention by the ambulance officers. When the body was rolled over, Dr Robertson could see the wound that had killed the young woman. A single stab wound in her upper back, which measured just 1.9 centimetres across, had proved fatal.

The internal examination revealed the exact damage the wound had caused. The weapon had penetrated into the right thoracic cavity and punctured her right lung to a depth of six centimetres. Robertson noted that the wound was consistent with being caused by a knife. She also noted that there were no defence wounds on her arms or hands to suggest that Gong Qi had fought off her attacker. The doctor found no evidence of a struggle prior to the stabbing – apart from the position of the jumper. A toxicology screen showed no trace of alcohol or drugs in the young woman's system.

When the post-mortem examination was over, Dr Robertson handed forensic samples as well as the victim's effects to Senior Detective Phelan.

While Shelley Robertson was doing the post-mortem examination on Gong Qi, crime scene examiner Tony Kealy was back in
Levanto Street coordinating the daylight search for any evidence
that might help the investigation. He and local uniform police
searched all footpaths, gardens, nature strips and stormwater
drains in streets close to where Gong Qi lived. Given the nature of
her stab wound, police knew the attack must have happened quite
close to where she lived, or she would never have made it home.
This kind of line-searching was vital because there was always
the possibility that a fleeing offender might discard a weapon, or
inadvertently drop something that could help police identify him.
However, in this case, searchers found no sign of a weapon, or
even any blood on nearby footpaths to indicate where the stabbing
might have taken place.

After giving the line-searchers parameters, homicide detectives
assigned to the investigation, Detective Senior Sergeant Bob
Ryan, Detective Sergeant John Robertson and Detective Senior
Constable Peter Wheeler, met at the Mentone police station. They
would use this as a base for the duration of the investigation. They
were then joined by Detective Senior Constable Peter Phelan
after the post-mortem examination had finished.

With the search failing to turn up any evidence, the homicide
crew realised that at this early stage of the investigation, they had
no primary crime scene, no witnesses, no motive, and no suspect.

As soon as the International College of English opened for
business the morning after Gong Qi died, detectives contacted a
Chinese-speaking college official and explained what had happened
to Gong Qi. Helpful employees at the college offered to telephone
Gong Qi's parents in Shanghai and break the news to them. They
also offered to arrange for the parents to fly to Australia. The
detectives were grateful for their support.

At 2.30 pm, the detectives went to the Mordialloc police
station and spoke to an officer whose job it was to collate details

of local crime patterns. The collator told them that local police were investigating a series of attacks on women in the area. The culprit was a young man who rode a bicycle and attacked women from behind. Usually he touched them on the breasts or genitals before riding off.

Around 4 pm, the detectives visited the Chinese Consulate in St Kilda Road to officially alert them about the murder of a Chinese citizen. The detectives then headed back to the Homicide Squad offices and discussed the case till 7.40 pm. After working 32 hours straight, they called it a day. Peter Phelan wanted to get home to his wife – it was their fifteenth wedding anniversary.

The next step in the murder investigation was to try to retrace Gong Qi's final movements. Homicide detectives appealed through the media and set up a police information caravan outside the Mentone railway station. A police artist sketched a picture of a Chinese woman wearing the same clothes as Gong Qi and carrying the same handbag. The murdered woman's mustard-coloured jumper with the brown floral design was unusual, and the detectives hoped that the sketch would jog people's memories. The sketch was publicised through the media and given out on flyers at the caravan and at both Mentone and Flinders Street railway stations.

After news of the murder spread, a distressed friend of Gong Qi's contacted police. Fellow Chinese student Hong Tang had met Gong Qi at the International College of English, and the two women had become friends. On the day Gong Qi died, they had caught the 7.16 pm Frankston-bound train from the city with another friend, Ping Gui. They had sat together and chatted on the journey. Ping Gui had left the train at Glenhuntly station and Hong Tang had alighted at Ormond. Gong Qi had appeared normal and hadn't said she was worried about anything.

Hong Tang told the detectives that Gong Qi was a very innocent and trusting person, and that she was very moral and intended marrying her fiancé when she returned home to China.

On the same train as the women that night was a man called Douglas, who worked for Telecom in Spring Street. When he had entered the train carriage, there were few seats left and he approached three Asian women who were sitting together. One of the women had a black fabric handbag on an empty seat and he asked her if she could move it, which she did. He sat next to the women, who were chatting together in Chinese. He watched as one left the train at Glenhuntly and then the other left at Ormond. When the third woman got off the train at Mentone station, he noticed her walking up the platform towards the gate. Although there were other people around, no-one approached her and he saw her walk off alone. It was around 8 pm.

When the news of the murder hit the press the next day, Douglas was certain that the dead woman was the one he had sat next to on the train. He rang the police and gave a statement. He was shown a photo of Gong Qi and identified her as the woman on the train.

Once it was established that Gong Qi had definitely caught the train home from the city, the next step in the investigation was to find out how she came to arrive at the Levanto Street flat with a fatal stab wound. Had someone picked her up at the station? Or had she walked home and been attacked on the way?

A young man called Grant came forward to say that he had pulled up at the lights on the Nepean Highway near the service station on the corner of Warrigal Road, some time between 8.10 and 8.30 pm on Wednesday 26 April. He had seen a woman fitting Gong Qi's description standing at the pedestrian crossing on the median strip. He didn't pay much attention to her but noticed she had a light-coloured top and carried a dark-coloured shoulder bag over one shoulder. Grant was driving with his brother and a friend and the trio had continued up the highway towards Lower Dandenong Road. He told the detectives that the Shell service station towards which the woman was heading was busy with customers at the time. Chances were that nothing would have happened to her till she was well clear of so many witnesses.

Once the detectives knew that she had in fact walked home from the Mentone railway station, most probably past the Shell service station, they set about finding out what route she had taken from there. The route from the station itself was direct; down Balcombe Road to the Nepean Highway. After crossing the highway and turning left into Warrigal Road, there were a number of streets that Gong Qi could have taken to get to her home in Levanto Street. It was up to the detectives to anticipate all the routes and then canvass every house on every possible route, which in the end meant covering six suburban blocks.

Detectives began door-knocking houses the day after the murder using the same opening lines: 'We're investigating the murder of the Chinese girl yesterday. We're canvassing the area in the hope that someone may have seen something ...' Every detective knows that there are always people who, despite media blitzes, will not ring police with information but rather wait for the police to come knocking on their doors, so the door-knocks, although time consuming, were important. Detectives carefully noted down which occupants were home and which houses they had to go back to. Long days ensued for the detectives because some neighbours weren't home until evening, while some could only be caught early in the morning.

A man who lived in nearby Albenca Street reported hearing a woman scream some time between 7.45 and 8.15 pm. The scream seemed to come from Levanto Street and did not seem that far away. It lasted for a few seconds. He took little notice of it, thinking that someone was 'mucking around' outside.

A local woman had heard an argument in Levanto Street some time between 8 and 8.30 pm on the night Gong Qi was stabbed. Another neighbour remembered hearing a loud scream and the sound of someone running down Levanto Street between 8.15 and 8.30 pm. None of the neighbours had gone outside to see if anything was wrong.

Other detectives from the Homicide Squad liaised with local detectives to see who they had on their books who might be capable of this type of offence. They were looking for offenders who had priors for violent assaults against women. A police collator gave the detectives a list of twelve offenders who lived in the Mentone area who had a criminal history of such a nature that would make them possible suspects. Detectives began to contact each person on the list and soon narrowed the list down to four, but none of the leads panned out.

Speaking with Ben and his fiancée, with whom Gong Qi had boarded, detectives found out that she was an ordinary young woman, and the couple could shed no light on her murder.

Suspicion after a murder falls on anyone in the circle of the victim. Because Ben lived with Gong Qi, the shadow of suspicion automatically fell over him. His fiancée wasn't home on the night Gong Qi died, and he had no-one to vouch for his movements. His flat was the only place the victim had bled and the detectives couldn't discount the possibility that she might have actually been stabbed inside the flat.

Soon after the murder, Ben agreed to undergo hypnosis just in case he remembered anything else. Under hypnotic questioning, he could add nothing else to his account. He became so upset during the procedure that the doctor stopped the session; Ben had relived the whole traumatic event. The detectives discounted him as a suspect.

The case was as puzzling as it was tragic. Gong Qi had only been in the country for six weeks, and there was no reason to think that she had met anyone and formed a relationship. She didn't seem to be frightened of anyone. Could it have simply been a random attack? Could a stranger have simply come up behind her, struggled with her, pulling up her jumper in the process, and stabbed her in the back? She hadn't been sexually assaulted, and there was nothing missing from her handbag. No motive. No evidence.

Meanwhile, information from the public flooded in. Mentone is one of Melbourne's quiet bayside suburbs and the crime rate was relatively low. The seemingly random murder of a woman walking home from the railway station made local residents nervous.

A worker at the Ampol service station on Balcombe Road in Mentone contacted police saying that he knew of a male person who police had arrested at Mordialloc about eight weeks before the murder. The man had said that he wanted to kill Asians. Another report came in that a Seaford man was telling people that he was the one who had stabbed the Chinese girl. A man from Hawthorn reported being harassed by two men in a blue 1972 HQ Holden on Warrigal Road a week before Gong Qi was murdered. Someone reported that they had seen a man running along Como Parade near the station at 6.50 pm on the night of the murder. And two women who worked at the Tuckerbag supermarket reported that they had seen a man talking to girls outside the supermarket last November.

A number of people rang the police to tell them about a man who had been seen recently walking around the Mentone Safeway supermarket with scissors in his mouth. One of the cops from the Transit police reported that a man had been seen recently staring at Asian students at the International College of English. A Mentone woman rang and said that she'd had a Chinese student living with her for six months in the previous year, and the student had been approached by a man when she was walking home from the railway station. That Chinese student had attended the same International College of English that Gong Qi had attended. This lead was worth following up, even though the woman and the Chinese student lived on the beach side of Mentone, a couple of kilometres from the other side of the highway where the murder took place.

Sergeant John Robertson found out that Cub Scouts met on Wednesday evenings at the Scout Hall that was across the street from where Gong Qi lived. He organised a list of all members; any member who attended the 13th Mordialloc Cubs on the night of the stabbing had to be interviewed. Someone might have seen something – but it turned out that no-one had.

The media blitz was so successful that anyone who had seen anyone acting suspiciously in the last year, or thought anyone's behaviour was in any way odd, rang the police, and the information piled up. In some ways this was good for the detectives but conversely, it muddied the waters. Members of the public nominated many suspects and each of the suspects had to be checked out and eliminated.

Within days of the murder, Gong Qi's parents, Li Zhen Chen and Zhao Rong Gong, arrived from China. The detectives met them at the International College of English with an interpreter. Gong Qi's parents were an elderly couple. Her father was a successful businessman in Shanghai and had sent his only child to Melbourne to study English so that one day she might take over his business. While the dignified couple held their emotions in check, they were clearly distraught at their loss. Speaking through the interpreter, they urged the detectives to find the person responsible for taking their daughter's life. They explained that according to their beliefs, their daughter's soul could not rest until her killer was found.

The emotional meeting with Gong Qi's parents added a sense of urgency to the investigation. The couple couldn't stay in Australia indefinitely and would soon have to return to China. The detectives knew that while an arrest wouldn't bring Gong Qi back, it would ease the pain a little for her devastated parents, knowing that her soul could rest in peace.

On Tuesday 2 May, Peter Wheeler and John Robertson continued canvassing the neighbours. Parallel to Levanto Street was Albenca Street and the detectives knocked on the door of a flat there, in a cream-brick, nondescript, single-storey block with a carport on either side of a waist-high brick wall housing six letterboxes. This was the fourth visit to this particular flat. No matter what time the detectives had called, the occupant either wasn't home or hadn't answered his front door. They had spoken to his neighbours, who reported that the young man who lived in the flat often sat outside on the brick letterbox smoking cigarettes. If this was true, then the detectives wondered if he might have seen something on the night of the murder, and could have information for them.

'We're from the Homicide Squad,' said Peter Wheeler to the young man who finally answered the door of flat four. Wheeler showed the man his identification badge. 'We're investigating the murder of the Chinese girl on 26 April.'

'Yeah,' said the man. 'I heard about it on the radio.'

'We're just canvassing the area in the hope that someone may have seen something on the night.'

'I didn't see anything,' said the man.

'Were you home on the night?' asked Wheeler.

'Yes. I got drunk and went to bed.'

'Do you recall what time you went to bed?'

'About 8.30.'

'So you didn't hear anything?'

'No. I sat out on the letterbox for a while and went inside about 5 o'clock. I had a few cans, got well and truly pissed and went to bed about 8.30.'

The young man was of medium height and slight build. He had shaggy dark brown hair and didn't appear nervous. When he spoke, he dropped his 'g's and said 'anythink' instead of 'anything'. He didn't make eye contact with the detectives.

What made the man's story suspicious was that one of his neighbours had already told police that he had seen the young man sitting out on the front letterbox between 6.30 and 7 pm on the night of the murder. So right from the start, the detectives knew he was being less than honest.

For the record, the detectives asked the young man his name and date of birth. His name was Mark Hastie Brown. He was 22 years old. Wheeler and Robertson got the feeling there was something not quite right about the young man. Both men had been in the force for years and prided themselves on having an instinct for these things. They resolved to run his name through the system and see if Brown had been in any trouble with the police before.

When the docket sheets that listed prior convictions came back from the check on Mark Hastie Brown, the detectives knew they could be on to something. Even though he was only 22, Brown had been in trouble with the police on several occasions.

When he was around fifteen years old, he had coaxed a young girl on her way home from school into a shed on the pretext of showing her a kitten. Inside the shed, he sexually assaulted her. The arresting officer had written: *The foster mother provides a good home for the child. It is clean and warm and he has a room to himself. They are concerned for his future. He seems to be a loner and has difficulty making friends.*

Brown denied the offence when first spoken to but when he realised that he'd been seen, he agreed substantially with the girl's account.

Just over a month after that assault, Brown was again charged with indecent assault. He had chased a thirteen-year-old girl, and when she fell to the ground, he had sexually assaulted her. The girl managed to run away from him. The offence was committed in broad daylight and in front of witnesses. On the back of the docket sheet, the arresting officer had written: *His foster parents with whom he is now living have brought him up as their son since he was six, however they are elderly and have trouble controlling him. He has obvious mental problems as this is the fourth reported case of indecent assault committed by him, and this offence was committed while on bail. When interviewed, he admits everything but the indecent part of the assault and it appears he will not admit that he has a problem. He needs psychiatric treatment and will continue to be a danger to young girls unless he can be cured.*

But the prior conviction of most interest to the detectives happened in May 1983. Mark Brown had attacked an elderly woman as she was walking down the street. He grabbed her from behind, forced her to the ground, then looked at the lady for a short time before running off. Again, a comment by the arresting officer gave the homicide detectives further insight into Brown: *This child is the subject of an extensive effort to assist him and establish him as a normal member of the community. It remains to be seen whether the efforts of a number of agencies will be enough to bring this about. This child is asking for help and believes he has a mental disorder that causes him to act in this fashion.*

For the detectives, the fact that Brown had priors for sexual offences against women, and the fact that he had attacked a woman from behind, took him from a letterbox-sitter who was hard to locate to a suspect high on the list. It was definitely worth taking a closer look at Mark Hastie Brown.

Of course, Brown wasn't their only lead. As well as looking into his background, the detectives had a number of other suspects who had been named by members of the public; some were brought in for questioning, and others were put under police surveillance.

On Thursday 4 May, the detectives met with Gong Qi's parents again, this time at the Chinese Museum in the city. There, police had set up a press conference and they were surrounded by TV cameras and journalists. Through an interpreter, the parents made an emotional plea for people to come forward with information about their daughter's murder. The following day, Peter Phelan met the parents again, this time at their hotel. He returned a ring that was taken from Gong Qi's body during the post-mortem examination. It was the only piece of jewellery she was wearing when she died.

On Thursday 11 May 1989, the day before the Homicide detectives would finally make an arrest in the murder of Gong Qi, an unrelated incident happened to detectives Peter Wheeler and Peter Phelan that has echoes to this day. The police doorknock had extended to streets surrounding the Mentone railway station, and Wheeler and Phelan made their way up the driveway of a house in Elizabeth

Street, Mentone. Suddenly, Wheeler heard the crack of a projectile hitting the bricks of the house.

'Did you hear that?' he asked, looking around, trying to make sense of the noise.

Phelan had heard it. The two police were suddenly on high alert. Scanning their surroundings, they both spotted the barrel of a firearm being raised over the top of a tall set of gates across the road. Before they had time to react, another projectile was fired their way. This time, it was so close, Wheeler felt it whizz pass his head and strike the brickwork on the house behind him.

'We're being shot at!' Wheeler yelled.

Both men dived to the ground and crawled on their stomachs to take cover behind the low brick fence of the house they were door-knocking. Through a hole in the fence, Wheeler had a line of sight to the gates across the road. Again, he saw the barrel rising above the gate and again heard a shot being fired. The gun barrel disappeared behind the gates again.

'Looks like a single-shot rifle,' Wheeler told Phelan. 'They're lowering it to reload.'

While they could see the barrel of a firearm and hear the projectiles hit the house, the sound of gunfire was muffled. In a frantic whispered conversation, the two cops wondered if the gunman was using some kind of silencer.

Wheeler saw a couple approaching from up Elizabeth Street, walking a dog. 'Turn back!' he yelled at them. 'Someone's firing a gun!' They turned and hurried back from where they came.

Another rise of the barrel. Another shot fired.

The two detectives were stuck. They were unarmed – no firearms were carried during routine doorknocks. They had no radios. The only communication device they had was a pager, but it only received messages, not transmitted them.

Two more shots were fired, with the same time gap between them.

The two cops were safe if the gunman stayed where he was and they stayed behind the fence, but that could change any moment. The shooter need only open the gate and cross the road, and they would have no way of escaping.

Wheeler measured the time between shots. He turned to Phelan. 'I reckon we've got enough time between shots to get across the road and grab the shooter.' Phelan agreed. It was their only way out. The moment the next shot was fired, the two men scrambled to their feet, sprang across the low fence and bolted across the road to the house with the high gates. Just as they reached the gates, the ominous barrel appeared again, pointing towards the wall where they'd just come from.

A split-second decision to keep moving towards the gun.

'Police! Drop the gun!' yelled Wheeler as he launched himself against the gates. He could hear Phelan yelling too.

Just as the barrel of the firearm was levelling to fire, they both hit the gates with considerable force. The gates smashed into two men on the other side, knocking them off the milk crate they were standing on. The men were pushed backwards and the gun dropped to the ground. Wheeler secured the firearm – which turned out to be a .22 calibre high-powered air rifle.

'Why were you shooting at us?' yelled Phelan.

'We thought you were Mormons!' said one of the young men, who smelt of alcohol.

'We were only trying to scare you,' said the other. 'We're sorry!' He'd been drinking too.

Sorry or not, they had chosen to fire on two men in suits from across the road with reckless regard for the safety of two fellow human beings. Wheeler and Phelan couldn't believe the stupidity of the men. Both men were from New South Wales. One was eighteen. The other was 22. Old enough to know better. Wheeler and Phelan seized the firearm, remaining ammunition and questioned both men for various assault- and weapon-related offences.

They then conveyed the rifle and ammunition back to the Homicide Squad office in Melbourne and told their colleagues of the door-knocking shooting. After such a harrowing experience, the two detectives felt strangely let down by their colleagues, who seemed to shrug off the incident.

'It's only a .22 calibre air rifle,' one detective said.

Wheeler felt he missed the point. They had been shot at, crawled to safety, kept the dog walkers away from harm, then risked their lives to bring down the shooters – all the while not knowing that the firearm wasn't of the most lethal kind. And even if it wasn't lethal, air rifles were well known for their ability to take out an eye and cause severe injuries if fired up close, or even from the distance that the detectives had been fired at. But with the pressure to make an arrest in the Gong Qi case, the incident was pushed to the background while the detectives got on with the job.

The following day, at 6.50 am on 12 May – seventeen days after Gong Qi's murder – the four homicide detectives, Bob Ryan, John Robertson, Peter Phelan and Peter Wheeler, arrived at Brown's flat. The day was significant for the detectives because it was also the day of a funeral service for the victim. None of the investigators had forgotten what her parents had told them about her soul not being able to rest until her killer had been caught. Gong Qi was being cremated so her parents could take her ashes back to China.

They knocked on Brown's door, but there was no answer. The door to the flat next door opened and a woman called Kate came out. The detectives told her they were looking for Mark Brown and she told them that he was in her flat. Soon after, Brown appeared. Detective Senior Sergeant Ryan did the talking. He introduced himself and his fellow officers and asked if he minded them coming into his flat. The police were shown inside. Phelan stayed near the front door in case Brown tried to make a run for it.

'Who do you live here with?' asked Ryan.

'I live on my own,' Brown said.

The detectives all noticed a newspaper lying on the coffee table in the lounge room dated 9 May. It was open at page three and the main article was headed: 'Police step up hunt for girl killer'.

'We are investigating the death of a Chinese girl on 26 April, just down the road from here.'

'I read about it in the paper,' said Brown.

'Do you mind if we have a look around the flat?' asked Ryan.

'No,' said Brown. 'Be all right if I have a cup of coffee and put some other clothes on?' The suspect was in his pyjamas at this early hour of the morning.

Ryan said that it was okay for him to change. Brown went into his kitchen and put the kettle on, then into his bedroom to dress. He came out of his room soon after wearing a tight blue jumper and tight acid-wash jeans with a rip in the right leg.

When he returned, Ryan cautioned him. 'Do you understand that you do not have to say anything but whatever you say will be taken down and may be given in evidence?'

'Yes,' replied Brown sitting down on his couch with a cup of coffee.

Significantly for the detectives, Mark Brown had not asked what they wanted to talk to him for, or why they were there. The detectives knew that most people when questioned by police are full of questions themselves: Why do you want to talk to me? Why would you think I had anything to do with this? But Brown didn't ask anything at all. It added to the feeling there was something amiss, something about him that wasn't right.

Ryan checked the cutlery drawer in the kitchen and saw a number of knives and two pairs of scissors.

'Who owns these?' he asked.

'I do,' Brown replied.

Ryan bagged them all as evidence as he explained to Brown that he wanted to ask him some questions about the death of the Chinese girl. Brown agreed to accompany the detectives back to the Homicide Squad offices at the St Kilda Road police complex.

Wheeler sat with Brown in the back seat of the car while Phelan drove. Again, even though he had ample opportunity, Brown asked no questions, expressed no surprise that the police wanted to take him to the Homicide Squad to interview him, and most importantly, made no denials about any possible involvement in the murder of Gong Qi.

Having deposited him into the interview room, the detectives met to discuss an interview strategy. They knew from the notes on his docket sheets that Brown had a history of denying offences that he had committed, and they figured he would probably do the same thing in this case.

Wheeler looked around at his colleagues and said, 'If this bloke didn't do it, I'll eat my hat!'

After the preliminaries were over and the caution was given, the questioning began in the interview room at 7.45 am. Wheeler and Phelan were given the task of conducting the interview.

Phelan asked Brown to repeat what he had told Wheeler and Robertson when they'd knocked on his door on Tuesday 2 May.

'What did you tell them on this occasion?'

'That I heard about it on the radio but didn't see anything. I was home that night, got drunk and was asleep in bed by about 8.30.'

'We have been told that you had been out the front of your flat sitting on the letterbox.'

He replied, 'Yes, I was out there for a while having a drink, sitting there. I went back inside for a while and remembered that I had forgotten to check the letterbox, so I went out again and sat for a while longer.'

'What time did you go inside from the letterbox?'

'I got a phone call from a mate around 10 past 8.'

'What is the friend's name?'

'I haven't known him for long. Tony. I don't know his last name.'

Brown said the friend lived in Black Rock. He said that he went to bed after the phone call around 8.30 pm.

'What happened after 8.30 pm?'

'I heard police sirens everywhere.'

'What time did you hear the sirens?'

'At 8.30, just after I got into bed. I saw blue lights flashing up my room.'

'Were your blinds open or closed?'

'Closed.'

'How did you see the blue lights then?'

'Over the top of the blinds.'

'What happened then?'

'I went to sleep.'

At this stage, Phelan called a break in the interview and asked Brown if he'd like something to eat. It was normal police procedure that suspects be given food and drink during the interview process. Brown ordered a bacon and egg sandwich and a coffee.

After eating his breakfast, Brown was ready to resume the interview. Phelan decided to play hardball.

'I'm not happy with your story so far, Mark. How could you see the blue lights in your bedroom? You would have to be outside in the street.'

'No, I was in bed.'

Phelan persisted. 'What I'm saying is that there was no reason for police cars to be in the street outside your address.'

'There was a reflection on the roof.'

'The police cars didn't go past your flat, and if they had, the carport out the front of your flat would have stopped the light entering your room. What do you say to that?'

Brown began to look very nervous. 'I thought I saw lights,' he replied uncertainly.

Phelan kept his own voice steady. 'Take your time and think about what actually happened that night between you and the Chinese girl.'

Now Brown looked visibly upset and Phelan used that. 'Mark, you are upset for some reason?'

'I don't want to be charged with murder. I'm not a murderer. It's all an accident. No-one will believe me.'

'How was it an accident?' asked Phelan knowing that he was about to get an admission of some sort.

'It was an accident, the knife fell out of my pocket and she fell on it. I have been getting threatening phone calls and I had to get out of my flat.'

Phelan cautioned the suspect again and asked him to explain what had happened. Brown said that he had gone for a walk and armed himself with a knife for protection against someone who had rung him and threatened him. He said that he saw the Chinese girl and asked her for a cigarette. She hadn't understood him and pushed him.

'The knife fell out of my pocket; she slipped, fell over backwards on the knife. It was an accident.' Brown told the detectives that he'd tried to help her when he saw that she had the knife in her back, but she couldn't understand him. He said that he took the knife out of her back and she ran off into Levanto Street.

'What did you do?'

'I was scared and didn't know what to do. I just wanted to get away. No-one's going to believe me.'

'What did you do with the knife?'

'I took it home and washed it.'

'Where is the knife now?'

'You people have it. You took it from my flat this morning.'

'Mark,' said Phelan, 'we will just take a break. Another coffee?'

'Yes, please. I'm not a murderer.'

During the break, detectives Wheeler and Phelan told John Robertson and Bob Ryan that Brown had admitted having a role in the stabbing. Robertson and Ryan got straight into a car and drove to the funeral service to break the news to Gong Qi's relieved parents. The man responsible for their daughter's death was in police custody and now her soul could rest in peace. It was a positive moment in an exhausting investigation.

Phelan organised for the formal interview to be recorded on video. Brown drank coffee and sat patiently smoking a cigarette, waiting for the detectives to come back into the room.

When the detectives were ready to resume the interview, Brown sat on a chair at the interview table. Phelan led the questioning with a legal caution, and asked for Brown's full name, address and occupation for the record. Brown said that he was a process worker at a business in Mentone.

'How do you feel at the moment?' asked Phelan solicitously.

'I feel a little bit ... much better than I was before,' replied Brown. It was as if he had got the incident off his chest, and now all he had to do was convince the detectives that it was all just an accident.

Phelan asked him to go over his story once again.

'I was gettin' threatenin' phone calls ...' began Brown.

'Now, where were you getting threatening phone calls?'

'At my place.'

'Do you know who was making these phone calls?'

'No, I've only had the phone on for a short while.'

'Right. Is there any reason for these phone calls?'

'Not that I know of. I've hardly got any enemies ... I was getting 'em on Wednesday night. I got a threatenin' phone call so I decided I had to get out of me flat, so I went for a walk. Um ... but I took a knife with me.'

Phelan showed Brown a map of Mentone and asked him to indicate the street where his flat was, which he did. Brown said that on the Wednesday that Gong Qi had died, he had received another threatening phone call and the person had allegedly said, 'We're gunna get you'. After the call, he told the detectives, he had changed his clothes and left his flat wearing blue jeans, white runners, a navy top and a tracksuit top.

Using the map, he indicated that he had walked up Savona Street to Warrigal Road, then up Warrigal to Cervara Street, and that was where he had seen the girl.

'Did you take anything from the flat with you when you went?'

'Er ... the only thing I did take was the knife.'

'Right.'

'Because ... er ... that night, when I got the phone call, er ... to me ... er ... with the crank telephone calls I was getting – this one was serious. In case I got attacked, well, I took the knife so I can protect myself ... er ... and that's how the accident happened.'

Phelan got the bag of knives that Ryan had collected at Brown's flat. Earlier, Brown had told the detectives that the knife he had taken on the night of Gong Qi's death was in the bag. He indicated the knife to the detectives.

'How did you put that in your pocket?' asked Phelan. The black-handled knife wasn't that long; in fact, it looked much like an ordinary steak knife that would be found in most kitchens. Still, it was a bit too long to fit comfortably in someone's pocket.

'Well, I had it in me pocket this way, but me pocket only came up to here but I had me hands in me pockets,' said Brown, holding his hand to the side of his jumper.

'Right,' said Phelan. 'So you actually had your hand on it ... so it wouldn't fall out.'

Soon after came the event that Brown referred to as 'an accident'.

'Er ... I left my smokes at home ... um ... with the state I was in with the phone call, I just completely forgot me smokes. Er ... I saw the young lady there walkin' in the street so I went up to 'er and asked 'er if she had any smokes. Er ... She pushed me backwards ...'

'Where on the map did this take place?' asked Phelan, passing Brown the map again.

'It was in Levanto Street, opposite the park.'

Phelan asked Brown if he'd approached the girl from in front or behind.

'Walking behind 'er but I did ... um ... sort of ... I didn't scare 'er or anything ... I said, "Excuse me," you know ... pretty loud so she can hear me, so she wouldn't, you know, think I was gunna attack her. Um ... what happened was that um ... I asked her if she had any smokes. I couldn't understand what she was saying. Er ... and all ... I just repeated, you know, "Look, I just want one smoke if you got it," and she was speaking Chinese as far as I know.'

'Right.'

'Er ... I couldn't understand the language ... um ... she pushed me backwards and the knife fell out of me pocket ...'

'Were you standing on the footpath?'

'Sort of on the road and she was on the ... sort of ... pavement ... er ... I think it's called the pavement where the gutter is.'

'The nature strip?'

'Where the gutter is ... she was on that and as she pushed me, she slipped as well and the knife went on the ground and she fell on the knife.'

'The knife's fallen out of your pocket?'

'Yeah...'

'... and she's fallen over at the same time?'

'She fell backwards on to the knife.'

'Right. Did you realise at that stage that she'd hurt herself?'

'Um, she got up and then I saw the knife, er ... in 'er back. Um ... I was scared at the time. I didn't know what to do ... All I could think of is to get out ... um ... I moved the knife gently from her back and ... um I was just that frightened, I ended up running away.'

'Did she scream?' asked Phelan. Several neighbours had reported hearing a woman scream around the time Gong Qi was stabbed.

'Um, it was sort of a mumbled scream, but I thought that, you know, just fallin' back ... er ... I didn't think that the knife went into 'er or anythink.'

'Now, when you stood up, the knife was in her back?'

'Mmm.'

'You must have been fairly close to her, is that right?'

'Ah, yes I was. I ... I was gunna start walking away but she got up. I saw the knife and um ... I thought that um ... it wasn't in 'er back fully. Er ... when I took the knife out gently ... um ... I said to her that, "Look, I'm gunna get the knife out".' When Brown repeated the words he allegedly said to Gong Qi, he spoke as if he was her rescuer, not her killer.

Phelan handed Brown a pen and asked him to indicate how far the knife had gone into the woman, which he did. Then Brown described taking the knife out.

'When I was takin' the knife out ... um ... she was in agony. Well, that's understandable ... er ... and I sort of took the knife out and I ended up running up the street.' Brown told the detectives that he'd run back to his flat and washed the knife in boiling water. He told how the next day, CIB detectives had knocked on his door. Since Peter Wheeler first spoke to him on 2 May, obviously, Brown hadn't opened his door when the CIB came calling.

'And I was still frightened. I didn't know what was gunna happen or anythink. I was sort of frightened of myself mainly, because I heard that ... er ... she died and ... um ... it was an accident and ...

um ... I thought I'd be charged with murder and I was sort of a little panicky.'

Phelan asked Brown if he had tried to help the girl in any way before he'd run off. Brown said that he'd tried asking her where she lived, but she just pushed him away. He said that when he got back to his flat, he had tried to call triple 0 but the number was engaged. He said that he'd then heard ambulances and he knew that someone must have called them for her.

The detectives turned the questioning back to how Gong Qi had actually fallen on the knife. Brown tried to describe how when she had pushed him, she had lost her balance.

'When I did actually see the knife as she was fallin' back, I tried to grab it but I was too slow.'

Brown admitted having had two cans of beer two hours before his encounter with the Chinese woman. But, he said, it didn't have any effect on him. He was simply upset after having received the threatening phone call. He told the detectives that he wasn't the only one to have received threatening phone calls. He said that his next-door neighbour, Kate, had gotten them too.

Wheeler asked Brown again about how Gong Qi might have fallen onto the knife. Mark Brown's convoluted story sounded highly unlikely. When the interview was finished, Phelan said, 'Mark, as a result of what you've told us, you're going to be charged with causing the death of Gong Qi in Mentone on Wednesday night the 26th day of April 1989.'

When asked if he had anything to say, Brown replied, 'I was just walking along this street and ... and it ... it was an accident and ... er ... I'm sorry.'

The interview concluded at 10.36 am – it had lasted 36 minutes.

After the interview, the two detectives and the police video operator drove with Brown back to his flat in Mentone. Brown found the clothes he had been wearing on the night he stabbed Gong Qi and gave them to the detectives. Then he was allowed to shower and change his clothes. Looking refreshed and relaxed, Brown stood outside his flat with Peter Phelan. The clothes he'd worn on the night of the stabbing were laid out on the boot of a car parked in the driveway of his block of flats. With the video running, Brown indicated the clothes for the camera, and then he, Wheeler and Phelan walked the route he said he'd taken on the night of 26 April.

When the three men got to the place where Brown said he had approached Gong Qi to ask for a cigarette, Wheeler walked ahead and mimicked the actions of the dead woman, according to the instructions of her killer.

When Brown tried to show his scenario of how Gong Qi had pushed him, he made Wheeler stand side-on because he kept insisting that he never saw her face. Wheeler tried to simulate a push from that position, but he looked awkward. Brown described how the knife had fallen from his pocket and said that Gong Qi had somehow fallen onto it so that it penetrated her to cause the fatal wound. In the re-enactment, the story seemed even more unlikely. The detectives didn't question him about the improbability of what he was saying because they wanted the implausibility to speak for itself when the video was shown in court.

When the video re-enactment was over, Phelan asked Brown if he had anything else to say to the camera.

'It was an accident,' said the young man. 'I just hope people don't take me the wrong way. The only reason why I'm doing this is to let people know that I'm not a murderer; it was an accident.'

Brown and the detectives arrived back at the Homicide Squad at 1.30 pm. It had been a long day for all of them. By 2.30 pm, Mark Hastie Brown was charged with murder and brought before a magistrate at the Melbourne Magistrates' Court. He was remanded into custody.

Wheeler and Phelan joined Ryan and Robertson at the funeral. Held at a hall in Lennox Street, Richmond, the Buddhist service was over by the time they got there but they were able to see how relieved the parents were at the news of an arrest.

The interpreter spoke to Peter Phelan: 'The parents are happy that Gong Qi's killer has been caught and are looking forward to watching his execution on TV on Saturday night.'

'You did tell them that we don't do that in this country?' Phelan asked.

The interpreter nodded. Yes, he had tried to explain that.

Discussing the case after the confession of sorts, and the unlikely re-enactment, the detectives concluded that Brown had most probably approached Gong Qi with the view to sexually assaulting her. Most important to their conclusion was the fact that when her body was examined, and the pathologist had lined up her shirt and jumper with the stab wound, it was obvious that she had been stabbed after someone had tried to pull up her clothing. Nothing in Brown's re-enactment accounted for this. It was unlikely that robbery was a motive since her handbag hadn't been taken, and Brown's prior convictions had involved sexual assault when he attacked women – not purse-snatching.

A confession is not enough in a case like the death of Gong Qi. Police still need to build their case for court. All of the physical evidence was lodged with scientist Jane Taupin at the State Forensic Science Laboratory in Macleod. Taupin examined the knife that Brown said was the murder weapon, forensic samples taken from Gong Qi during the post-mortem examination, the white and blue tissues that crime scene examiner Tony Kealy had found in the street on the night of the murder, a blood sample from Brown, and the jumper and shirt Gong Qi had been wearing when she was stabbed.

Taupin found that the knife was capable of producing the cuts that she found in the shirt and the jumper, but she was unable to find any traces of blood on it, which wasn't surprising considering Brown said he had boiled it for fifteen minutes. She was unable to type the blood found on the tissues, so was therefore unable to say whether or not they were connected to the crime. Taupin came to the same conclusions as Dr Shelley Robertson with regard to the stab wound not lining up with the normal hang of the jumper and shirt. She also examined Brown's clothing but found no blood on it. This wasn't unusual since most of the bleeding from Gong Qi's single stab wound was internal, and any external bleeding had soaked into her own shirt and jumper.

Mark Brown's next-door neighbour, Kate, was interviewed following his arrest. He had been in her flat on the morning the detectives came for him. She was six years older than Brown and described herself as an invalid pensioner. She told Wheeler that she had lived in the flat in Albenca Street since June 1988, and thought it was sometime in January 1989 that Brown had moved in next door.

'Basically right from the time that Mark moved in, we established a good relationship with each other. Our relationship was platonic,' she explained, 'we never went out on any dates or anything like that, but just kept each other company at home.'

Kate explained that the two friends spent a lot of time together. 'Nearly every night when he came home from work, Mark would come into my unit. He sometimes would bring his own food and watch television and it was basically a good, friendly relationship.' He had even helped her put new locks on her door after her flat was broken into in March. After the break-in, she had asked him to spend more time with her because she was scared to be on her own.

'Mark would often fall asleep on the couch in my flat and from March 1989, we spent a lot of time together. Because I spent so much time with him, I got to know him fairly well with regard to his behaviour. He never really drank alcohol. Only on one occasion when we were having a barbecue, we both shared a bottle of Southern Comfort. I have never seen him drink beer before and he has never brought beer or alcohol into my unit at all. On a few occasions, I spent time in Mark's unit, and I have never seen beer or alcohol in there either. Mark has never come into my unit smelling of alcohol or in an intoxicated state.'

Kate explained to Peter Wheeler that she had gone into hospital in April for two weeks. On the night of the murder, she rang Brown from the hospital and told him that she was coming home the next day. She couldn't remember what time she had called him, but he had told her that he really wanted her to come home because he was lonely. He also told her that he had received a threatening phone call. Kate said she didn't know what it was all about; she didn't ask and he didn't tell her. Even though Brown told the detectives that Kate too had received threatening phone calls, she didn't mention them in her statement to the police.

Kate had returned home from hospital the following day and it was then that she'd heard about the murder in the next street. When Brown got home from work that evening, the two had talked at length about the murder of the Chinese girl. Kate was frightened and did most of the talking. A couple of days later, the two spoke again about the murder. Kate had commented that you couldn't trust anyone nowadays, and Mark had said, 'How do you know it wasn't me?' She had told him not to talk like that because she was really scared.

Kate finished her statement by saying, 'I always felt completely safe in his company and he never gave me any reason to think that he was involved in the incident with the Chinese girl.'

Shortly after the arrest, detectives Bob Ryan, John Robertson, Peter Phelan and Peter Wheeler were invited to a Chinese banquet in their honour to thank them for the work they'd done in arresting the man responsible for Gong Qi's stabbing. At the dinner, Gong Qi's parents presented each of the detectives with a framed message written in Chinese characters. They read: *Maintain justice, drive away evil.* A larger plaque was presented that was hung on the walls of the Homicide Squad offices in St Kilda Road.

On 29 September 1989, a committal hearing and inquest were held into Gong Qi's death. The coroner found: 'Brown approached her from behind where the deceased had received a fatal knife wound to the back. I further find that Mark Hastie Brown contributed to the cause of death.'

In March 1990, Brown stood trial for the death of Gong Qi. He had been charged with murder under section 3A of the *Crimes Act 1958*, which covered unintentional killing in the course or furtherance of a crime of violence. The Crimes Act says that a person convicted under 3A can be sentenced to level one imprisonment (life) or they could be 'imprisoned for a term of ten years or more [and] shall be liable to be convicted of murder as though he had killed that person intentionally'.

Outside the courtroom, Detective Peter Phelan sat with all the witnesses. The prosecutor approached him and told him that Brown would plead guilty to a 3A murder charge. He asked the detective if he agreed to that.

Phelan was happy to agree and told the witnesses that they wouldn't have to testify. It also meant that both they and the detectives could go into the courtroom to watch the trial since they were no longer witnesses.

Between being charged and the trial, Brown's story had changed. He pleaded guilty to murder, but to the surprise of the detectives who had charged him, his lawyer explained to Mr Justice Hampel that 'during the course of the robbery, Mr Brown produces a knife and there is a struggle and the deceased falls whilst Mr Brown is holding [her] from behind, and he falls as well, and it is that action, sir, that the knife enters the deceased from the back'. This was the first time any of the detectives had heard that Brown had attempted to rob Gong Qi. It was like the docket sheets from Brown's youth; he admitted the assaults, but strongly denied that his attacks against females were of a sexual nature.

Brown's lawyer, Mr R Lopez, told the judge: 'Your honour, there is a fair amount of support in relation to that situation through the evidence of the pathologist which does not suggest any other injury apart from some bruising to the knee, and it is on that basis that Mr

Brown pleads guilty and that plea is accepted on that factual basis.'

Phelan tried to get the attention of the prosecutor. None of the detectives could understand this new reference to robbery. There was no way that any of them believed that Brown had set out to rob Gong Qi. But the wheels of justice had started to move and the trial proceeded in that direction.

And so began three days of testimony and legal discussion. Lopez told the court of Brown's deprived childhood, and the fact that he had gone to live with an aunt and uncle when he was six. The year before the murder, he had met up with an older sister that he hadn't known existed and had been embraced into her family. The lawyer then went on to detail the conditions that Brown was experiencing in prison.

'He has been in custody since [the time of his arrest] and has been what is referred to as in "lock-up", because of some apprehension about his safety. I am instructed, Your Honour, that on 18 May, he was transferred to Pentridge, his arrest being on the 12th. He was placed in a lock-up situation on 12 June 1989 where he remained until 16 August when he was removed to the new remand centre, returned to the lock-up on 29 October '89, and has been in that condition, Your Honour, since then, and it is envisaged, sir, that that type of incarceration will continue. There has been some fear in relation to his safety.

'Now, I am instructed, sir, that being in the lock-up means spending 23 hours a day in your cell and you do have one cell-mate and it is not a large cell – in other words, you can't very well move because of the items of furniture in it. There is not too much room in which to move – and you are let out one hour a day. Sometimes, depending on the demands and other pressures at Pentridge, you sometimes remain more than one hour in the exercise yard.' Lopez felt that the conditions in which Mark Brown was 'doing his time' should be taken into account at sentencing. He explained that Brown's need for prison protection came from a rumour that had apparently spread through the prison system that he had been involved in several rapes and had in fact raped Gong Qi after he had stabbed her.

'I am instructed, Your Honour, that ... he had been the subject of threats and it got to the suicidal stage. So, Your Honour, as at this stage, this is the reality of his incarceration. Whether, at a later stage, things will change, one does not know, but it is my submission, sir, that Your Honour ought to take the view that these sorts of conditions are likely to continue, certainly for the foreseeable future.'

Brown's sister gave evidence that she had seen her brother drink socially on a few occasions and three times had suspected that he might have taken drugs because his eyes were glassy. She described her brother as a 'very kind-hearted person who would give you the shirt on his back and the last twenty cents in his pocket to try and help you out, and he is very loving and caring'. She had continued to see him after his arrest.

Next, the court heard from Brown's probation officer who had become friendly with the young man. And then a psychiatrist, who had seen Brown for a total of four-and-a-half hours in order to assess him, described his background and how he was abused by his biological mother before being fostered by his aunt and uncle when he was six. He detailed the accused's past difficulties and his stay in a psychiatric unit for over eight months before he was eighteen. The psychiatrist told the court that Brown had admitted using drugs from about the age of seventeen. He reported him saying he was in a relationship with the woman in the flat next door – Kate had denied this in her statement – and that he found himself unable to cope and began using marijuana and abusing amphetamines. Interestingly, Kate had made no mention of Brown being under the influence of anything and he spent most nights in her flat.

If Brown had indeed been in an intimate relationship with Kate, it seemed to be more than a coincidence to the detectives watching in the courtroom that Gong Qi was attacked after Kate had been away for a fortnight. When the judged asked about the exact nature of the relationship, the psychiatrist said: '... he described to me [that] it was a supportive relationship ... but there were also phases of intimacy in their relationship.'

The psychiatrist finished his testimony by saying that he didn't think Brown would be able to cope too much longer in the isolated setting of prison.

The next phase of the trial dealt with the problematic application of Section 3A of the Crimes Act, which hadn't really been tested in sentencing. Despite a search, lawyers for the defence and prosecution couldn't come up with case law that could be applied to the killing of Gong Qi. There were a few cases with some similarities, but nothing really to guide the judge.

On 15 March 1990, eleven months after the murder, Mr Justice Hampel read his sentence in court. 'Mark Hastie Brown, on the 26th of April last year, you attacked the victim Miss Gong Qi in the street whilst she was on her way home. During this attack, she received one stab wound from which she later died. You have now pleaded guilty to the charge of murder. The contention on your behalf is that your motive was robbery, that you threatened her with a knife, a struggle ensued, you both fell to the ground, and the stabbing was accidental.

'There is no evidence of any relationship between you and the victim, and the medical evidence accords with your version of events. There is not sufficient evidence from which an inference can properly be drawn that you intended to kill her or inflict serious injury. In those circumstances, the Crown, I think quite properly, concedes that I should treat this killing as one of a kind envisaged by Section 3A of the Crimes Act, namely an unintentional one in the course, or furtherance, of a crime involving violence.

'At the time that you committed this crime, you were 22. You were living alone and using drugs. You had been, since an early age, the victim of a disturbed and unhappy background. You were a neglected child who ran away from terrible home conditions and became a ward of the state by the age of six. You were looked after by your aunt and uncle but later spent much of your time in institutions. You have a number of prior convictions and you have spent time in youth training centres and on probation. Given those circumstances, your record is not as bad as that of some people in your situation.'

Justice Hampel gave an overview of how Brown had met up with his sister but started using amphetamines again. 'You have been in custody in most difficult circumstances since your arrest. There is apparently a misconception by other prisoners about the nature of your crimes and you have been threatened. As a result, you have been in protective custody and significant isolation throughout and may well be in that position for some time to come.

'The sentence which has to be imposed must be substantially reduced by reason of your plea of guilty, your relative youth and some prospect of rehabilitation, which, of course, is not only in your interest, but in the interests of the community. Although the sentence must have a component of general deterrence, that is minimised because of your disadvantages and disabilities with which you could not cope and which have contributed to your personality disorder. However, despite the various mitigatory factors personal to you, the killing of an innocent victim in the circumstances in which it occurred is a very serious crime indeed, although it must be distinguished from an intentional killing.

'Since the change in law which has enabled the fixing of determinate sentences for murder, there have not been any cases which have been drawn to my attention where the sentencing judge proceeded on the basis that the killing was unintentional that the murder was of the category contemplated by Section 3A of the Crimes Act ...' Justice Hampel spoke of *The Queen v. McInnis*, in which a judge found that the defendant had deliberately shot a service station attendant in the course of a robbery. The defendant had been given an eighteen-year sentence.

After balancing the various sentencing considerations, Brown was sentenced to twelve years in jail with a minimum of nine.

Melbourne's *Sun* newspaper reported that Gong Qi's parents in China were devastated with the leniency of the sentence and were horrified that Brown hadn't received a life sentence, which they had lobbied for at the Australian Consulate in China. Kelly Ryan, a journalist at the *Sun*, wrote: 'Mr Justice Hampel said he had taken into account Brown's neglected childhood, his drug use, his limited intelligence and his few convictions. He said he was satisfied Brown had not intended to kill Miss Qi.'

Other newspaper accounts quote unnamed police as being 'outraged' at the leniency of the sentence.

According to Peter Wheeler, many police see their job as investigating a crime, catching the culprit, and gathering evidence for the case in court. What happens after that is in the hands of the lawyers and the judges. In the case of Gong Qi, however, Wheeler felt compelled to make his concerns known to the then Director of Public Prosecutions. Because Brown had been sentenced under Section 3A of the Crimes Act and his case was the first of its kind to be tried under changes to the Act, the leniency of the sentence formed a worrying precedent. Wheeler and his colleagues were concerned that future sentences could be based on that imposed on Brown.

Nothing came of the detective's concerns.

What happens to an offender like Mark Hastie Brown, constantly in trouble, and an ongoing threat to women? He served out his minimum sentence of nine years and then got out of prison, enrolled in a TAFE course and went to live with a family member about 20 minutes' drive from Mentone. Five months after he was released, Brown was riding his bike along a bike track and passed an eighteen-year-old girl wearing a school uniform walking the other way. He got off his bike, and ran up behind the girl, put his arm around her neck, forced her to the ground, and forced his hands into her underpants while lying on top of her. The victim screamed and Brown let her go. The girl ran to her house, which was nearby, and Brown followed her home, claiming that she had stolen his mobile phone. He was arrested a short time later.

On his latest docket sheet, the arresting officer wrote: *The defendant stated that he had accidentally fallen off his bike and onto the victim and that the whole affair was an accident. Offender stuck to story throughout even though inconsistencies in same were made apparent to him. Offender remained very calm throughout and appears to talk himself into believing the story he concocts.*

The officer might as well have written: *a leopard doesn't change its spots.*

Mark Brown was given a six-and-a-half-year sentence with a five-year minimum. Because he violated his parole conditions by reoffending, he had to serve the final two years of his original sentence before beginning his new sentence.

In 2002, Peter Wheeler, who was by then a detective senior sergeant in charge of the Computer Crime Squad and the chairman of the Australasian Computer Crime Managers' Group, attended an Interpol forum in Seoul in South Korea. He had been asked to present a paper on the experience of emerging trends and initiatives developed by Australian jurisdictions in combating computer-related crime.

On the flight over, the movie screen would periodically switch to an aerial map with a small computer-generated graphic showing where the plane was. Not long before he landed in Seoul, the map showed that it was flying over Shanghai. Memories of the Gong Qi investigation came flooding back thirteen years after it had happened.

Wheeler remembered thinking that her parents would have no idea that one of the policemen responsible for capturing their daughter's murderer was in a plane flying overhead. It was tragic to think of how their lives would have changed forever when they lost their only child.

Every time Peter Phelan leaves his house, he walks past the plaque that Gong Qi's parents gave him. He thinks about the phrase, *Maintain justice, drive away evil*, and is reminded of how the system failed her. He believes that if Mark Brown had pleaded guilty to a Section 3A murder and it had been established that he had tried to sexually assault her, then his sentence might have been harsher.

'It's about the dignity of the victim and the truth,' he said, some sixteen years after the murder. He strongly believes that because the truth didn't come out, the system failed her and her family. And he thinks about this every day.

Sometimes trauma can take a long time to bubble to the surface and for many police officers, a single incident of jeopardy can pierce the internal armour of invincibility and leave a gap that can't be plugged. On the day Peter Wheeler and Peter Phelan were shot at while door-knocking in Mentone, the incident was trivialised back at the Homicide offices for two reasons. Primarily, the weapon turned out to be 'only' a .22 calibre air rifle and in the minds of some, it seemed hardly worth worrying about. The fact is that shots fired by the gunmen with the .22 calibre weapon, initially at head height, could have caused serious injury if either of the detectives had been struck. And secondly, the pressing matter of making an arrest in the Gong Qi murder case was the only priority for all those working it. Pressure had come from the Chinese consulate and force command to solve the case with an arrest. Detectives had planned the dawn arrest for the next morning.

A process was not initiated to recognise the bravery under fire and the incident was lost in the passage of time.

Thirty years after being shot at, Peter Wheeler and Peter Phelan applied to police command to be recognised for their actions that day. Both men felt the long-term effect of the incident, and both men felt their response amply reflected the criteria laid out in the Australian Honours and Awards guidelines: ... *a deliberate choice to go from a place of safety to danger.*

Let's hope their actions of bravery that day are finally rewarded.

Chapter Eight

❖

FOUR-CAR, SINGLE FATAL, DOUBLE HIT-RUN

Nick and Garry were driving too fast – 100 kilometres an hour in a 60 zone. A white car ahead loomed in the distance. Garry veered onto the wrong side of the road to pass it, crossing double white lines in the process. He wouldn't see the oncoming red Holden over a crest in the road – until it was too late. The crushing impact sent his car spinning back onto the left side of the road, coming to rest against the gutter. The red Holden swerved to its left and was hit in turn by the car behind it. The driver of the red Holden died instantly, leaving his heavily pregnant wife screaming by his side.

Garry was injured, but not badly. His mate Nick pulled his green Holden Commodore up onto the nature strip next to Garry's gold Ford, and then walked back to the other two cars. He surveyed the damage, noted that the driver of the red Holden looked dead, and returned to Garry. Nick helped Garry out of the wreck of the gold Ford and drove him home. They didn't call the police. They didn't try to help the pregnant woman, nor the mother and son in the white Ford station wagon that had rammed into the red Holden as it spun across the road. They merely surveyed the devastation they had caused and left the scene.

Two months later, the young widow would give birth alone.

Senior Constable Chris Field of the Accident Investigation Section was called to the scene, along with Sergeant Tony Hill and Senior Constable Geoffrey Exton. Field had been working an afternoon shift and had received the call at 8.30 pm. He and his colleagues had hurried to the accident scene with lights flashing blue and red, and siren blaring.

Chris Field says that an accident scene is like a crime scene. Evidence needs to be gathered and preserved with the least possible delay. Their specially equipped police Land Cruiser was known as the 'crash truck', and one of the police vehicle's most important features was the light on top of the roof, which could be extended on a pole to a height of four metres to illuminate accident scenes at night. Before long it would be illuminating the scene of carnage left by this latest collision.

The accident scene in the south-eastern Melbourne suburb of Heatherton was littered with debris from the mangled remains of three vehicles – two on one side of the road and the gold Ford further down on the other side. Having been attached to the Accident Investigation Section for five years, Field was used to such scenes. His first duty was to speak with uniformed officers already at the crash site. Half an hour had elapsed since the collision and the only remaining victim at the scene was the dead man in the red Holden. His body would remain in the car until the on-site investigation was complete. In death he had, in a sense, become a piece of evidence.

The first officers to arrive at the scene had taped off the accident site with crime scene tape and they relayed all the information they had gathered from witnesses to the accident investigators. The pregnant woman had been taken by ambulance to hospital for observation and sedation, and the woman driving the white station wagon had been picked up, together with her young son, by her husband after giving police her version of what happened. She had told officers that she had seen the oncoming car speeding down the wrong side of the road and she had realised well in advance that it was going to hit the car in front of her. She had heard a loud crash and then felt the impact of her car careering into the car in front.

The woman explained to the officers that she was temporarily dazed after the impact and then she had heard a woman screaming for help. She and her son got out of their badly damaged vehicle and had gone over to the red Holden. They both helped the distraught woman out of the car. In the darkness, they couldn't see the woman's husband, who had fallen back between the two front seats. In the confusion, it had appeared that the expectant mother was the only occupant of the car – until she began screaming for someone to help her husband.

It was around this time, the woman had told police, that a man had appeared and looked inside the red Holden. He told her that the man 'didn't look too good' and then he walked away.

After the man left, the woman remembered people coming and going, but delayed shock had set in and her memory of subsequent events was hazy. Her young son had run across the road to call an ambulance from a nearby house.

Officers at the scene also informed the members of the Accident Investigation Section that the third car – the gold Ford – was empty. Immediately, Field notified the police helicopter to begin a search of surrounding market gardens knowing that the driver couldn't have walked away from the twisted wreck uninjured; he could have suffered a head injury and wandered off in a daze. He had to be located as soon as possible. State Emergency Service officers, together with the police and sniffer dogs, joined the search on the ground. When they didn't find him, police had to consider another possibility: the driver had left the scene of the accident deliberately in order to avoid the consequences.

Field and his colleagues began their investigation at the red Holden. The signs were easy for the trained officers to read. Skid marks told them the direction in which the vehicles had been travelling, the shape of dents told them the angle of impact and flakes of paint told them which vehicles had collided. The red Holden was a wreck. The front end on the driver's side was completely smashed in, as was the driver's side door. The dead man lay back against the seat – his face covered in blood. Field concluded that the dead man was definitely the driver of the red Holden; as further proof, they discovered his feet had been jammed under the pedals on impact. Field noted that the red Holden had come to rest on the nature strip at right angles to the white station wagon driven by the woman and her son. Scuff marks in the grass indicated to the investigators the direction in which the car was spinning prior to coming to rest.

Field noticed gold flecks of paint adhering to the red Holden at the point of first impact. The accident investigators checked the front dashboard in case the speedo had jammed on impact to give a clue as to how fast the car had been travelling, but the needle sat on zero. The dead man's seat belt hung slackly around his body. He had been wearing it and on impact it had locked in position as the man had been thrown forward. But no seat belt could have saved him.

A check of the inside of the red Holden revealed nothing to suggest that the dead man and his wife were anything but a regular, law-abiding couple. There were no beer cans, stolen property or drugs. It was the experience of the investigators that fatal accidents such as this often involve drunk drivers, drug addicts or burglars more concerned about absconding than keeping their eyes on the road. Every possibility had to be covered.

Rather than call upon forensic science photographers, the Accident Investigation Section take their own photographs and in this case, Field took pictures of each car as he walked around the scene.

Next, the accident squad investigators examined the white station wagon. It wasn't as badly damaged as the red Holden but they could easily see the point of impact at the front where the collision had occurred. Field photographed the car from a number of different angles, capturing all of the damage on film.

When this examination was complete, Field, Hill and Exton made their way to the third car, further down and on the opposite side of the road. The gold Ford had come to rest against the gutter and it, too, was very badly damaged.

Immediately the crash investigators noticed tyre marks on the nature strip next to the car. The scuff marks were fresh and couldn't have been made by the Ford because it had not mounted the curb. The Ford had telltale flakes of red paint from the Holden lodged in its front grille.

Field walked around the car and looked at the nature strip. He bent over and picked up a bit of plastic moulding and looked at it carefully. The moulding was part of the bumper bar of a late-model Holden – possibly a Commodore.

Field surveyed the scene. Something was amiss. Why were there pieces of Holden Commodore near the wrecked gold Ford? On closer examination, he noticed a dent in the gold Ford that didn't seem to be associated with the damage caused by the collision with the red Holden. There were pieces of green paint lodged in the dent and Senior Constable Field put two and two together.

He figured that a green Holden Commodore had driven up onto the nature strip after the collision and then in its haste to leave the scene had tried to drive forward along the nature strip to get back onto the road. However, there hadn't been enough room to pass between the wrecked gold Ford and a power pole on the nature strip. Apparently, the green Holden Commodore had clipped the Ford, leaving behind part of its bumper bar and paint work.

Common sense told the investigators that the driver of the green Holden Commodore had collected the driver of the gold Ford and driven him away. That made the collision a hit and run, the official title being a 'Four-car, single fatal, double hit-run'.

Senior Constable Field immediately put out a 'keep a look-out for' bulletin for a late-model green Holden – possibly a Commodore with front end damage. He put a call through to D24 to summons an officer from the Victoria Police forensic science laboratory to come to the accident scene and gather soil samples and make casts of the tyre marks from the missing car. Such samples may be needed later in court to link the missing vehicle with the accident scene – in case the owner of the car denied ever being there.

The next step in the investigation was to find the owner of the gold Ford. Registration details were taken from the smashed window of the car and a check was run on the owner; Garry's name was soon known to police. Field sent uniformed officers to check the address, only to find that Garry hadn't lived there for some time. Field ran an Information Bureau of Records (IBR) check on Garry and wasn't really surprised to find he had a long list of prior convictions, most of which were for driving and drug offences. The IBR check also listed his known associates. Four addresses would be checked before police officers located his mother, who gave them his current address – he was living with a mate called Nick.

Field left his colleagues, Exton and Hill, at the accident scene and went with uniformed officers to the house in Noble Park. Using their powerful police torches, Field and the other officers illuminated the green Holden Commodore in the driveway of the house. It had obvious recent front-end damage.

It was now six hours after the collision and Chris Field felt the car's bonnet, which was still vaguely warm. His examination was interrupted by loud barking and the arrival of two dogs, one of them a bull terrier. He recalls bluffing the dogs with his drawn police baton before making his way to the front door of the house.

A woman had come out onto the front porch when the dogs started to bark, and Field asked to speak to the driver of the green Commodore. Going into the house, he heard the woman tell two men to say nothing and proceeded to give the police officers a concocted story. She told them that her boyfriend, Nick, and his mate Garry were at the pub watching a strip show when they noticed that Garry's car was being stolen from the car park. They took off in pursuit until Garry's car had been involved in the accident. Nick had driven home and, according to the woman, was going to report the whole thing to the police the following day.

Understandably, Senior Constable Field was sceptical. He asked to see Garry and was led into the lounge room. A man in his mid-twenties was lying prone on the couch covered with a blanket. Field asked him to stand up, which he did reluctantly and with great difficulty. He could see that Garry's legs were severely bruised and one of his wrists was swollen enough to suggest it was broken.

Ironically, Garry was in the middle of denying that he was driving his car and denying that he was in the accident when Field noticed the glint of broken windscreen glass caught up in his tracksuit. Indeed, glass began dropping from his clothing as soon as he stood up. He began to repeat the story the woman had told.

Field cut him short. 'Don't insult our intelligence, mate. Tell us what really happened.'

Garry and Nick finally admitted to their part in the fatal collision. Field asked the two men if they had been street racing. They both denied this. He then told Garry and Nick that the driver of the red Holden had died. Neither of them showed any obvious signs of regret or remorse. Field was used to such reactions. The police officer cautioned the two men and took them to the Cheltenham police station to be interviewed. Worried about taking a statement from Garry, who was injured, Field called in the police surgeon to examine him. The doctor recommended that Garry be taken to hospital for X rays. Nick was later released pending further investigation.

Back at the collision site in Heatherton, Sergeant Tony Hill and Senior Constable Geoffrey Exton supervised the removal of the smashed cars. The gold Ford was sent by tow truck to the Victoria Police State Forensic Science Laboratory, while the other cars went to local police compounds to be sealed until examination by police mechanics attached to the accident squad.

Exton and Hill used a geodometre to measure the distance between the vehicles and any skid marks at the accident scene in order to prepare a detailed scale map for future reference. The first part of the job was finished and now officers were faced with the painstaking examination of all the evidence collected, as well as gathering witnesses and taking their statements. The pieces of the puzzle had to be put together.

The first 48 hours following any collision are crucial. Both evidence and witnesses need to be fresh. Field had appealed through the media for the driver of the car that Garry was trying to pass just before the collision to come forward. The man rang police the next day. He told them that he had been driving along the road in Heatherton when he had noticed two cars in his rear-vision mirror speeding towards him. They were going so fast, he told police, that he was sure they were going to crash into the back of his car. He had seen Garry's car swerve onto the wrong side of the road and hit the oncoming red Holden. The man told police he had panicked and was unable to stop – possibly for fear of what he would see. He went home, had a stiff drink, and telephoned police the following day to offer his assistance. He was a valuable witness.

Garry was charged with culpable driving, recklessly causing injury to the wife of the deceased, negligently causing injury to the wife of the deceased, recklessly placing the wife in danger of death, recklessly placing the woman and her son in danger of death, failing to render assistance at the scene of the accident, failing to give name and address at the scene of the accident, driving in a manner careless, driving in a manner dangerous, driving while disqualified, crossing double lines, and exceeding 60 kilometres per hour. His alleged speed according to complicated calculations performed by crash investigators was 100 kilometres per hour.

When his case finally came to court, Garry pleaded guilty to the charge of culpable driving – giving him an automatic one-third reduction of any possible sentence. Field says that Garry 'cried like a baby' when the judge gave him a 30-month jail sentence.

Senior Constable Field says that people never get the full penalty for culpable driving, which is fifteen years in prison. He tries to distance himself from the sentencing process, which he feels is a societal responsibility. He does his job, which finishes when he gives evidence. It is ironic, however, that a man like Garry was given such a relatively light sentence considering his list of prior convictions.

He had lost his driver's licence almost as soon as he got it. In 1987 he had been convicted of unlicensed driving and exceeding .05 – his blood alcohol reading was .170. He had also been convicted of dangerous driving and speeding. In 1988, Garry had been convicted on a number of theft and drug trafficking charges. In addition to his considerable list of prior convictions, he had continued to offend after the fatal collision. Field believes that Garry was given enough warnings, but perhaps nothing will ever change him.

Chris Field and his fellow officers at the accident squad thrive on their work. Their squad is largely independent and an aspect that Field enjoys is that they follow an investigation from beginning to end. Officers from the squad attend accidents and post-mortem examinations, gather evidence, take their own photographs, collate evidence and appear in court as expert witnesses.

Most cases fail to touch the hardened investigators. They refer to those who drive dangerously as 'customers' and periodically throughout a shift, members look out the station window onto busy Springvale Road, see a speeding car and say, 'There goes another customer.' Indeed, an altered sticker on the office wall reads: 'If you drink and drive, you're a bloody customer'. Seeing so much death on the road, mostly through alcohol and speed, officers at the accident squad feel that the messages of road safety generally mean little to the public.

'People think it won't happen to them,' says Field, whose work proves it can happen to anybody.

Time after time, they are called to collisions involving young drunk men with prior convictions, their cars wrapped around poles. One collision that stands out particularly in Field's memory was a triple fatality where one young man's body was found in the car's boot. Investigators had been called to the collision scene and found two dead young men in the front seat of the car. Empty beer cans had spilled out of the wreck onto the ground.

The back of the car was jammed against a stone fence and it wasn't until the wreck was being moved that the police found the third body. Investigations revealed that the young man had jumped in the boot 'to be with the beer', which was also in there. For a lark, his friends had sped around the streets to throw him around inside the boot. They were all drunk and they all died. It's such a waste.

Field says that it is usually the death of children that break through the emotional barrier. He says children are innocent victims. One Christmas Eve, he was called to investigate a two-car collision near a small country town in Victoria. Five people had been killed. It transpired that a woman had been driving to New South Wales to visit her mother-in-law for Christmas. Her passengers were her two children aged six and two. She was following her husband and father-in-law, who were travelling in their own car. Inexperience with country roads and possibly fatigue were blamed for her missing a bend and colliding head-on with a car containing two people – also on their way to visit relatives for Christmas. The scene was utter carnage.

Not only did Field have to thoroughly investigate all aspects of the accident, but he had to deal with the distraught husband who had pulled his car over when he noticed his wife was no longer following him. The hardest task for Chris Field was to look at the bodies of the two children and then to see the back of the car full of Christmas presents with cards handwritten in a childish scrawl: 'To Dear Granny ...'

Field finished his lengthy investigation at 3 am, returned home to catch a couple hours' sleep and was woken by his own small children opening their presents.

'All I could think about were the two little kids who wouldn't be opening their presents that morning,' he says. 'It ruined Christmas.'

Another tragic case involving a tiny baby made a lasting impression on the senior constable. A woman had hit a tree, dying on impact. The car roof had folded in, trapping her baby in its capsule in the back seat. People rushed over to try to free the baby, but soon smoke began to billow from underneath the car. The would-be rescuers tried to shield the trapped baby with blankets but were soon driven back by the flames. The police officer shrugs sadly. There was nothing anyone could do.

Because cars have a tendency to burn following a collision, Field has a number of tragic stories forged forever in his memory. A case he was called upon to investigate involved a man who had lost control of his car on a corrugated country road. The car careered into a small bridge, trapping the driver. A private security officer saw the accident and stopped to help. He couldn't free the man's leg, which was caught under the dashboard, so he began running to get help at a nearby farmhouse. He heard the man yelling and turned back to see smoke coming from the car's engine. The security man continued running to the farmhouse but help didn't arrive in time.

The driver's charred body was later found still in the car, his arms raised defensively in front of him to shield his face. The security man later told Field, 'I would have given a million dollars for a fire extinguisher that day.'

Not all road fatalities are added to the state's annual road toll – some are suicides and some are murder – but any involving a car or a road may be investigated by the accident squad. Field says that investigators always need to have an open mind. It is easy for experts to tell the difference between someone who has been hit by a car and someone who was run over while lying on the road to make it look like an accident.

Pedestrians hit by cars typically suffer similar injuries. Damage to the victim's legs at the height of the car's bumper bar is usual, as are head injuries where the victim is thrown up onto the bonnet and smashes the windscreen.

He says that the function of the accident squad is to investigate any road fatality with three or more victims, any case involving police – on or off duty – and any case of criminal negligence. According to Field, police are just as accountable as everybody else and the accident squad is always called in as an independent investigator when police are involved in serious collisions. Field lectures occasionally at the police academy and tells new recruits bluntly of their responsibility on the roads. He calls it 'double jeopardy' if police are involved in a collision. He says that not only are they investigated by the accident squad, but they are also investigated by the police internal investigation department. The case is then passed to the state ombudsman for independent review. These exacting standards mean that the public can be assured that police neither receive nor expect special treatment.

The success rate of the accident squad is high; 95 per cent of hit and run cases are solved with the examination of physical evidence and the help of witnesses. One of the few unsolved hit and run cases on file concerned a drunk who had fallen asleep on a road in Dandenong. A car had run over him and killed him. The only piece of physical evidence was a smear of grease – probably from the car's handbrake spring – on the dead man's sleeve. The car itself would probably have suffered no damage but Field is reasonably sure that the driver would have known he had run over something. There were no witnesses, owing to the fact that the hit and run occurred in the small hours of the morning, and the case remains unsolved.

The investigator is understandably cynical about the general messages of road safety. He says that most people are eternal optimists and they live in a fairyland world, thinking that it won't happen to them. He concedes that innovations such as speed cameras have slowed traffic, but concludes that any messages to the public must go through the so-called 'hip pocket nerve'.

Field believes that road safety is ultimately society's responsibility. If our society believes drink driving is wrong, then its members will actively encourage each other not to drink and drive. He says that 20 years ago, it was considered normal – even humorous – for a drunk to stagger to his car to drive home. This attitude has clearly changed. Death on the roads is no longer considered an inevitable part of driving.

One thing that Chris Field is certain of is that while people continue to flout road rules, drink and drive, speed, and drive while tired or under the influence of drugs, the accident squad will never be short of 'customers'.